POETRY
and STORY
THERAPY

Writing for Therapy or Personal Development Series
Edited by Gillie Bolton

Writing for Therapy or Personal Development, a foundation library to a rapidly developing field, covers the theory and practice of key areas. Clearly exemplified, engaging and accessible, the series is appropriate for therapeutic, healthcare, or creative writing practitioners and facilitators, and for individual writers or courses.

other books in the series

Therapeutic Journal Writing
An Introduction for Professionals
Kate Thompson
Foreword by Kathleen Adams
ISBN 978 1 84310 690 6

Writing Routes
A Resource Handbook of Therapeutic Writing
Edited by Gillie Bolton, Victoria Field and Kate Thompson
Foreword by Gwyneth Lewis
ISBN 978 1 84905 107 1

Writing Works
A Resource Handbook for Therapeutic Writing Workshops and Activities
Edited by Gillie Bolton, Victoria Field and Kate Thompson
Foreword by Blake Morrison
ISBN 978 1 84310 468 1

POETRY
and STORY
THERAPY

The Healing Power of
Creative Expression

Geri Giebel Chavis

Jessica Kingsley *Publishers*
London and Philadelphia

For full details of permissions granted please see page 10.

First published in 2011
by Jessica Kingsley Publishers
116 Pentonville Road
London N1 9JB, UK
and
400 Market Street, Suite 400
Philadelphia, PA 19106, USA

www.jkp.com

Library of Congress Cataloging in Publication Data
Chavis, Geri Giebel.
  Poetry and story therapy : the healing power of creative expression / Geri Giebel Chavis.
    p. ; cm.
  Includes bibliographical references and index.
  ISBN 978-1-84905-832-2 (alk. paper)
  1. Graphotherapy. 2. Creative writing--Therapeutic use. I. Title.
  [DNLM: 1. Poetry as Topic. 2. Psychotherapy--methods. 3. Writing. WM 450.5.W9]
  RC489.W75C53 2011
  616.89'165--dc22
                            2010035224

British Library Cataloguing in Publication Data
A CIP catalogue record for this book is available from the British Library

ISBN 978 1 84905 832 2

Printed and bound in Great Britain by
MPG Books Group

This book is dedicated to my father, William Giebel, affectionately known by his co-workers as 'Willie G.' I owe to him my love of traditional poetry, my appreciation for the sheer joy of word-creation, my reverence for the natural world and the priceless gift of unconditional love. This book is also dedicated to my mother, Ray Schiffman Giebel, who modeled generous giving, the ambition and fortitude to finish a challenging task and careful attention to detail.

Contents

Acknowledgments

I wish to express my sincere appreciation to all the clients, growth group participants, students, poetry therapy trainees, co-facilitators, and poetry therapy colleagues in the National Association for Poetry Therapy who have taught me so much about the healing power of human creativity, compassion and resilience. I wish to pay special tribute to Arleen McCarty Hynes with whom I began teaching poetry therapy in the 1980s. Her graciousness, modesty and wisdom will be forever memorable to me. Together, Arleen and I founded the Minnesota Poetry Therapy Network, a group that continues to flourish and keep the fires of poetry therapy burning brightly in the Midwest because of its wonderfully creative and supportive members. I am indebted to St. Catherine University in St. Paul, Minnesota. Since the late 1970s, it has been a place where I have been free to develop and pilot so many innovative courses related to the substance of this book. I acknowledge with gratitude the organizing efforts and generosity of the following individuals who made possible my teaching of poetry/bibliotherapy workshops in Cornwall, Ireland and Scotland: Victoria Field, Niall Hickey, Liam McCarthy, Josephine Murphy, Ruth MacNeely, Jean Tuomey, and Larry Butler. I also wish to express a special thank you to my dear friend and teaching colleague, Gay Herzberg, for her encouraging words and belief in me, and to thank Gillie Bolton and Kate Thompson for initially encouraging me to write this 'primer of poetry therapy' primarily for readers outside of the United States. While not directly related to the writing of this book, my husband, Ken Chavis, deserves special recognition for being the loyal, loving mainstay of my life during these past 40 years.

Copyright Acknowledgments

Introduction

The Transformative Power
of Word and Image

Words are powerful, and words matter to people. When words embody sense imagery, they conjure up visions in the imagination and affect us on a visceral level. When we embrace special words of our choosing to soothe or inspire us, they often function like a companion or a talisman. This book focuses on the act of reading word combinations found in poems and stories. It also highlights the act of writing creative pieces in response to these literary works and to a rich variety of other stimuli. This book is even more about how the acts of reading and writing personally meaningful words can act as springboards to growth and healing through the guidance and encouragement of a skilled helper.

Since the late 1970s, I have felt privileged to meld my love of literature and creative expression with my desire to help others heal or pursue their journeys of self-discovery. With their evocative images, striking characters, dramatic situations and powerful phrasing, the literary works we respond to or the creative pieces we write can help us lead better lives. They can nurture us, enlighten us and enable us to cope more effectively with everyday challenges and major crises.

The acts of reading and writing constitute powerfully transforming experiences for the human psyche. We tend to feel less alone when we read or listen to others' words, or when we physically experience images from evocative poems and stories. We enter a community of creative minds and voices. While some works present striking parallels to aspects of our own lives, others offer material quite different from that which is familiar. Sameness helps us affirm our reality, while difference challenges us to grow. We also can discover insights in a non-threatening context. Although we might at times resist what our therapists, parents or teachers tell us, we do not need to be defensive with the narrators of creative works or with the characters we meet there. We can be one step removed, even as we identify with some element of a literary work.

When we express our truths in our own writing, either in response to literary works or to other prompts, we empower and develop our voice. We provide a concrete record we can reflect upon and put form to the chaos of raw emotion and sensory experience. Through the act of arranging words on paper, we forge new meaning out of the feelings, images and memories that shape us. As D.H. Lawrence (1962, p.234) puts it, 'one sheds one's sicknesses in books—repeats and presents again one's emotions, to be master of them.'

Anne Lamott, in *Bird by Bird* (1994), recounts the answer she gives her students when they ask the question of why our writing matters. In doing so, she captures the therapeutic power of not only writing but also reading what others have written:

> Because of the spirit, I say. Because of the heart. Writing and reading decrease our sense of isolation. They deepen and widen and expand our sense of life: they feed the soul. When writers make us shake our heads with the exactness of their prose and their truths, and even make us laugh about ourselves or life, our buoyancy is restored. (Lamott 1994, p.237)

Like Lamott, I have witnessed, over the years, how words and images speak directly to the soul and heart. They etch paths to self-awareness and help bring about relief from sorrow and confusion. They provide links between our past, present and future and between the people in our lives.

Several years ago a friend of mine was driving her daughter to a college she would begin attending in the upcoming months, when they suddenly encountered a field abundantly spread with daffodils swaying in the breeze. In response to this dazzling array, both mother and daughter instantly recalled and recited in unison these immortal lines of William Wordsworth (1965b, p.191): 'I wandered lonely as a cloud / That floats on high o'er vales and hills,/ When all at once I saw a crowd,/ A host of golden daffodils.' The mother had introduced this poem to her daughter when she was a child, and at this moment, their shared heritage of inspiring words came back to vivify their experience and unite them at a crucial time of impending separation.

A more recent event also vividly illuminates the healing quality of words. A few months ago, a colleague of nodding acquaintance stopped by my office to thank me profusely for a quote she had repeatedly noticed on my office door. The quote, from Mary Oliver's poem 'The Summer Day' (1992, p.94), poses a simple yet potent question. We as readers are asked what we intend 'to do with' our 'one wild and precious life.' My colleague was enormously grateful for the inspiration these words provided. She claimed they gave her the courage to follow her heart and make significant changes in her job situation and place of residence. Her expressions of appreciation were actually a gift to me, affirming once again the power of language that has been such a bountiful feature of my personal and professional life.

As both these vignettes suggest, poetic words not only forge links between the writer's voice and the mind and heart of an individual reader, but also provide connection among members of a community. Evocative language builds bridges not only between levels of a single individual's consciousness but also between people. While words can bring us together, they also often carry ambiguous, multiple meanings that foster diversity of response, thus broadening each individual's perspective and helping us learn from one another. My colleague's reaction to Oliver's poetic lines now amplifies the resonance these words will have for me in the future.

Obviously, Oliver's words were evocative enough for me to choose them for my office door. In fact, they have often brought tears to my eyes, for they capture the extraordinary essence of our mortal existence in a single, intensely viable question. In responding to Oliver's words, my colleague brought her own life situation, memories and sensory awareness to what is a quite abstract and ambiguous sentence. However, the words 'one,' 'precious' and 'wild,' arranged as they are by Oliver, have the power to amaze and even call us to action. The word 'wild' in itself evokes a wide range of responses from various individuals; yet, when combined with 'one' and 'precious,' it tends to suggest wonder, possibility and freedom of choice.

I could go on to guess all the possible reactions that Oliver's set of words, arranged as they are, might elicit from all readers, but it would be impossible to do so. The beauty of facilitating and witnessing the response of others to magical words such as these is that we can never predict their idiosyncratic reaction. What we can do, if we commit to using poetry, story, and/or creative writing in our role as helpers, is provide the initial stimulus, establish a tone of trust, and encourage fruitful dialogue. In this way, we help set in motion a therapeutic process.

While the individuals in the above incidents experienced transformation as readers largely on their own, this book is designed to introduce a modality that involves interactive dialogue in psychotherapy groups, in community-based growth and educational groups and in therapeutic settings with individuals, couples and families. This book is therefore addressed to mental health professionals, educators, writing workshop facilitators, medical personnel, clergy, life coaches and students in helping professions who are ready to explore a fresh approach to their work with others.

The following two experiences helped forge, in very direct ways, my personal belief in the therapeutic modality that I am presenting in this book. These anecdotes convey how responding to literary expressions and engaging in creative writing in a supportive atmosphere of structured interactions result in personal benefit.

The first incident highlights the impact of interactive responses to Leo Tolstoy's story, 'Family Happiness' (2003). I was teaching this work at a medical center in a literature course where most of my students were 18- or 19-year-olds pursuing a two-year degree in nursing. After an intense discussion of the struggles that Tolstoy's young heroine and middle-aged hero go through, as they progress from courtship to marriage, four female students, who were all engaged to be married, came to talk with me after class. Overloaded with the stress of preparing for a demanding career, these women lacked the opportunity to reflect upon their personal lives. Expecting to simply fulfill a course assignment, they were surprised to discover that our class on Tolstoy's story was so profoundly illuminating for them. All four students animatedly expressed their appreciation for the insights that the reading and particularly the interchange of ideas had brought them. They were struck by how much they had learned about the expectations and disappointments that couples experience. They gained hope from seeing how conflict can lead to growth and reconciliation and felt increased confidence in their ability to negotiate with their partners when differences arise.

The second experience shows how creative writing is a fundamentally affirming activity that has ongoing beneficial effects. I was presenting a workshop for a woman's organization when I saw an individual who had participated in a growth group I had facilitated about 12 years earlier. She was glowing with her memory of a food metaphor writing activity she had completed in this past group and indicated how writing in this context had unleashed her personal voice. She had begun writing poems on a regular basis over the years and was even considering publication of her work. She recalled vividly the poem that provided the catalyst and light-hearted energy for this writing activity. It was Gladys Wellington's 'I Wanted to Be a Cauliflower' (1977), a short provocative work which uses food imagery to capture a daughter's changing identity in relation to her mother and sister.

In this earlier group, after leading a discussion of Wellington's poem, I had invited participants to create their own poetic expression, using food images, as does Wellington's persona, to describe herself and family members. I suggested the following two-stanza form:

> Stanza One: I am… (choose your favorite food and free write on whatever this metaphorical link suggests)

> Stanza Two: But my mother, sister, or father, etc. is… (select their favorite food and free write on whatever this link suggests)

Standing before me 12 years later, the woman who had written in response to this prompt indicated how that first excursion into spontaneous self-expression had given her permission to pursue a path that would greatly augment her self-esteem and sense of purpose.

Through the years, I have introduced food and other everyday imagery choices, to help individuals bypass their inner critic and set into motion a flow of words that, to quote Robert Frost (1972, p.440), may begin 'in delight' but 'ends in wisdom.' When clients have written to the above prompt in a variety of settings, they have not only enjoyed selecting and developing their food metaphors, but also begun an illuminating process of defining the differences and similarities between themselves and a significant family member. As they relish and elaborate on the food they love, they are usually quite edified by what they discover.

The above recounted experiences suggest the fundamental beliefs that undergird the work I do and the material presented in this book. These are:

- that reading poems and stories and writing personal reactions to literary and other forms of stimuli affect emotions, cognitions and behavior

- that guided discussions with others on our reading and writing experiences enhances the processes of healing and growth

- that we can modify our feelings, attitudes and actions to attain more healthful functioning

- that we are all capable of being creative when given opportunity and encouragement

- that we are each the best storytellers of our own lives

- that capturing our memories, sensory experiences and personal metaphors in written form increases our self-worth, helps heal psychological wounds and brings fuller meaning to our lives.

In the pages to follow, you will have the opportunity to learn about the practice of *poetry therapy*, or what Arleen McCarty Hynes has called the *interactive process of biblio/poetry therapy* (Hynes and Hynes-Berry 1994). As a practitioner of biblio/poetry therapy, I harness the power inherent in creative writing and shared responding to lyric poems and stories, in order to improve the quality of clients' lives. While lengthy literary works, such as novels and plays, can be quite therapeutic, this book focuses on more concise works that the facilitator can introduce or that participants can write within the therapeutic setting, for a more immediate, spontaneous effect.

I invite you in the pages of this book to discover the rich possibilities of this modality, with its unique features and strategies, and to integrate it into your work responsibly and wisely, taking into account your own levels of training and the particular populations you serve. The material here is meant to be an introduction to the exciting potential of the above mentioned materials and is not intended to provide training in poetry/ bibliotherapy, which involves supervision and guided study.

PART ONE

Poems

Springboards to Growth and Healing

CHAPTER 1

Poetry's Special Healing and Inspirational Role

Healing Poetry and its Historic Roots

The special place of poetry in the history of healing is well established. The shamans and medicine men and women of ancient civilizations chanted poems as a part of their healing art. In ancient Greece, Apollo, the patron god of poetry and music, is also recognized as the divinity of medicine and healing not only in his own right but also through his son, Aesclepius. Through the multifaceted Apollo, poetry is associated with light, sun and prophecy. The Biblical David soothed the cares of Saul with his psalms. Early dramas that provided inspiration and catharsis for entire communities also were performed in poetic form. At the beginning of the early nineteenth century, British Romantic poets such as William Wordsworth, John Keats and Percy Shelley re-energized the deeply inspirational role of poets and poetry.

Poetry's Power in the Present Day

In our own time, there seems to be a resurgence of poetry's presence in the popular imagination and in popular culture. Poetry is alive and well in emotionally charged spoken word competitions, in coffee house gatherings where poems are recited against musical or visual backdrops, in the increasing popularity of poem memorization, and in the growing presence of poems on city streets, nature trails, buses and trains. Almost every time we attend a wedding, funeral or prayer service, we hear aptly chosen, evocative poems, and we repeatedly read newspaper accounts of how catastrophic events elicit poetic outpourings to memorialize and help us cope with trauma.

Rose Solari (1996) conveys a strong sense of the ever widening net poetry is casting for growth and healing in our own time. Solari (1996) points out that:

> poetry is making its way into a number of new fields: Poems and poets can now be found in corporate training sessions, in educational programs for at-risk groups, and in therapy sessions, where social workers, psychologists, and psychiatrists have discovered the healing power of a well-made poem.

According to Solari, 'many seem to agree' that:

> Good poetry, in whatever form, can provide the means for exploring the psychological complexities of our lives, as well as our spiritual yearnings. Today those in psychology and spirituality circles often turn to poetry for enlightenment and guidance. (Solari 1996, pp.25–26)

Poetry as a Vehicle to Insight

Throughout the years, many writers have claimed that poetry provides significant insight into the human psyche and human behavior. For example, in concluding his essay on 'The Psychology of Women,' Sigmund Freud (1933, p.185) asserts that 'If you want to know more about femininity, you must interrogate your own experience, or turn to the poets.' Both Freud's and his disciple Carl Jung's respect for poetry as a cornucopia of significant personal knowledge is eloquently embellished in our own time by two authors whose goal is to bring poetry to the people. In *Poetry for Dummies*, John Timpane and Maureen Watts (2001) describe the wonder of poetry in a way perfectly fitting the world of poetry therapy:

> Suppose you invented a way to concentrate all the best things people ever thought and felt into a very few words. And suppose you *did* something to those words to make them

pleasant, beautiful, unforgettable, and moving. Suppose this invention could get people to notice more of their own lives, sharpen their awareness, pay attention to things they'd never really considered before. Suppose it could make their lives— and them—better. You'd really have something there... What is this fantastic creation? Poetry. (Timpane and Watts 2001, p.1)

Romantic Poets on the Mission of Poetry

The ambitious mission of poetry implied in the above words mirrors the strong messages of English Romantic poets like Keats, Shelley and Wordsworth. In their own ways, chiefly through their poems but also in their prose writings, these authors affirmed poetry's power to guide, illuminate and heal.

In his 'Preface to the Second Edition of Lyrical Ballads,' William Wordsworth (1965d) sets forth the poet's mission as he sees it: to convey the truth of human experience empathically and in accessible language and to 'describe objects, and utter sentiments, of such a nature, in such connection with each other, that the understanding of the Reader must necessarily be in some degree enlightened, and his affections strengthened and purified' (Wordsworth 1965d, p.448).

In Canto One of John Keats' narrative poem, *The Fall of Hyperion: A Dream* (1990a), the poet-persona asserts to the goddess Moneta, mother of the Muses and divinity of memory, 'sure a poet is a sage / A humanist, a Physician to all Men,' and Moneta supports the truth of his statement by fervently replying that the poet is the one who 'pours out a balm upon the world' (Keats 1990a, pp.295–296). When Keats decided to devote himself to poetry instead of medicine, he ended up becoming a poet-healer. He realized that he needed to incorporate pain into his work and transform it through the alchemy of his artistry, into beauty that is truth. His commitment to this task is suggested in these words he wrote to his brothers, George and Tom Keats, in an 1817 letter: 'the excellence of every Art is its intensity, capable of making all disagreeables evaporate, from their being in close relationship with Beauty and Truth' (Keats 1990b, p.370).

After the persona in *The Fall of Hyperion* convinces Moneta that he is indeed a poet, he not only is allowed to ascend the colossal stairway, but also reaches a height from where he views a vast arena of grief. As he watches the fallen Titans, he is seared by his empathetic response. The poet's reaction is viscerally captured in the following lines describing Saturn:

> *Degraded, cold, upon the sodden ground*
> *His old right hand lay nerveless, listless, dead,*
> *Unsceptred; and his realmless eyes were clos'd,*
> *While his bow'd head seem'd listening to the Earth,*
> *His ancient mother, for some comfort yet.*

(Keats 1990a, p.299)

Nearly two centuries after these lines were written, they eloquently embody the pain of individuals who have lost their 'kingdoms' in one way or another. When I was counseling a young man who was experiencing his mother's lengthy battle with cancer, he resonated deeply with the above depiction of Saturn's state. Like Saturn, he too was losing his realm of the familiar.

Keats' contemporary, Percy Bysshe Shelley, defined his role as poet-healer or guide in a more overt way than did Keats. In his essay, *A Defence of Poetry*, Shelley (1967) focuses on the regenerative force of poetry for individuals and entire societies. He claims that 'Poetry is ever accompanied with pleasure: all spirits on which it falls, open themselves to receive the wisdom which is mingled with its delight.' He adds that poetry 'awakens and enlarges the mind' and 'lifts the veil from the hidden beauty of the world' (Shelley 1967, pp.11–12). At the conclusion of his 'Ode to the West Wind,' Shelley's (1993) poet-persona suggests his role as master-therapist when he prays for the power to disseminate seeds to regenerate new possibilities in humankind. Shelley's metaphor is particularly apt when we consider the fact that the original Greek root of the word, therapist, is linked to the midwife role in the birthing process.

Poets and Their Poems as Counselors

These words of Elizabeth Drew (1959) help to explain why poems can be so empowering: 'The poets find the right words in the right order for what we already dimly and dumbly feel, and they also fertilize in our consciousness responses which were lying inert and cloddish' (p.32).

Like Drew, poetry therapists recognize that untold numbers of poets are unwittingly acting as counselors for people they will never meet or see.

Wordsworth, in fact, functioned as an unwitting therapist for the famous essayist statesman, John Stuart Mill. In his *Autobiography*, Mill (1993) recounts details of the severe depression he experienced when he was a young man in the years 1826 to 1827. Alarmed at his extreme dejection and total lack of emotion, he turned to the poets, Wordsworth and Coleridge, in particular, to help himself. Mill was relieved to discover fitting descriptions of his own suffering in Coleridge's 'Dejection Ode,' a somber yet moving poem that captures its creator's own despair and loss of creativity. More importantly, Mill's reading also included the emotional utterances of Wordsworth, through which Mill tells us, he discovered a cure. Although he 'took up his collection of poems from curiosity, with no expectation of mental relief from it' (Mill 1993, p.1027), he found to his surprise that Wordsworth's poems, especially those conveying the beauty and grandeur of Nature, helped him regain hope (p.1028). He pays homage to the effect of these poems in the following terms:

> What made Wordsworth's poems a medicine for my state of mind, was that they expressed, not mere outward beauty, but states of feeling, and of thought colored by feeling, under the excitement of beauty. They seemed to be the very culture of feelings, which I was in quest of. In them I seemed to draw from a source of inward joy, of sympathetic and imaginative pleasure, which could be shared in by all human beings; ... And I felt myself at once better and happier as I came under their influence...I needed to be made to feel that there was real, permanent happiness in tranquil contemplation. Wordsworth taught me this. (Mill 1993, p.1028)

In asserting the healer's territory for the poet, American literary icon, Robert Frost, is akin to his Romantic predecessors and Mill, even if his claims are more moderately expressed. Frost (1972) tells us that a poem 'ends in a clarification of life' and can be 'a momentary stay against confusion.' But Frost goes further in asserting a powerful connection between poet and reader, when he notes that a poem 'must be a revelation, or a series of revelations, as much for the poet as for the reader' (Frost 1972, pp.393–4).

The Intimate Link Between Poet and Reader

In *How to Read a Poem*, Molly Peacock (1999) also captures the link between poet and reader when she notes that we are sometimes 'attracted to a poem because it makes us feel as if someone is listening to us.' She describes the effect of reading poems special to us in these words: 'As you meet your own experience through someone else's articulation of it, you are refreshed by having a companion in your solitude' (Peacock 1999, p.14). Peacock articulates what I and so many individuals doing similar work encounter repeatedly. Clients and group members will often say with wonder and relief, 'Wow, this poem is about me,' or 'This is my life described here!'

Throughout the centuries, poetry has occupied a special place in the human psyche. Individuals living in different times and places have highlighted the unique ways in which poems forge deep connections with their readers, arousing them on many different levels. Repeatedly and in passionate terms, poets and other writers have attested to the power of poetry to awaken our minds and spirits, soothe our hearts and even transform the course of our lives.

CHAPTER 2

Therapeutic Features of Poetry

An Authentic Voice Inviting Reader Engagement

The intimate connection between the poet's voice and the reader or listener is at the core of what makes poetry such a valuable resource for helpers in the service of their clients. The persona of so many poems seems to communicate directly with us in passionate conversation. Poems embody the presence of an authentic voice speaking to us across time and space, often in throes of emotion and at an important juncture.

Concise lyrical expressions, confessional and personal in tone, tend to grab and hold a reader's attention as they speak to the senses, mind and heart. There is an immediacy to so many poems that causes many to refer to them as *experiences* rather than works of art. The active experience of poetry reading is well captured by Nikki Giovanni (2003b, p.221) when she defines a poem as 'pure energy' that is 'horizontally contained / between the mind / of the poet and the ear of the reader.'

The instant establishment of a connection between the persona's voice and the reader is well illustrated in 'Marks,' which Linda Pastan, in her 2009 keynote address to the National Association for Poetry Therapy, described as her 'most popular poem.' In it, the speaker confides in us as readers, immediately allowing us into her world. With a healthy blend of humor and serious content, she employs an everyday metaphor that anyone who has received grades or been judged can appreciate.

My husband gives me an A
for last night's supper,
an incomplete for my ironing,
a B plus in bed.
My son says I am average,
an average mother, but if
I put my mind to it
I could improve.
My daughter believes
in Pass/Fail and tells me
I pass. Wait 'til they learn
I'm dropping out.

(Pastan 1982, p.69)

From the very first line, readers usually sign on to the persona's situation, living through their own experiences of being evaluated by others. Reacting to the last line, readers almost always exclaim with laughter, relief or surprise. The journey to which this poem summons the reader proves irresistible time and again.

The reader's immediate personal engagement with Pastan's speaker can be illuminated in terms of a phenomenon that Norman Stageberg and Wallace Anderson (1952) call 'The Poem Within,' described as follows:

> When we read a poem something happens within us. The words on the page awaken a response: they bring to life a group of images, feelings and thoughts. The nature of these is determined (1) by our own past experiences with the words, and (2) by our present mental and emotional set. This response within us—the experience caused by the words—*is* the poem. (Stageberg and Anderson 1952, p.5)

While neither of these writers are counselors, they pinpoint a crucial fact for us to keep in mind when we use poems for growth and healing, that the 'real' poem is the one 'experienced within the reader' (Stageberg and Anderson 1952, p.5).

When participants in my groups read Pastan's 'Marks' (1982), the 'poems within' are richly varied. While one self-satisfied individual sees her past self who used to worry about what everyone thought, another sees his present anxious self who wishes to perform perfectly in every situation. For some, this poem evokes images of an overloaded schedule or the bitterness of a legacy left by an overly critical family, while for others, 'the poem within' primarily engages the rebellious self who stands ready to defy others' expectations. Pastan's ending invites explorations of what 'dropping out' of a world dominated by judgments can look like. When Pastan discussed this poem in the above mentioned talk, she noted that it actually inspired one reader to leave her marriage and that she did find happiness in a second marriage. While responders to this poem that I know have not had such a dramatically life-changing reaction, they do find relief in the possibility that one doesn't have to take others' 'grading' so seriously. If we consider that getting grades is about someone else's power in our lives, the words, spoken in a confidential whisper to the reader, 'wait 'til they hear I'm dropping out' (Pastan 1982, p.69) overturn that power differential. This recouping of one's equality with others perhaps explains why these lines, more often than not, have such an energizing effect.

A Concise Form Loaded with Choice Words

As concise forms, lyric poems are loaded with a rich loam of language. We can read or listen to a poem within a few minutes, caught instantaneously by its shower of words. Yet, we can also savor it, reading or hearing it repeatedly, so that it delights and enlightens us again and again. A poem introduced to me by one of my poetry therapy trainees provides a good example here. Entitled 'Love the Winter' (2009), it is an anonymous, simplified spin-off of Thomas Merton's 'Love the Winter When the Plant Says Nothing' (2005) and can be found on the internet (Anonymous 2009). Using Merton's evocative title words, this poem, reprinted below, contains images which are both luminous and instantaneous in their effect, particularly for those of us who are not fond of winter. Even though there is an ostensible lack of vitality in the season described here, we can still use our senses, move our bodies to its rhythm and find much to celebrate.

> *Love the winter,*
> *when the plant says nothing.*
> *In this mystic season, I want to remember*
> *to unplug the flashing lights*
> *and sip the long evenings,*
> *to breathe in the moon,*

dance in the dark,
to love this winter nothing.

(Anonymous 2009)

Merging the Mundane with the Marvelous

Another definitive and potentially therapeutic element of poetry is its ingenious way of forging links between the mundane and the marvelous. For Dennis Patrick Slattery (1999, p.41), 'Poetry has the capacity and power to focus the imagination on the particular and specific things of the world and through its language, stir the soul to see the ordinary in extraordinary ways.' Slattery's words call to mind Emily Dickinson's definition of the poet as one who 'Distills amazing sense' from 'ordinary Meanings' and an 'Attar so immense' from an often unnoticed 'familiar species' of flower growing right by our door (Dickinson 1961b, p.106).

Evocative Sense Images and Figurative Language

One of the reasons why poetry is so at home in the therapeutic setting is that everyday material is transformed, in often surprisingly delightful ways, through the alchemy of sense images and figurative language. The essence of poetry's power to grab our attention, in my opinion, stems from its striking word combinations and the ways in which it evokes sights, sounds, smells, tastes and visceral reactions. Poems thus tend to engage not only our intellect but our emotions and physical being, all at the same time.

In his 'Ars Poetica,' Archibald MacLeish (1987) captures poetry's sensory vitality and highlights the condensing power of figurative language, when he compares a poem to 'a globed fruit' and epitomizes a world of sorrows with images of 'an empty doorway' and 'a maple leaf' (MacLeish 1987, p.140).

Like image, metaphor itself can be considered the essence of poetry and viewed as the crossroads where image and idea intersect. As a Greek word, metaphor means to 'carry over.' The connotations and features of an image 'carry over' to color the idea in innovative and vivid ways that drive home its meaning to the reader. Carl Sandburg (1969a, p.319) tells us that 'Poetry is the establishment of a metaphorical link between white butterfly wings and scraps of torn-up love-letters.' As this metaphor shows, the image-idea link activates both our sense perceptions and our imaginations.

Poetry's characteristically metaphorical language forges unusual links, often catapulting us into new awareness and bypassing the logical, walled-up self. For example, when we read of Sandburg's 'torn-up love letters,' we simultaneously envision graceful, fluttering, free-wheeling butterflies. In an instant, the sorrow and anger of lost love magically merge with joyous, carefree movement. Without thinking, we experience how renewal is possible.

Fresh metaphors, like the one created by Sandburg, shake up our old ways of seeing things and thus are very effective agents in the therapeutic process. According to Richard R. Kopp (1995), 'metaphoric interventions are especially well-suited to the therapeutic task of creating new patterns and connections' and metaphors are 'powerful vehicle[s] for therapeutic work' because 'they combine two modes of cognition— logical and imaginal' (Kopp 1995, pp.97, 94).

Patricia Fargnoli's 'Going' (1999), quoted below, provides an excellent illustration of a poem combining sense imagery with original, accessible metaphors that evoke feelings, thoughts, and memories. On a first reading, it grabbed my attention. Here lucid and vivid images capture elements of a family drama that reach across time and space. The direct address to 'you,' the parent, heightens the effect of this poem's captivating imagery. Conveying the parents' experiences directly and depicting the children's lives somewhat less directly, this poem spreads a wide net in terms of the audience it reaches. Over and over again, I have witnessed a degree of reader engagement with it that seems to match my own.

> *The children walk off*
> *into crowds of strangers,*
> *their laces are tied,*
> *their backs straight.*
> *They wave to you*
> *from platforms you cannot reach.*
> *You want to hang on.*
> *Running after them,*
> *you thrust out small packages:*
> *vitamins, a new blouse, guilt,*
> *But they keep discarding*

your dreams for their own.
They carry your admonitions
in their pockets
and their children will sing
your lullabies,
so that, finally, knowing this,
you let go.
They blur, fade.
You settle back.
The years pass, silent as clouds.
Sundays, they come for dinner,
serve up slices of their lives,
but it's not the same.
Sometimes, in a crowd,
You will catch a glimpse
of long braids,
a ribbon streaming,
and you will remember—
a head beneath your hand,
a quilt tucked in,
small things snapping on a line.

(Fargnoli 1999, p.10)

If we look for a moment at the images in the above poem, we see that the power lies in the unique combinations of ordinary words, combinations that grip our senses, taking us physically to concrete places and times of life's developmental transitions. For example, the experience of maturing offspring no longer needing daily parental care is immediately evoked when we see these 'children' walking off into 'crowds of strangers' with 'laces' that are 'tied' and 'backs' that are 'straight.' The blending of 'vitamins,' 'a new blouse' and 'guilt' as parting parental gifts encompasses a heady brew in which family nurturing, legacies and dysfunction comingle. When the young people 'carry' their parents' 'admonitions in their pockets,' these warnings take on a presence at our finger tips, and when the sons and daughters 'serve up slices of their lives' at weekly dinners, leaving the whole rest of the pie off the table, that sense of so much withheld, is palpable. When the parents 'catch a glimpse of long braids' and recall 'small things snapping on a line,' readers are invited into a sensory experience that smacks of grief and wistful remembrance.

The Resonance and Repetition of Rhythm and Sound

Like images and figurative language, the rhythm and sounds with their pitch, resonance and repetition also powerfully act upon us when we are introduced to a poem. A poem's rhythms catch us unawares below the surface of the intellect. In the same way that our breathing and heartbeats give life to our body, so too does the rhythm of a poem animate its words. In *Responses to Poetry*, Alberta Turner (1990, p.129) tells us that 'Rhythm and the variations of rhythm have worked to emphasize feeling ever since human beings have had bodies to move and feelings to move them in repeated patterns.' Turner also refers to 'emphasis' achieved through 'sound repetition' and points out that 'The sounds of words affect feeling more than meaning' (1990, p.154). In summarizing the responses they received on the beneficial effects of poetry, Robin Philipp and Imogen Robertson (1996, p.332) report that 42 percent or 83 out of 196 respondents 'spontaneously reported that reading poetry helped them by incantation of rhythm, silent or aloud.'

The attraction of the lines from 'Love the Winter,' quoted earlier in this chapter, comes not only from its images but also from its sound effects and subtle rhythms. When we savor the liquid music of the words, 'sip the long evenings' and vicariously move to the tranquil pace of the phrase, 'dance in the dark,' we have a chance to discover joy even in the dreariest of seasons.

In Pastan's poem, 'Marks' (1982), one of the reasons why the ending almost always elicits a strong reaction also relates to rhythm. While virtually the whole poem lists, in an almost monotone way, situations where the persona is being graded, the last sentence, spread across the final two lines, grabs our attention because of the way the words are placed and the rhythm pattern our voice creates when we read them:

> ... *Wait 'til they learn*
> *I'm dropping out.*

> (Pastan 1982, p.69)

White Space and Silence

The set up of lines upon a page, with white spaces and pauses created by punctuation and line endings, is important in subtle ways. These determine the very tempo of our breathing, invite us to stop and contemplate, live in the silence, or fill in a gap. The significance of white space is highlighted by Gillie Bolton (2004, p.110) when she notes that 'These white spaces are silences which contain elements of the explored images and metaphors which could not be written.' Her words suggest why it is important to give readers of a poem in a therapeutic setting both time and space to read between the lines.

Through what is present and what is left to the imagination, poems open up a magical universe to their readers, one that interweaves the ordinary with the extraordinary in unique and striking ways. In the presence of a poetic speaker who voices his or her truth, readers take part in an intimate conversation and experience language that appeals to their senses, feelings and thoughts. Poetry derives its distinctive therapeutic power from several salient characteristic features involving choice of speaker, sense imagery, metaphorical links and various types of sound effects.

CHAPTER 3

Choosing Therapeutic Poems for Your Files

The features that help define the power of poetry, as described in Chapter 2, are all taken into account when we make decisions on what poems to include in our therapy files and what poems best fit the people we are helping. As Arleen McCarty Hynes and Mary Hynes-Berry point out in their book, *Biblio/Poetry Therapy: The Interactive Process* (1994), the selection process is a significant aspect of the biblio/poetry therapist's responsibilities and actually consists of two separate processes. The first is the act of choosing *potentially* healing and growth-enhancing materials as resources to draw upon. The second is what Hynes and Hynes-Berry (1994) call the 'strategic choice' of materials for specific populations of clients. Both types of activities require reflection, judgment, patience, time, and knowledge of various resources and search engines.

Those of us who introduce selected poems for growth and healing build up an extensive collection of healing poems to draw upon in our work. You may choose to have electronic files and/or paper files, but either way, it is crucial to find an organizational scheme that works for you. I organize my files by themes and emotions, and when poems fit into a variety of categories, I make duplicate copies to place in separate files. Having ready access to these materials when you need them is crucial.

Questions to Ask When Evaluating Poems

When evaluating which poems are appropriate ones for your therapy files, there are two basic questions to ask:

1. What qualities does a therapeutic poem have?

2. What do you imagine is this poem's potential as a therapeutic tool or catalyst?

In *Poetry Therapy: Theory and Practice*, Nicholas Mazza (2003, Appendix A) presents a list of 16 useful questions that he recommends practitioners ask themselves about specific poems and other literary works, as a part of their training, their own self-awareness work and their readiness for the important selection process. Besides asking about your own 'personal reaction' to the work, Mazza includes such questions as 'What types of problems does this poem address?' 'Is there a part of this poem that you would like to change?' and 'Can you identify any potential harmful effects in using this poem with a client?' In his list, Mazza even invites poetry/bibliotherapy trainees to draw a picture in response to the poem and write a letter to the poet (Mazza 2003, p.149).

Criteria to Consider

According to Hynes and Hynes-Berry (1994, p.65), desirable poems for your therapy or support group files are succinct and of manageable length, convey universal experiences or emotions, offer some degree of hope and contain sound effects, striking imagery and clear language.

Alberta Turner's (1990) list of 'the universal reader's request of poets' is also useful as criteria for choosing growth-enhancing poems:

1. Tell me about something that I have already experienced and therefore I am already concerned about.

2. Tell it in such a way that you stimulate my feelings.

3. Tell me in a way that I can understand and remember.

4. Show me by the way you tell it what kind of person you are, so that I can decide whether I can trust you.

(Turner 1990, p.6)

Accessibility and Universal Appeal

As the above lists of criteria suggest, a poem that is accessible, clear, emotionally engaging and memorable will be one that you want to include in your files. Gladys Wellington's 'I Wanted to Be a Cauliflower' (1977), mentioned in the Introduction, provides an example of a poem with widespread appeal, compelling imagery and attention-getting metaphors:

> I wanted to be a cauliflower
> when I was a child
> so my mother would love me.
> I too, was bland
> like her favorite vegetable,
> with no hollandaise
> to give me verve,
> but she looked past me
> to my sister
> who led a pastrami life
> all over the world.
>
> Years have passed,
> the pastrami's turned green,
> and I've found a bit
> of sauce for myself,
> so now when my mother
> comes to visit,
> I offer her hot chili peppers.

(Wellington 1977, p.92)

This poem occupies a special place in my poetry therapy files because it is filled with potential material for a therapeutic discussion of identity issues and relationships between family members. The division between the past and present self sets up a very useful distinction, inviting the reader to perceive the place of change and maturation. With its playful and accessible figurative language, it mixes the serious with the humorous. Its ambiguous ending, which raises the question of what it means to 'offer' your 'mother' 'hot chili peppers,' fosters a range of responses that more often than not reflect readers' backgrounds and biases. For example, while some assume the daughter is punishing her mother, others view her as adding excitement to a parent's drab life. The latter group of readers may even see the daughter as trying to enrich her mother's life with extra flavor. While some imagine that the daughter remains hurt by her past neglect or may still be trying to catch her mother's attention, most readers express their view that the daughter has discovered her own personality and is simply sharing her new spicy element with her mother.

While some readers, attuned to classic literature, initially find the previous poem frivolous in its image choices, it does seem to regularly elicit significant personal reactions. In contrast, obscure materials with esoteric word choices and archaic allusions will tend to deaden the effect of a poem and even more seriously feed the fears and aversions that so many people have acquired from poetry classes in their academic background. Since promoting self-esteem and fostering empowerment are crucial to any helping process, introducing poems difficult to understand will be counterproductive. Moreover, very complex poems tend to encourage intellectualized responses. Participants may start working hard to figure out the puzzle of the poem's meaning, and as they display their mental prowess, forget or avoid their personal reactions.

William Butler Yeats' 'Sailing to Byzantium' (1996b) is a good example of a poem whose allusions and complexities make it inappropriate as therapeutic material for most readers. While it may be a brilliant poem in many ways, much of its content makes it inaccessible to a great many people. For example, encountering such phrases as 'Monuments of unageing intellect,' 'perne in a gyre' and 'artifice of eternity' (Yeats 1996b, p.193) the average reader can get lost in the poem's heady intellectualism. Words such as these tend to block our spontaneous, personal reaction to the poem.

There are, however, poems, that despite some complex word usage, have so many other redeeming qualities. With poems such as these, readers may have a strong intuitive, emotional reaction that they do not fully understand, and they can be encouraged to trust the 'poem within' that emerges.

Hy Sobiloff's 'My Mother's Table' (1954), reproduced here, provides a good example of a complex poem that we may not comprehend in its entirety, yet contains enough positive features to make it a worthwhile addition to the poetry therapist's files. The poem's speaker begins with an evocative image of his mother's table and presents a family in which the children seem to be hungry, demanding and competitive. In this crowded and perhaps suffocating household, the speaker craves privacy, jealously guards his desserts and invents a language of his own. The poem's final ten lines begin to become more elusive in meaning as the speaker refers to leaving home. He mentions an unidentified 'they' who 'erected fences.' He subtly suggests his adult years when he speaks of having 'crossed out chimneys and attics,' but the reader is left to puzzle over exactly what he means. The poem's final two lines also contain imagery that may be difficult to grasp; nevertheless, they provide a closing that is both powerful and thought-provoking.

> *My mother's table was round like her face*
> *Round and covered with fingerstains*
> *And crumbs that stuck to my fingertips.*
> *At that table each child wanted everything:*
> *My father gave everything, emptied himself*
> *Into the pockets round my mother's table.*
> *We ate hard crust and made a hatbrim of hard crust,*
> *Ate each other around my mother's table.*
> *Ashamed to age alone,*
> *My sister cried for too many dresses,*
> *Grabbed for my dessert,*
> *But I hid my chocolate under my pillow,*
> *Stalked about the bedpost*
> *Disappeared among the beams in our attic.*
> *I counted my fingers and toes like a miser*
> *Shouted to myself in my own language.*
> *I grew by making promises to myself;*
> *In lonely baths the fear of love became my religion.*
> *Then one year they erected new fences for me to climb,*
> *Prepared sticks and stones to destroy me*
> *And I flew off at a tangent from my mother's round table.*
> *The hobby horses were playing*
> *And my childhood carousel*
> *Was still a familiar wonderland,*
> *But when I crossed out chimneys and attics*
> *The world became a strange neighborhood*
> *Where I climbed a ladder of birthdays,*
> *Reading my father's face.*

(Sobiloff 1954, p.15)

Years ago when I first introduced this poem in a class on family relationships, I was struck by how fully engaged the readers were, despite their lack of total understanding. Many of these students came from large families, and when they read Sobiloff's lines, they conversed energetically on how they learned to share or hoard attention and possessions in their families of origin. They visualized their family tables, and the roles that each family member played as they sat eating dinner. A great many students responded to the image of the father 'empty[ing] himself' into metaphorical 'pockets' gathered at the table. These words elicited personal discussions of childhood allowances, times of financial scarcity and parents' sacrificing behavior. When students addressed the poem's final ten lines, they began attempting to solve an intellectual puzzle instead of staying on a personal level. However, even these enigmatic lines came alive for them in a more meaningful way when I invited them to react to the sensory words there, with their physical being and imagination, rather than their intellect.

The Issue of Originality

At the other end of the spectrum from complex poems, are those that are overly simplistic and filled with clichés. We are all probably familiar with such works, ones that tell us that if we maintain a positive attitude, the sun will shine for us always, or use words like 'stop and smell the roses' to encourage us to bring balance into our lives. Like the very esoteric poems with their formidable allusions and archaic language, these too are not usually appropriate for effective therapeutic change. While such works are not likely to endanger a client's self-esteem, they do not tend to engage clients in ways that help them grow. Alberta Turner (1990, p.62) tells us, 'A felt idea that you consider too shallow or obvious or overfamiliar will probably not receive your admiration.' While Turner seems to focus here on a poem's literary quality, we can view the superficial or unoriginal work as not evoking much reaction and not challenging the reader to think in new ways.

Stageberg and Anderson (1952) suggest the therapeutic power of original, evocative poems as opposed to hackneyed ones in the following words:

> Poems that are stock responses in themselves are often popular
> with uncritical readers. They touch off familiar feelings that

are pleasant to experience; they require no troublesome mental adjustments; they are easy, lazy reading. The objection to them is that we are no better off after having read them; they do not help us to escape from an experiential and emotive rut; they do not provide us with new norms of perceiving and feeling that make possible finer experiences in the future. (Stageberg and Anderson 1952, pp.25–26)

To illustrate the shortcomings of cliché, let us think of words many of us have heard, such as 'you have to learn to love yourself before you can love others or be loved by others.' While there is sound advice here, these words do not tend to stir us at all or have much impact. But if we are presented with a poem like Lucille Clifton's 'what the mirror said' (1987), we hear the speaker tell herself she is 'a city / of a woman' with 'a geography' for which 'somebody' will 'need a map' and 'directions' (Clifton 1987, p.169). With simple yet creative language, Clifton gives the reader a unique image of positive self-regard to visualize and enjoy.

As Stageberg and Anderson (1952) suggest, cliché poems with a simple message can comfort, and as such, they cannot be categorically ignored by the poetry therapist. Often clients will bring in such works, indicating that they display them on their wall or refrigerator, to be read as often as possible. They also state that these works have helped them through a tough time. As counselors, we need to respect these choices.

Keeping an Open Mind

I have learned to keep an open mind when considering which works to add to my pharmacy of poems. There are some poems that I have not initially considered appropriate for growth and healing, but through the years have noted the positive reactions of others to these works. Two examples of such poems are William Ernest Henley's 'Invictus' (1965) and Dylan Thomas' 'Do Not Go Gently' (1957).

As a student and specialist of nineteenth-century British literature, I had read 'Invictus' but never resonated with it personally. While vaguely recognizing its inspirational tone, I, along with many of my peers, considered it pompous and melodramatic. Yet as my father grew older, experiencing much loss and distress, he repeatedly referred to this poem, focusing in particular on the lines, 'Under the bludgeonings of chance / My head is bloody but unbowed' (Henley 1965, p.794). As he recited

Henley's poem from memory, he also found the notion of 'Being the captain of [his] soul' (p.794) enormously appealing. This poem was so special to him that I chose to have it read at his funeral. Since that time, I have learned that a good friend's father felt equally moved by this work, citing it as one of his two favorites. Recently, my growing positive evaluation of this poem returned to me in full force when I was viewing Clint Eastwood's film, *Invictus* (2009), which focuses on Nelson Mandela's life. The poem constitutes the centerpiece of this film, for it was one that particularly inspired Mandela. The special place of this poem in his life is captured by the actor (Morgan Freeman) playing Mandela. He says that its words 'helped me to stand when all I wanted to do was lie down.' Mandela asserts that its powerful sentiments helped him survive his 27-year incarceration. He even gives the South African rugby team's captain a copy of the poem to help him defy the odds and bring home a victory for his nation.

The second poem, 'Do Not Go Gently,' has always conveyed to me images of an anguished son or daughter telling his or her father to fight oncoming death. For me, this poem was primarily a series of pleas uttered in distress and conjured up pictures of a very unquiet passing. However, because this poem has repeatedly turned up as the centerpiece of memorial services and funerals through the years, I have had to ask myself what constitutes the comfort emerging from Thomas' words. While I have not fully answered this question, I recognize that the poem vividly captures what so many mourners experience—a passionate craving to keep a beloved person away from death's door. At one time or another, we all find ourselves 'raging against the dying of the light' (Thomas 1957, p.128), and words such as these can be enormously cathartic and appealing in ways we may not fully comprehend.

The Usefulness of Ambiguity

At times, we might question using poems whose ambiguity leaves us with more questions than answers. However, poems whose words carry multiple meanings are often quite therapeutic because individual readers can apply their own interpretations. An example of such rich ambiguity occurs in Robert Frost's poem, 'The Road Not Taken' (1979b), an American classic that has been used countless times in a therapeutic context. When readers respond to the last two lines, 'I took the road less travelled by,/ And that has made all the difference' (Frost 1979b, p.105), some view the choice that the persona made as positive while others hear regret. The ambiguity in these words is even more pronounced when we consider earlier lines where the two diverging paths are first described. The fact that both paths are 'worn…really about the same' (p.105) suggests that both the alternatives faced by the persona may have actually involved charting new ground, in spite of the wording he uses in his conclusion.

Free Verse and Traditional Forms

Modern and contemporary poetic expressions written in free form constitute the bulk of choices for my poetry therapy files. However, lyric poems written many years ago or those written in traditional forms such as sonnets, villanelles or odes can be appropriate therapeutic choices if they present universal themes and do not distract readers with their archaic word order or language.

For example, my files include William Wordsworth's sonnet, 'The World Is Too Much with Us' (1965g), which begins with the evocative lines, 'Getting and spending we lay waste our powers,/ We see little of Nature that is ours / We have given our hearts away' (1965g, p.182). While there are several allusions to pagan gods and a few old-fashioned words, these can be readily explained, and the sonnet's opening lines make the poem both powerful and accessible to many audiences. In today's world, where so many people suffer stress from overly full schedules and crave a return to a simpler life, Wordsworth's poem remains quite relevant.

Another poem that is useful for today's readers in spite of some archaic wording is John Keats' ode entitled 'To Autumn' (1990d). With its calming tone and rich sensory images of 'mellow fruitfulness' it provides a useful model for individuals creating their own written accounts of this season. For participants coming from a farm or rural community, Keats' images of 'moss'd cottage-trees' that 'bend with apples' and a season that 'swell[s] the gourd, and plump[s] the hazel shells' are familiar in spite of the poem's conventional form and somewhat formal language (Keats 1990d, pp.324–325).

One of the most frequently used villanelles in my poetry files is Elisabeth Bishop's 'One Art' (1983). The line repetitions and rhyme scheme of this elaborate form intensify the dramatic presentation of the poem's major theme, which in this case is loss. As Bishop's persona ticks off a list of things lost from personal items to countries to a special person, the repeated line, 'The art of losing isn't hard to master,' subtly morphs into 'The art of losing's not too hard to master' (Bishop 1983, p.178). This refrain, along with the persona's matter of fact tone, highlights the poem's central irony. While readers are told that coping with life's losses is an easily learned skill, the underlying message is quite the opposite.

Finding a Middle Ground: The Presence of Hope and Mood-Matching

Since poems can be so powerful, it is crucial to avoid using ones that are totally hopeless or likely to augment life-defeating ruminations. For example, works that convey unrelenting despair, cynicism or guilt, or glorify suicide or other forms of violence are not recommended for the poetry therapist's list. However, while poems without any shred of hope are to be avoided in a therapeutic context, effective materials often depict quite a bit of life's pain and contain only a faint modicum of hope. The isoprinciple concept, borrowed from music therapy, involves selecting materials that match the client's mood or state of being. This principle is quite a sound one, for troubled readers usually experience great relief when they encounter a poem that captures so well the tenor of their emotional state. Cheery, overly optimistic poems are likely to be quite inappropriate when chosen for individuals who are hurt, disappointed, angry, anxious or depressed. In fact, such materials tend to discount the reality of these individuals and augment their sense of isolation.

In keeping with the isoprinciple, I even, at times, select a poem that presents raw images of pain, such as Elizabeth Zelvin's 'Coming Apart' (1981). This work is an important addition to my files, despite the fact that it contains some highly unpleasant imagery. What makes this poem so useful is the progression of images that move from disturbing to calming. While the opening stanza bombards us with gut-wrenching details, the second tones down the pain somewhat. And the final stanza presents an almost comforting, yet very physical image of how two people ever so gradually progress toward healing from their separation from one another.

Sometimes it feels
like cutting:
the scalpel peeling back the flesh
slicing away the connective tissue
baring the bones

sometimes it feels
like falling:
a star wrenched from its socket

sometimes it feels
like rubbing:
patient gentle fingers
on the seam that joins us
over and over and over
letting the old glue crumble
so we can come apart.

(Zelvin 1981, p.33)

The isoprinciple in relation to dark material is well illustrated by a vignette that Linda Pastan told during her keynote address at the National Association for Poetry Therapy's conference in April 2009. According to Pastan, a poetry therapist informed her that a Vietnam War veteran was moved to begin telling his traumatic narrative upon hearing Pastan's poem, entitled 'Why Are Your Poems So Dark?' (2003). In this poem, the persona affirms the place of darkness along with the light in our world, and in answer to the question of 'Why are you sad so often,' replies with the words, 'Ask the moon./ Ask what it has witnessed' (Pastan 2003, p.249). With its suggestion that the somber side of our world needs to be acknowledged comes the permission to tell one's own distressing tale.

Poems Chosen as Springboards or Models for Therapeutic Writing

While most of the poems I choose for my files are organized by their predominant mood or subject matter, there is a category of poems in my collection that function primarily as evocative springboards for clients' expressive writing. Because of their basic structure, framework, title, or particular image motif, they provide excellent models. For example, I have works in my files that provide examples of list poems that clients are invited to write in a number of different contexts. One entitled 'Reflections' by Henry Bobotek (2003) contains a long series of 'I prefer...' statements completed with such diverse words as 'tea,' 'birds that cannot fly' and 'uncertainty' (pp.189–190).

Another list poem that I find particularly useful is Anne Waldman's 'Fast Speaking Woman' (1996). This is a lengthy work, so I usually introduce only about 20 lines of it. In rapid tempo, the speaker reels off an abundance of statements beginning with the words, 'I'm a _____ woman' and inserts a wide array of unrelated and often illogical descriptors such as 'abalone,' 'vagabond,' and 'shouting.' She varies this framework with another set of words, 'I'm the woman with _____,' also completing each of these sentences with a string of disconnected and thought-provoking words, such as 'keys,' or 'glue' (Waldman 1996, pp.3–5). This poem's breathless, freewheeling, and disjointed quality, along with its simple framework, leads to spontaneous outpourings that are almost always both playful and illuminating. For males in my practice, I find that modifying the Waldman's sentence stems to 'I'm a _____ man' or 'I'm the man with _____' works very well. In my practice, I also have discovered that this poem effectively functions as a model for individuals from a wide range of age groups as well.

Somewhat akin to the list poem, Miroslav Holub's 'Door' (1990, p.64) contains five repetitions of the line, 'Go and open the door.' This work occupies an honored place in my files because the door image is such a fruitful and universal one. Opening doors is a fertile metaphor for those adjusting to life transitions, exploring risk-taking behavior, or focusing on privacy or boundary issues.

Built on repetition like the 'Door' poem is Rudyard Kipling's 'If' (1989). Addressed to the speaker's son, Kipling's poem is comprised of twelve 'If' statements and a two-line conclusion which sums up what can happen if the listener takes his father's advice seriously. For example, the poem's opening statement is 'If you can keep your head when all about you / Are losing theirs' and its closing words promise a great deal: 'Yours is the Earth and everything that's in it,/ And—which is more—you'll be a Man, my son!' (Kipling 1989, p.578). When I use this poem in my practice, I present it as a model, not for an advice poem like Kipling's, but for a poem of personal empowerment. I present Kipling's 'If' to illustrate the writing of an 'If You Can' list poem that repeats a series of sentences using the framework, 'If you can... then...' For each of these sentences, the writer inserts a different verb to follow the word 'can,' wrapping up each thought with a conclusion that begins with the word, 'then.' When I invite clients to generate this series of hypothetical or wishful statements, their imaginations are engaged in their own option-building or dream-making process.

The following anonymous poem called 'Then and Now: The State of Things' employs a very useful framework. The words, 'I used to be…' introduce the first stanza, while the words, 'Now I am…' begin stanza two. In this sample, the predominating metaphors are place names.

> I used to be California. I was everything
> to everybody except something to myself.
> I used to be New York. I was tiringly
> impressive, pretentious, hard metal, too busy.
> I used to be Alaska. I was hard to get to,
> unapproachable, they only guessed at how wild.
>
> Now I am Columbus, Ohio. I am comfortably
> cultured, a healthy mix of cow and opera; I
> have everything and I'm discovering myself,
> and being discovered.

In a playful yet meaningful way, the writer of the above 'Then and Now' poem embellishes his or her chosen location metaphors within each stanza. While participants may wish to also use place names in their own writings, I often provide additional options. I suggest categories of metaphors, such as types of vehicles, buildings, foods, colors, or articles of clothing. When clients create their own two-stanza poetic expressions modeled after the above poem, they have an opportunity to embody and discover significant change in themselves.

Charles R. Brown's poem, 'We Are Not Hen's Eggs' (1974) is a very apt work for introducing a color metaphor that nearly everyone can appreciate. Brown's work celebrates the fact that we are all unique and valuable, as together we comprise a rainbow of hues. Its concluding lines constitute the perfect writing invitation:

> Take your own color
> in the pattern and be just that.

(Brown 1974, p.76)

Like color images, food images are accessible to all and readily engage most individuals. 'Parsley' by Jeannette Ferrary (2004) provides a model for using food metaphors in order to pursue a poetic journey of discovery. Beginning with the line, 'I wouldn't want to be Parsley,' the speaker describes this bit of greenery as sitting on 'the edges of platters' and being 'picked off' as it lies 'seductively on the carrots.' While poor 'parsley' is relegated to a life of secondary roles, the creator of this image can blatantly reject parsley's world when she concludes her writing with the words, 'I wouldn't want to be her' (pp.170–171).

With its blend of humor and defiance, this poem seems to resonate with most readers, and when they are invited to use its framework 'I wouldn't want to be...' along with a disliked food of their choosing, they usually mobilize their feisty side. Time and again, I have seen individuals energized, relieved and edified by this writing activity as they create their own scenarios with entertaining food imagery. For example, in one staff group at a psychiatric clinic, participants chose foods such as lima beans and tofu and were delighted to vigorously reject what they found disgusting. Others, however, could see how the personal features they assigned to these unsavory foods were ones they had spent time denying in their lives. Some even realized that these traits were elements of a shadow side they needed to explore more fully and incorporate into an expanded view of self.

The last type of poem that functions for me primarily as a resource to stimulate therapeutic writing activities involves a focus on objects. Ruth Fainlight's 'Handbag' (1983) is an excellent resource, recounting, in a rich, sensory way, the items that the persona finds in her mother's worn purse. I frequently employ this poem as a springboard to a writing activity inviting participants to capture an item belonging to a significant person from their past. Respondents to this poem often begin sharing their own vivid childhood memories of playing with their mother's purse and discovering the treasures it contained. Others focus on the wartime letters that the mother in the poem kept for many, many years. Fainlight's work illustrates how we can write in a detailed way about seemingly ordinary things to arrive at deeply held truths and feelings about people in our lives. It suggests that a person's belongings can tell us so much about that individual and also about our own attitudes toward that person.

As you can see from the above criteria for including or excluding particular poems for your therapy files, the process of collecting appropriate materials is complex and multi-faceted. As we discover poems drawn from a variety of sources, it is important to keep in mind the basic therapeutic features of poetry set forth in the previous chapter and to take into account each poem's degree of complexity, universality and originality. In our role as helpers, we need to walk the middle ground between choosing materials that elicit some degree of hope and materials that affirm the reality of life's most trying times. While we basically test the poems we find on our own pulses, imagining, in a very personal way, how effective each one will be for growth and healing purposes, we also need to stay open to others' opinions. We need to take into account our knowledge of the ways in which specific poems have been received over the years and to respect the wide range of tastes in poetic material. It is also useful to have an array of poems on hand that function primarily as models or vehicles for stimulating meaningful creative writing activities.

CHAPTER 4

Selecting Poems for Specific Participants and Settings

Identifying Selection Criteria

With a treasure trove of poems to draw from, the poetry therapist or facilitator goes through an important decision-making process in selecting poems for particular clients. This is a different process than simply gathering poems that you consider inherently or potentially healing. Hynes and Hynes-Berry (1994, p.83) offer very sound advice on the criteria for what they call the 'strategic choice of materials.' Factors to keep in mind include the therapy or growth group goals and participants' developmental stage, present situation, emotional state, predominant set of symptoms, ethnic background, socio-economic status and significant family of origin issues. In addition to these factors, I have found that we, as helpers, also need to take into account the stage of therapy or how long a growth group has been meeting, in order to gauge the degree of trust and safety that has developed.

When selecting poetic materials, it is also important to keep in mind the age range of the population you are helping. For instance, when working with senior citizens, the poems of traditional authors whose words trigger recall are often very welcome. Many elderly individuals have enjoyed reading and even memorizing the work of such poets as William Wordsworth, Henry Wadsworth Longfellow, Alfred Lord Tennyson and Robert Frost, to mention just a few. Since many senior citizens have cultivated gardens in the past, I find that poems with flower imagery are also often good choices. With adolescents, popular rock or rap songs are often quite evocative, with the music adding impact to the printed lyrics.

Matching Poems to Specific Therapeutic Goals

The immediate and long-range goals developed for particular clients or growth groups are key determining factors in the selection of poems. For example, you may be facilitating a support group for recently widowed individuals where the primary goals are to express grief, begin healing from the wounds of loss, reminisce about a deceased family member and begin adjusting to a new life style and sense of self. A poem such as Dorian Kottler's 'LIST For My Father' (1979) is very appropriate for beginning the reminiscence process in the above mentioned group. In it, the speaker tells her deceased father that since he has died, she has 'been coming across' a variety of items that she knows 'would interest [him],' including a magazine article on a topic of scientific interest, a 'gadget for making coffee' and a 'Vivaldi concert.' As she predicts that this list 'will grow longer,' she resolves to keep it available at her desk 'on grief's tall spindle' (Kottler 1979, p.14).

In my opinion, Kottler's poem is congruent with the goals of the grief group because it invites participants to make their own lists of objects, interests and talents that honor the deceased person. This focus constitutes a healthy way of coping with loss. In a gentle way, this poem also suggests how grief comes at us in intermittent flashes when we encounter reminders of the person we have lost. The concluding image of 'grief's tall spindle' affirms how gradual the grieving process can be and debunks those artificial time limits on mourning that do not fit for so many who have lost loved ones.

Denise Levertov's 'Talking to Grief' (2002) is another appropriate choice when the goals relate to grieving. I have used this poem several times in my work with individual clients suffering from the death or terminal illness of a close relative or friend. The speaker of Levertov's poem addresses grief directly with the words, 'Ah, grief, I should not treat you / like a homeless dog' and suggests what she needs to do in order to care for this creature, to claim it as her 'own dog' (Levertov 2002, p.120). With its animal imagery, this poem animates grief and, in an evocative way, recounts how we accept or stifle our emotions when we are wounded by loss.

When I work with individuals who are missing a sense of balance and suffering from fatigue or anxiety due to overload, the goals usually involve reducing stress by exploring ways to prioritize and by discovering tranquil spaces in a hectic daily schedule. In today's world, I find that so many individuals recognize the need to change an unhealthy pattern yet feel stuck in their demanding life style.

Barbara Crooker's 'In the Middle' (2005) is an excellent poem for setting up the theme of time and how we view it. In her opening two lines, she immediately connects to readers in acknowledging how 'complicated' all our lives are and how we are 'struggling for balance, juggling time' (Crooker 2005, p.265). She provides images of stopped clocks, removed watches and seasons speeding by. She also introduces food, pets and the people we love, all in the context of time's rhythms. When I choose this poem to begin a discussion of how we can relax and gain control of our stressful lives, I recognize how Crooker's personification of Time as a live being 'urging us on faster, faster' engages clients to explore the pace of their own lives.

When the specific goal is to help stressed clients or group participants identify their abundant responsibilities and begin the process of prioritizing, Robert Frost's 'The Armful' (1979a) is an ideal choice. 'The Armful' provides an intimate first person voice, is replete with accessible images of overload and is gently forgiving in tone. In this poem, there are crucial details for burdened clients to consider in their own lives. There is the very human and comical, Charlie Chaplin-like image of a person trying to carry too many diverse items. As the speaker tries to add one more, he or she finds that the 'whole pile is slipping' yet expresses reluctance to relinquish any of them. The symbolic quality of these 'parcels' is suggested when the character in the poem refers to 'holding' them with his 'hand' and 'mind / And heart.' After trying to 'prevent' them from tumbling about, this overloaded individual simply sits down in the 'road' right in the midst of all the packages, ready to consider how he or she might 'stack them in a better load' (Frost 1979a, pp.266–267). This unexpected and strangely freeing image brings relief to many individuals and provides a rich source for the poetry therapist to use in his/her facilitation process. Time and again, individuals exclaim with delight and surprise that Frost's words 'tell the story' of their own lives.

Natasha Lynne Vodges' 'Snowbound' (1980) adds another dimension to Frost's poem, so the two are quite complementary in my work. With a set of very accessible images Vodge's poem presents the option of creating space and time for yourself:

> *There is time to stop traveling...*
> *to get off other people's subways*
> *to halt airplanes from landing in your life.*
>
> *A time to refuel yourself.*
>
> *A time to be snowbound*
> *within your own private space*
> *where the only number you dial*
> *is your own.*

(Vodges 1980, p.67)

'Snowbound' is a particularly apt choice if you are working with people who have difficulty saying no to others' requests and have taken on an over-responsible pattern in their lives. In this case, the therapeutic goal involves helping the client develop a sense of balance between the need to help others with the need to care for self.

When I recognize that perfectionism is driving my clients' tendency to over-schedule their days, and the therapy goal is to temper this perfectionism and explore its role in the client's life, I often choose Kate Green's 'Don't Make Your Life Too Beautiful' (1983). This poem asks us not to always rush to fix the broken household items or make everything in our world clean and neat. It invites us to 'Look out the cracked window' for 'There are heartaches enough to live for.' It tells us to 'Live out your ecstasy on earth' (Green 1983, p.62) amid the messes and unfinished business surrounding us. While the unsavory details of this poem may cause the perfectionist to feel discomfort, they provide an effective catalyst to a discussion of whether or not we can tolerate a life with untidy loose ends. It also sets in motion a process whereby the perfectionist can assess the cost of excessive worry over getting things right all the time.

Where the primary goal for anxious or overburdened individuals is to stimulate reflections on calming environments, I find these three nature poems to be particularly appropriate: Wendell Berry's 'The Peace of Wild Things' (1980), William Butler Yeats' 'The Lake Isle at Innisfree' (1996a) and William Wordsworth's 'I Wandered Lonely as a

Cloud' (1965b) discussed in the Introduction and sometimes called the 'Daffodil' poem.

Berry's poem addresses the 'despair' and 'fear' that we need to escape from, and the invitation here is to 'come into the peace of wild things,' where there are herons, wood drakes and 'the presence of still water' (Berry 1980, p.30). 'The Peace of Wild Things' invites us to find our own unspoiled place, an environment where we can enjoy tranquility if even for a short while.

Yeats' poem takes us on a journey to an idyllic place where honey bees, linnets and lapping waters reign, and 'peace comes dropping slow' from the 'veils of morning.' The persona's decision to 'arise and go now' lures us into the poem immediately, and in the end, the persona's memory of this special place stays in the 'deep heart's core' (Yeats 1996a, p.39), even when physically he cannot be there. The effect of bringing a hallowed place of restorative beauty into our daily lives is also present in Wordsworth's (1965b) 'Daffodil' poem, and both works can be used effectively in tandem to help anxious clients find their own special places to carry like a talisman.

When I work with parents of adolescents in either a growth group setting or in individual therapy, there are often these two primary goals: first, to help them balance their desire to be protective with their teen's need for independence, and second, to help them constructively deal with their own and their teen's anger and frustration. In these particular instances, Patricia Goedicke's poem 'Circus Song' (1992) fits both these goals well. Told from the mother's viewpoint with attention-getting imagery, 'Circus Song' presents the struggles and ambivalence of both mother and daughter. The mother describes the daughter as yeasty, sticky dough in her hands but also as a raging circus cat ambivalent about leaving its cage. While the daughter is described as 'trying out [her] weapons,' the mother conveys to her this wise message: 'Sharpening your claws on me first / is how you begin to grow' (Goedicke 1992, pp.23–24).

I found this poem particularly apropos for my family intervention work within a county court system. There I counseled a single mother in her early thirties with a 14-year-old daughter who was already involved in the court system for petty crimes and numerous episodes of running away from home. The mother felt powerless as a parent and was searching for the confidence and information she needed to effectively fulfill her mother role. I decided to share this poem because the persona shows perspective and acceptance while recounting, in a realistic manner, the troubling interactions and power struggles mothers and teen daughters so often experience. My client resonated with the poem, feeling that she was not alone in her plight with her daughter. She was able to articulate how difficult and yet how important it was to allow her daughter to find her unique identity. She was also motivated to talk about ways she could take care of herself when her daughter was lashing out in rebellion.

Although the persona of Goedicke's poem is the parent, I use it at times with adolescent females who are dealing with issues of dependency and individuation and experiencing a mixture of anger, guilt and frustration in their interactions with one or both parents. I ask the client to narrate the poem's scenario from the daughter's point of view, creating a story that not only employs images from the poem but also includes others of her choosing.

When in a couples session, I counsel parents who are primarily concerned with their teenage son's or daughter's rebellious behavior, I often select Kahlil Gibran's poetic piece 'On Children' from *The Prophet* (1971a). I find this poem particularly appropriate for parents who experience difficulty relinquishing complete control over their children's lives and who have very high expectations regarding their children's academic, athletic, and/or social accomplishments. While Gibran's piece tends to be more didactic than poems I usually use, its teaching tone is soothing and self-assured rather than aggressive, as seen when Gibran tells parents: 'You may give them your love but not your thoughts' (1971a, p.18). This line is quite useful for stimulating a discussion of privacy and control issues. Parents of 'acting-out' teens tend to feel threatened by secrets or intentions being kept from them. Yet, they often discover that their most rigid and angry attempts to violate their child's privacy lead to the most extreme forms of defiance.

The chief attitude fostered by Gibran's poem is acceptance of life's natural rhythm, the releasing of rigid control in order to remain the healthy stabilizing force in the background. This is an appropriate poem for struggling parents because comfort and challenge go hand in hand here. While Gibran tells parents that children do not 'belong' to them, he also notes that our offspring are 'the sons and daughters of Life's longing for itself.' This last phrase fosters a sense of perspective, as 'Life' becomes a vital entity transcending everyday conflicts or power struggles. Also, while the line 'You may strive to be like them, but seek not to make them like you' (Gibran 1971a, p.18) may irritate parents focused on molding their children's lives, it can also tap parents' underlying desire to recover their lost youth. In voicing this desire, they may gain a revised view of their children's energy and aspirations. Also, in response to these last lines when I ask parents to name what features of their child they might want to emulate, I can help reframe their harshly critical stance.

In concluding his poem, Gibran (1971a, p.18) couches his advice in a bow and arrow metaphor, inviting parent-readers to visualize themselves as the 'bows' from which the 'living arrows' of children are 'sent forth' and assuring them that a divine force honors all generations. In this image, parents have their vital role to play but do not have to feel responsible for every decision their children make.

When I was facilitating 10- and 12-week women's growth groups, focused on the mother-daughter connection, I also carefully matched selected poems to goals. For these groups, my two primary goals were first, to foster awareness of and to normalize experiences and feelings in relation to one's mothers and one's daughters, and second, to foster empathic understanding of one's mothers and daughters. Women in these groups studied the mother-daughter connection across the life-span from birth to death, focusing on its various stages. Thus, the poems I chose reflected situations covering the spectrum of the mother-daughter life cycle and contained ones both from the daughter's and the mother's point of view. When poems depicted a struggle, I invited participants to explore the voice of both parties to the conflict, thus helping to increase understanding of the issues and feelings of both parent and child.

I have also facilitated groups for therapists designed to help them find ways to nurture themselves and increase their awareness of personal reactions to specific clients in their practice. In the early stage of these 'Oases for Therapists,' I usually introduce Rumi's 'The Guest House' (2006), which describes emotions and inner experiences such as 'joy,' 'shame' and 'meanness' as 'unexpected visitor[s]' arriving every morning (Rumi 2006, p.17). The poet invites the reader to greet every guest because we can learn from them all. I have found that this poem motivates the therapists in my groups to share what it is like for them to encounter a variety of clients in their work day.

In a later stage of these groups when participants are more comfortable with one another and more ready to reveal deeply personal material, I introduce a poem by D.W. Winnicott, which he titled 'The Tree' and sent in a letter to his brother-in-law. I consider this work to be an apt choice for this group because its author is a renowned psychoanalyst who seems to be recounting his own experience here. In this poem, which is reproduced in Adam Phillips' biography of Winnicott (1988), the poet repeats three times that his mother was 'always weeping' and concludes with the statement that 'to enliven' her was his 'living' (Winnicott 1988, p.29). In revealing his emotional role in relation to his mother, he also suggests how this role may have affected his work as a helper. I thus selected it as a catalyst to invite a similar exploration from the therapists in my group.

I chose to introduce this same poem during the middle stage of individual therapy with a woman in her thirties. I selected it because my client, as the only daughter in a family with three brothers, grew up enmeshed with her mother who was a very volatile alcoholic. As a child, my client continuously tried to placate her and was the one always apologizing after their savage battles. At this point in her therapy, she was eager to explore the impact of her relationship with her mother on her current marriage and friendships. I decided that Winnicott's poem could help her clarify the nature of her mother's influence and her own characteristic way of responding, if she, like the therapists in my 'Oasis' groups, used the basic structure of this poem. I asked her to write her own reflection, substituting for 'weeping' her own choice of a verb that best described her mother's habitual behavior. Then I invited her to supply another verb to substitute for 'enliven' in Winnicott's last line, in order to capture what had been her 'living' in relation to her mother. In creating her own version, she was able to sharpen her focus on key issues for our subsequent discussions.

Using the Isoprinciple

The mood-matching or isoprinciple, mentioned earlier (see pp.42–43), is also an important aspect of choosing materials for particular client and growth group populations. With this principle in mind, I have selected 'Island[1]' by Langston Hughes (2001) for several clients who are suffering from recent, severe loss and feel very distant from a time of relief. It is a striking little gem of a poem, only eight lines long, but replete with meaning and feeling. In this poem, Hughes directly addresses a 'Wave of sorrow,' beseeching it not to 'drown' him. While he can view an 'island' far off, he does not strive to reach it immediately but will wait for the 'Wave' itself to transport him (Hughes 2001, p.376).

The authentic beseeching tone of this work usually finds its echo within a grieving person's soul. Here, the bereft individual instantly discovers a fellow sufferer who is not uttering glib solutions nor suggesting emotional shortcuts. He is suggesting a way to heal, *through* the experience of sorrow, in a soothing rhythmic way that mirrors the ocean's ebb and flow.

About two years ago, a middle-aged woman came to see me to deal with her extreme grief over the sudden death of her younger brother. In the first two sessions, she cried bitterly and believed that she would never emerge from the dark cloud that was smothering her. It was at this time that I introduced 'Island[1].' I recognized that I needed to honor her intense grief in the holding space of our work together. At the same time, I wanted to suggest the ray of hope that was so elusive to her. Telling a client that the grieving process takes time and that one must sit in the place of sadness is important; however, the Hughes poem provides a visceral and elegant way to model a very difficult life experience. My client resonated immediately to the suffocation suggested by the word, 'drowning' and was moved to elaborate on the deluge of guilt, anxiety and sadness that she was experiencing. Moreover, with the help of this poem, she was also able to imagine her own 'island,' that place of peace she could look toward as she strove to survive this trying time.

Two other poems, akin to Hughes' (2001) work, that get right inside the heart of grief but offer hope as well, are Mary Oliver's 'Heavy' (2006) and Ellen Bass' 'The Thing Is' (2002). Clients suffering the anguish of recent loss find relief from these poems when they recognize that they are not alone in their unspeakable sorrow. Just hearing Oliver's persona say that she did not think she could 'go any closer to grief without dying' (Oliver 2006, p.53) or hearing Bass' speaker referring to everything she 'held dear' as 'crumb[ling]' like burnt paper' (Bass 2002, p.18) gives permission to voice the extreme despair that the grief-stricken person may be afraid to share with family members or friends. At the same time, both poems suggest the presence of a better life waiting in the wings. In Bass' work, the message comes couched in the tender image of the grieving person holding 'life like a face / between your palms' (Bass 2002, p.18). For Oliver's persona, 'laughter' coming out of her 'startled mouth' and admiration for 'things of this world' (Oliver 2006, p.54) merge with the searing pain she feels.

While you may assume that a poem primarily conveys a particular feeling state or mood, you can never predict clients' specific emotional reactions or know in advance what specific elements your clients will find most personally evocative or relevant. The magic of working with poems is that we are often surprised by the unexpected. A clear example of this turn of events involved responses to Theodore Roethke's 'Dolor' (1966), that I introduced to a group of college students in a poetry therapy course, in order to illustrate the isoprinciple for mood matching with depressed clients. Beginning with the line, 'I have known the inexorable sadness of pencils' (1966, p.46), Roethke's solemn persona refers to tedious afternoons, recounting a litany of everyday objects in a drab institutional setting. This list of cheerless ordinary items, suggesting a repetitive pattern, elicited a lively, fruitful discussion of the sometimes soul-deadening daily routine of paper pushing in their worlds of school and work. For these students, 'Dolor' functioned as a springboard for sharing primarily the time management issue that was uppermost in their minds and lives.

Taking into Account the Main Situation Within a Poem

There are times when the primary mood in combination with the focal situation of a poem helps determine your strategic choice. For example, Linda Pastan's 'Marks' (1982), included in Chapter 2, is a poem I selected for a long-term, psychotherapy group consisting of relatively high functioning, middle-aged males and females. I introduced this poem after a session in which most of the participants were focusing on their anxiety at the thought of being criticized at work or at home. I knew there were a number of individuals in this group struggling with perfectionism, fear of failure, task overload and lack of assertiveness. These issues were linked to therapy goals that these individuals had earlier identified. At this point I also recognized that virtually all group members possessed, in common, a strong sense of responsibility toward others, and had lost touch with their sense of playfulness. 'Marks' thus seemed like a very apt choice. First of all, it was likely to introduce some levity into the room. I also felt it could naturally lead to a detailed discussion of specific people who are currently being seen as judges. In addition, I envisioned this poem as a vehicle for exchanging ideas on how to cope with one's internal critic and how to deal assertively with others' putdowns or demands. Given its concluding words on 'dropping out,' 'Marks' offered permission to explore a wide range of creative options going beyond one's usual frame of reference.

I have also chosen 'Marks' when working with individual clients whose internalized negative parental messages result in critical behavior toward others. Since this poem suggests the consequences of being judged, it can be used to encourage individuals to explore the impact of their own judgmental behavior. In addition, it often elicits frank discussions of how our negative self-assessments can foster a belligerent or defensive attitude.

Selecting Poems for Couples Counseling

In marital therapy or in a couples group setting, goals often include improved communication and the ability to work through conflict constructively. Here carefully selected poems can help couples gain relief that they are not alone in struggling with these issues and can be used to elicit expression of feelings and expectations regarding one's marital situation or partner. A well-selected poem can also help provide couples as well as the therapist with much insight into the patterns characterizing the marital relationship. The manner in which two partners in a relationship discuss their different reactions to a poem's persona provides a snapshot of their characteristic communication style. Characters and situations within a poem can also serve as models of what to avoid or what to emulate.

The first stanza of a poem called 'Marriage' by Elaine Feinstein (1977) is an excellent choice for couples experiencing discord. Feinstein's words are likely to capture the essence of what couples in therapy feel and think about their relationship. The kinesthetic image in the line, 'every word has its ten years' weight,' can help couples get in touch physically with the burden of sadness and hopelessness they have been hauling around for years and can serve to open up discussion of the unproductive and circular patterns of arguments that are often so detrimental to the health of a relationship. The equally visceral image of one spouse or partner 'lurching away' from the other while being 'pushed to dance' can be a very effective vehicle for discussing the ways individuals in a relationship seek intimacy and distance (Feinstein 1977, p.24). It also is very appropriate for introducing dialogue on power and dependency issues.

There are many times when I have worked with couples expecting to get all their needs met from one another and struggling with how much time they 'ought' to be spending together. For these couples, I often choose Kahlil Gibran's poetic piece 'On Marriage' from *The Prophet* (1971b). While didactic poems, forcing value-laden messages on the reader, tend to elicit defensive responses and curtail participants' freedom to respond, Gibran's gentle tone and striking, yet down-to-earth food, musical instrument and tree images have the potential to open up, for a couple, new pathways to insight. In my opinion, this piece provides a model of what healthy separateness in a marriage looks like. One line here serves to provide the flavor of this work: 'Fill each other's cup but drink not from one cup' (Gibran 1971b, p.16).

Nikki Giovanni's poem, 'A Certain Peace' (2003a) provides an apt follow-up or alternative to Gibran's piece for couples or for individuals whose main issue is balancing independence with dependence in a relationship with a spouse or lover. It is an especially good choice for those who fear that their relationship isn't strong if each person has some interests separate from the other. The speaker of Giovanni's poem recounts a 'very pleasant' afternoon in which both she and her loved one pursued different activities that made them happy. Within the poem, it is clear that fulfilling their individual needs helped to make their reunion 'after midnight' (Giovanni 2003a, p.158) that much more satisfying. Like Gibran's work, this poem easily lends itself to a discussion of specific activities that each partner recognizes they enjoy doing alone rather than as a team.

Employing the Indirect Versus the Direct Approach

There are times when it is desirable to select a poem that is indirectly or tangentially related to your client's or group member's specific situation. For example, with someone who has suffered from childhood sexual abuse and is not ready to confront the issue head-on, the prose poem called 'Fear' from J. Ruth Gendler's *The Book of Qualities* (1988) is an appropriate choice. Personifying this emotion, Gendler tells us it 'has a large shadow' but 'is quite small.' Fear also thrives in a secretive atmosphere, so that when we begin 'to talk to each other,' he starts to seem artificial, fragile and even a bit ridiculous. He no longer looks like 'a puppet-maker,' and the speaker is no longer convinced that she is 'a marionette' (Gendler 1988, p.4). The piece concludes with encouragement to face down this demon directly.

Unlike 'Fear,' Lucille Clifton's 'to my friend, jerina' (1991) is a much more direct, situation-matching poem for sexual abuse survivors:

> listen,
> when i found there was no safety
> in my father's house
> i knew there was none anywhere.
> you are right about this,
> how i nurtured my work
> not my self, how i left the girl
> wallowing in her own shame
> and took on the flesh of my mother.
> but listen,
> the girl is rising in me,
> not willing to be left to
> the silent fingers in the dark,
> and you are right,
> she is asking for more than
> most men are able to give,
> but she means to have what she
> has earned,
> sweet sighs, safe houses,
> hands she can trust.

(Clifton 1991, p.55)

As you can see, this poem contains some images and references that may be too disturbing or raw for the sexual abuse survivor who has never shared the secret of her or his past. Knowledge of your client and appropriate timing are both crucial factors here. I have found that for clients in individual therapy, who have been openly exploring their past trauma within a trusting atmosphere, this poem is quite affirming. It helps traumatized clients realize they are not alone and provides a model of healthy assertiveness. It also acts as a catalyst for a therapeutic conversation on shame and the ways in which past abuse affects present relationships. I used this poem after six months of counseling a woman in her mid-twenties, who had been repeatedly molested by her stepfather during her childhood and teen years. She came to me when she began having recurring nightmares that flooded her with memories of her past victimization. She also had just ended a two-year marriage and sought to understand what went wrong in this relationship. In spite of past traumatic situations involving both her stepfather and her volatile mother, she was a strikingly resilient person who was ready to face her demons and very motivated to move forward toward healthier relationships. She was able to benefit from a poem such as Clifton's that came so close to her own experience and yearnings.

When I worked with breast cancer survivors in a hospital program, I chose poems that were both directly and tangentially relevant to group members' diagnosis and treatment. During one of the sessions, I presented a poem by Anita Skeen (1994), 'The Woman Whose Body Is Not Her Own,' which focuses, in an honest, moving way, on the aftermath of a mastectomy. In reacting to this work, participants began to recount how they coped with their own harrowing experiences involving surgery and chemotherapy. As they shared their stories, I was struck by the heroism of these women and decided it would affirm their journeys to introduce Denise Levertov's poem, 'Variation on a Theme by Rilke' (1987). This work tells of a 'day' which acts as a 'presence' to the speaker, 'confronting her' and treating her as if she were a knight, by 'granting' her 'honor and a task' (Levertov 1987, p.3). By the end of the poem, the speaker knows she can rise to the most difficult challenge to which she has been summoned. While this poem never mentions any medical conditions and was not in the set I had initially prepared for this group, I considered it to be a valuable selection for our subsequent session. This vignette illustrates how the decision to include a particular poem ought to emerge from the energy of the group process and the facilitator's intuitive sense of what will foster participants' self-esteem and wellbeing.

Choosing Poems for Getting Acquainted and Achieving Closure

In addition to strategically choosing poems such as those mentioned above for substantial exploration in a therapy session or growth group meeting, there are times when particular poems are chosen for their use as getting acquainted or closure activities.

I enjoy introducing Imelda Maguire's 'Origins' (2004) and Cheryl Parsons Darnell's 'The Lesson of Texas' (1994) for the getting acquainted phase in therapy, growth group and workshop settings. Both these poems invite participants to elaborate upon their early places of residence and what these mean to them.

'Origins' begins with the words, 'I come from a bog-cotton / hawk-cry, flat, plain place / from a father who was a motherless boy' (Maguire 2004, p.11). From these lines, you can get a sense of how this poem invites the reader to supply sensory details when they discuss their own 'origins,' the place they consider their first home. Sharing of such material not only helps participants relax and begin telling their stories, but also builds cohesion in a group setting, which in turn fosters safety and trust. Because there are fairly neutral scenic details and also other more provocative details on family members, Maguire's poem subtly signals to participants that they may choose to stay on the surface or go a bit deeper as they feel ready. This suggestion of choice is important because growing and healing are integrally linked to the sense of having options and the freedom to set your own pace and boundaries.

'The Lesson of Texas' begins with the line, 'I grew up in Texas' and proceeds to elaborate on the speaker's early world with a series of 'where' clauses focusing on tornadoes, floods, and droughts that became a fact of life. In this world, the speaker learned how to 'ride out' the storms of 'weather, love and life' (Darnell 1994, p.93). When I present this poem, I invite participants to share some details about an early place of residence. However, as with the 'Origins' poem, readers have a choice regarding the level of their disclosures. They can stay with the weather details of a childhood residence or include material of a more personal nature if they wish.

For the final phase of our work with others, there are a variety of poems that can help achieve closure. For example, the anonymous poem, 'Then and Now: The State of Things,' discussed in Chapter 3, is quite apropos for helping clients and group members assess and affirm their progress. As noted earlier, this poem is used primarily as a catalyst for participants' own creative expression using the 'I used to be... Now I am...' framework. Once they complete this review of where they have been and where they are presently, they can focus on ways to maintain their gains and move forward on their own. Since concluding a course of therapy or a group experience constitutes a transition, Miroslav Holub's 'The Door' (1990), with its repeated 'Open the door' phrasing, provides a stimulus for discussing future growth directions to pursue. Carl Sandburg's 'Different Kinds of Good-by' (1969b), which presents images of farewell and explores the variety of farewells we utter along life's path, is another work to use in a final session. It provides an effective vehicle for a conversation on the ways in which clients or group members wish to express their own goodbyes as a therapeutic experience comes to a close.

Dealing with Participants' Choice of Poems

While all the above examples involve the facilitator or therapist's choice of materials, there are also times when participants ask to bring to the therapeutic setting poems that they have found particularly moving or edifying. Teenagers and young adults, for example, are often eager to share the lyrics of a favorite song. In these cases, it is important to accommodate and even welcome such a request, and you need to be ready to facilitate discussion of material unfamiliar to you. If this is a group setting and you are concerned that such a poem or song lyric may be toxic for some of the other individuals, you may ask for a description of the work in advance or ask to read it before it is shared with the group. If you are counseling an individual who wishes to share a poetic piece, you can honor this request without such reservations. In fact, a poetic selection introduced by clients can enhance or vitalize their engagement in the poetry therapy process. Even if they bring in a poem that you would never consider choosing, therapeutic discussion can generate healthful possibilities that go well beyond the scope of the presented material.

Exploring Your Chosen Poem's Possibilities

As you can see from the above discussions, making poem selections for specific clients involves a wide variety of factors and can be a richly rewarding as well as challenging experience. While as facilitators, we may imagine, as fully as we can, the possible effects of poetic works on others, we ought to basically 'try out' each poem on ourselves, asking a set of questions such as the following:

- Does this poem move me?

- What feelings does it summon up?

- Can I relate to the persona's plight?

- Am I brought into a new view of something important by the speaker's tone, the poem's vivid sound effects or the poem's unique word combinations?

- Does the rhythm create welcome surprises and/or satisfying closure?

- Can I benefit from exploring the persona as a positive or negative role model?

- Does the poem's structure and subject matter provide a natural entry to a worthwhile writing activity, and what might that activity be?

By addressing questions such as those listed above, we gain important knowledge regarding the therapeutic possibilities of poems we are considering for specific individuals, couples, families and groups. As we carefully make selections, we are, above all, guided by all that we know about the people we serve. We take into account a wide range of psychological, social and cultural information about both the past and present of these individuals. We also recognize the full set of factors relating to the specific therapeutic context in which we are working. In choosing poems that we believe will be most beneficial, we pay close attention to the current emotional state of our clients, the tenor of the therapeutic relationship as well as the short and long-term goals that help structure our work together. This intricate process of choosing apt materials can be likened to the preparation of a gourmet meal. We assemble all the diverse ingredients, using our expertise to assess how these will work together to create the most savory and nourishing result.

CHAPTER 5

Facilitating the Poetry Growth and Healing Experience

While selecting specific poems involves imagining how we might lead a worthwhile discussion of that work, the actual facilitation of others' responses to poems is at the core of the poetry therapy process. While this task involves particular skills and techniques, it is primarily an art with a rhythm, a pacing, and intuitive, spontaneous elements. Essential to the facilitation process are respect, keen awareness and flexibility, as interactions among the client or group, the poem and the facilitator take place. As the session unfolds, the facilitator's interventions are primarily designed to encourage clients to *personalize* their responses to the literature and to further their self-understanding. The poems introduced are not discussed as literary products. The focus is not on the author's techniques or on the aesthetic value of the poetic materials.

Steps in the Poetry Therapy Process

The facilitator deftly guides participants—whether these are individuals, group members, families or couples—through a variety of steps involving personal connections to the poetic materials. In order to better understand what facilitation involves, it makes sense to recognize what usually takes place within participants when they read or listen to a poem in a growth group or therapy setting. Hynes and Hynes-Berry (1994, Chapter 3) thoroughly delineate several stages of this process. These are basically recognition or identification; exploration or elaboration; and the conscious decision to apply your discoveries or insights to your own present life situation.

Recognition or identification constitutes the initial phase upon which to build. After a poem is introduced, participants may clearly recognize some object, character, situation or feeling state within a poem that reminds them of something in their own lives. Or participants will have an emotional reaction that suggests their psyche has made a link of some kind to an aspect or several aspects of the poem. Participants may or may not yet be aware of what this link is. A blue sweater in a poem may remind one person of his father, or a golden peach may give another individual a sudden surge of joy that links her to grandma's garden from her past. Participants may get incensed by the attitude of the poem's persona because she/he reminds them of their past self or that part of the self they may be denying. Sighs, tears or exclamations all indicate that some form of identification is taking place. You know when these reactions surface that participants are not neutral in relation to the particular poem you have chosen.

Hynes and Hynes-Berry (1994) point out that 'At times, the recognition brought about by the literature is so strong as to bring about a catharsis,' which they define in 'psychiatric terms' as 'the surfacing of unconscious materials' that 'is accompanied by an emotional response and a release from tension' (pp.46–47). When a poem hits home in such a potent way, the sudden gust of emotion can be quite surprising and edifying.

When participants recognize some aspect of themselves or identify with a specific element in a poem, they are then in a position to elaborate upon that feature. Respondents may flesh out their initial reaction by narrating an incident, or reflecting on why they may have reacted with so much pleasure or anger to a particular metaphor. An example that immediately comes to mind here is a young group member's response to the last line of a short poem by Kathleen Wiegner called 'Autobiography' (1974). In this work, the speaker sums up her present life situation with the provocative words, 'I am at ease in the noose of my life' (Wiegner 1974, p.64). After exploring her outrage at this image, the participant was able to articulate that she used to feel trapped in her marriage and now gets very impatient with her friends when they act passive in their relationships. She concluded that she needed to be more understanding of these friends, because after all, she herself had 'been there.'

One very fruitful aspect of the exploration/elaboration stage in the therapeutic discussion of a poem is what Hynes and Hynes-Berry call 'juxtaposition' (1994, pp.43, 50–51). Like these authors, I have found that the juxtaposing of contrasting or similar responses to poems leads to positive growth and sparks new awareness. To juxtapose means to place next to, and when individuals hear the responses of others, they have the opportunity to evaluate their initial reaction and view something in a new way. If two individuals in a group react in a similar fashion, they usually form a bridge with each other that affirms their response. When participants place their initial reaction to a poem side by side with their own revised reaction, they can appreciate the journey they have taken. For example, with the Wiegner poem discussed in the previous paragraph, the woman who was so upset, at first, by the 'noose' image, was able to see, through others' very differing responses, how the poem's speaker could be accepting her lot with grace. Also, because others in the group focused on the persona's pregnancy, which is implied in the poem, and her ambivalence as a mother-to-be, the participant with the negative reaction was, by the end of the session, recognizing how sometimes we have to balance responsibilities with an idealized notion of total freedom.

If healing and real change are to take place, participants need to move beyond exploration. They need to incorporate new insights into their current life situation and *apply* what they have learned from the therapeutic dialogue. The above example of the woman who expressed her desire to be more patient with her passive friends was doing this kind of real life application. Through extended group discussion, she also was ready to imagine real life scenarios in which she could comfortably work out compromises, without sacrificing her autonomy.

Setting the Tone and Warm-Ups

When beginning a poetry therapy session, it is essential to establish an atmosphere where trust, respect, compassion, listening without judgment, spontaneity and openness are the norm. Participants are welcomed into a space where they can pay passionate attention to poetic creations, to their own reactions and, in a group setting, to one another.

Facilitators of poetry therapy sessions often use warm-up activities, especially in newly formed groups or when participants are weary or distracted from a long day of work. Warm-ups are also very appropriate when there is a high level of anxiety regarding new experiences, or when participants are unfamiliar with creative expression activities. In addition, warm-ups are effective for cohesion-building in a group and for introducing a topic that is controversial or challenging.

Some examples of warm-up activities include:

- free writing in response to relaxing music

- quick abstract drawing to capture how you are feeling at the present

- choosing one word to capture your present life situation or how you are feeling today and elaborating on this word, by creating a 'word tree'

- completing an acrostic, where you arrange the letters of your name or a key word vertically and use the beginning letter of each line to write a spontaneous poem.

The word you choose for this acrostic could reflect the particular theme for the session that is about to begin. To model spontaneity and risk-taking, I often complete an impromptu acrostic of my own in front of the group on a white board. If I allow myself to create without forethought or concern over the logical meaning of the result, it encourages others to follow my lead.

For example, for a recent group session focusing on current relationships with parents and siblings, I put the letters of the word 'FAMILY' vertically on the board and generated an acrostic that went as follows:

F or me today

A ll families

M anage to

I nstill

L onging for the

Y oung and the old

An acrostic based on the letters spelling 'WOMAN' provides a way to get the creative juices flowing on the subject of women's self-esteem and sets the tone for energetic conversation on a poem such as Maya Angelou's 'Phenomenal Woman' (1978).

Hynes and Hynes-Berry (1994, p.153) refer to a warm-up that involves a 'visual complement' to the poem chosen for a particular session. For example, you might bring in an assortment of sea shells, if shells are a primary image in the poem. If your poetic selection refers to a specific painting, a print of that work can be a welcome accompaniment. A discussion of Robert Frost's 'The Armful' (1979a), described in Chapter 4, could follow the facilitator's entry into the room laden with numerous packages of varying dimensions, in order to set the tone and stimulate interest. However, while these extra touches might enhance the process particularly for children or those reluctant to engage with poetry, they also might limit the ways in which individuals react to the poetic material.

Perhaps the most common warm-up activity involves checking in with participants, inviting them to bring up 'unfinished business' or insights gained during the interval between meetings. Providing this kind of continuity with a former meeting is important particularly when the previous session has dealt with very loaded material.

Introducing the Poems

When the facilitator introduces a poem, it is important for it to be read aloud, so that the sounds, silences, rhythm and tone can be fully experienced in the moment. The facilitator often reads the poem aloud or asks others to read it. It is quite effective to read a poem more than once and hear it read in different voices. Often group members, families, or couples take turns reading one stanza apiece, or all read in unison for a resonant choral effect. Usually clients find the group reading to be a powerful, even soulful experience. At times, if you have a high quality recording of an actor reciting a poem or the poet reading his or her own work, you may want to introduce your selection in this way. I enjoy using David Whyte's readings of Mary Oliver's poems, because he repeats key lines to achieve emphasis (Whyte 2009). A variation on Whyte's style of delivery involves reading every line twice when the poem is initially presented. There are times when the facilitator may decide to ask everyone to read the poem silently before all hear it presented aloud. In this way, quiet contemplation of the poem's spatial presence precedes the aural experience of the poem's sound effects.

In addition to hearing the poem, it should be available to all in a clearly printed form, so that participants can see it and refer back to it whenever they wish. For individuals whose eyesight is impaired or who cannot read, multiple vocalizations of a poem by the facilitator or another group member are highly desirable and even necessary. Whatever their reading ability, participants should always have a choice whether or not to recite a poem. While the people we are helping usually engage more fully with a poem and feel empowered when they articulate its words aloud, we, as facilitators, need to be sensitive to the fact that individual's reading backgrounds and public speaking abilities vary greatly. While we may wish to help people discover or celebrate their speaking voice, we also need to avoid intimidating them or setting up unrealistic expectations.

When participants generate a poem that becomes the text being discussed, they can be asked to make multiple copies for group members, if they wish to do so and if a copier is on hand. However, usually participants will simply be invited to read their work aloud slowly once or twice, before discussion ensues.

Another technique for introducing material in a group setting that I have begun to use lately involves physical enactments of a poem. Since many people are self-conscious about moving their bodies in front of others, I introduce this technique only if a strong sense of trust and comfort has already been established within a group. I invite participants to get into small units of three to five individuals, providing them with time to decide on how to enact a poem physically for the others. I ask each unit to choose the person who will recite the poem aloud as the others perform the enactment. At times, several different units work with the same poem, while at other times, each unit works with a different poem. In the latter case, the differing poems all usually deal with the same general subject. I have found that there is a great deal of excitement and energy in the room, as each unit plans its approach and performs for the rest of the group. As they perform their poem, I ask the observers to pay close attention, to monitor their feelings, thoughts and sensations. This request helps prepare for the ensuing therapeutic conversation on the enacted poem, a conversation that also involves asking the actors to share what their process was like. Translating a poem into bodily gestures and movements usually intensifies its effect on both performers and viewers. It also tends to highlight a poem's imagery and meanings in a unique and potent way.

Beginning Discussion: Encouraging Personal Engagement with the Poem

As the poem is introduced, the facilitator needs to pay close attention to the energy in the room and to both the verbal and nonverbal responses of individual participants. At this point, the facilitator focuses, in particular, on signs that indicate personal engagement with the material.

The facilitator may follow up on these observed signals by checking out what he or she has noticed. For example, the facilitator might say, 'I noticed you smiling broadly as this poem was being read. Can you tell us your reaction?' Or 'I heard several sighs while we were reading this poem. What are those sighs about?'

Open-ended questions, usually beginning with words like 'What,' 'Where' or 'How,' are very effective ways to elicit discussion regarding initial responses to a poem. Such responses may involve thoughts, memories or feelings. Examples of such questions include the following:

- Any reactions to the poem you just heard?

- How are you feeling right now after having heard this poem?

- Any striking images for you?

- Where did this poem take you?

- What do you think is going on here?

- How do you feel about this poem?

- What did you enjoy and not enjoy about this work?

- What is this poem saying to you?

In addition to these very broad questions, you may wish to garner more specific personal responses to various aspects of the poem, also using open as opposed to closed questions. Open questions are desirable because they leave room for extended response. Examples of such questions include the following:

- What is your personal response to the speaker's grieving process in this poem?

- What memory or current aspect of your life comes to mind when you think about the two people in this poem?

- What is your reaction to the speaker's statement at the end of the poem, and what statement would you make if you were in her situation?

- When you visualize and really physically feel the tree image in this poem, what comes to mind?

- How did all the pauses or silent intervals in this poem affect you when you were listening to it just now?

- When have you found yourself and/or someone you know in a situation like the one depicted in this poem?

Questions to encourage a more specific initial response may be as simple as 'Please tell us (or me) more about what you have said?' or 'Anything else to add?' You may also pose a question such as, 'You said that the poem's speaker reminds you of your sister—what particular traits were you thinking of?' If a client has just mentioned 'loneliness' or some other crucial word, you might simply repeat this word, using a gently questioning tone of voice.

While closed questions tend to elicit 'Yes-No' responses that curtail the flow of conversation, with a talkative group, these may work just fine. One example of a technically closed question that is quite useful for moving participants to a specific personal response is 'Does the poem's speaker resemble anyone you know?' If the forthcoming answer is a simple 'Yes,' the facilitator may elicit more information by directly asking the follow-up question, 'Who is the person you have in mind and what is he or she like?'

Closed questions that are value-laden are not recommended because they limit participants' freedom of response. An example of such a question would be 'Is the son's reaction to his father in this poem a good or bad one?' Or 'Do you think the husband in this poem is too domineering?' More open versions of these questions would be 'What do you think of the son's reaction to his father?' Or 'How do you react to the husband's behavior?'

'Why' questions, such as the following one, tend to elicit a defensive reaction: 'Why did you get so angry when you referred to the poet's lack of assertiveness?' Essentially the same question can be presented in a less threatening manner. For example, the facilitator might ask, 'When you spoke of the poet's unassertiveness, you showed a great deal of energy. Can you tell us more about your reaction?' or 'What do you think is going on for you when you express irritation over that image?' When facilitators phrase the question in these ways, they do not make assumptions and thus leave the door open to hearing the client's truth.

There are, however, some 'why' questions that can be effective, especially if they refer to the characters or situation in the poem and thus are not directly related to the participants themselves. For example, a question such as 'Why do you think the poem's persona feels the way he does?' could work very well. When participants are invited to freely speculate on the emotions of a poem's persona or author, they can respond without feeling judged yet often link their seemingly objective insights to their own life situation.

In a group setting, the facilitator can expand the range of initial responses while encouraging participation of reticent group members, by paraphrasing one participant's response and inviting others to add their own. For example, you might say, 'John has expressed a very strong opinion of the episode conveyed in this poem. Do the rest of you feel the same way or feel differently?' Another example of the same sort of question is the following: 'Mary has noted that this road image reminds her of her busy life right now? In what way does this link fit or not fit for the rest of you?'

Although questions designed to open discussion usually occur after the poem is read, at times the facilitator might choose to preface the reading with special encouragements or invitations. For example, when I initiate a therapeutic discussion of Gibran's poem, 'On Marriage' (1971b) for couples in counseling (previously discussed in Chapter 4), I invite the husband and wife to listen closely to the poem's words, to physically experience the many diverse images and to decide which of these they find the most congenial for them personally. Such preparation helps move the therapeutic process forward and subtly discourages an intellectualizing or impersonal response to the material.

At times, the initial responses to poems can be quite intellectualized. For example, if a poem focuses on choices, one participant might speak in generalities about how decision-making is a part of the human condition and begin expounding on the existential theories of Jean Paul Sartre. Another participant might distance him or herself from a poem by introducing irrelevant biographical information about the poem's author. A third might zoom in on the species of grape contained in the poem and begin telling everything that he or she knows about it. In the face of such intellectualized responses, the facilitator needs to gently move from the impersonal to the personal, asking some of the open questions cited above or focusing on the personal possibilities that may exist within the intellectualized response itself. For example, the client discoursing on existentialism might be asked if any aspect of this philosophy has meaning in terms of important choices he or she has had to make.

Besides the use of varied questions, productive nonverbal behaviors can be very powerful in eliciting specific personal responses to poems. If you, as a facilitator, detect that a participant seems ready or may need a bit of encouragement to say more, you can simply remain silent and wait, lean forward in the direction of the speaker, make eye contact, nod your head, or give a smile or exclamation of encouragement. You can also foster a spontaneous, non-intellectual response to a poem by providing paints, pastels, colored pencils, sculpting clay or collage materials and asking participants to render a visual equivalent of what they experienced when the poem was read aloud.

Encouraging Exploration and Self-Application Through Discussion

Once the participant has established and articulated some sort of personal link with the poetic material, the facilitator's primary role in the elaboration and self-application phase is to provide opportunities for a more fully developed exploration of immediate reactions. This exploration may include elaborating on an especially meaningful personal event, emotion or theme that has surfaced within the initial discussion.

For example, if the issue of rivalry between siblings emerges from the first responses to a poem, you may invite fuller elaboration by asking participants to recall the details of one memorable situation from their past that involved competition with a sibling. You can encourage an even more profound response, if you add the invitation to recount the specific thoughts and feelings experienced at that time and how these seem relevant in the present day.

To deepen and expand discussion in an individual therapy setting, therapists can help clients see parallels between their current responses to a poem and significant material that has emerged in past counseling sessions. Therapists can also gently direct clients' attention to discrepancies or changes in their reactions to a particular poem. For example, one of my clients had an immediate initial reaction to the words, 'chronic angers of that household' in Robert Hayden's poem, 'Those Winter Sundays' (1985, p.41). For years, she had been focusing on her own anger toward her hot-tempered father and automatically assumed that the father of the poem's persona was the only individual who was creating danger in the home depicted by Hayden. However, she changed her view of both the persona and the father in the poem, when she began responding to its last lines where the speaker regrets that he did not thank his father for all the positive things that he did. At this point, she stated that the 'chronic anger' may belong primarily to the poem's speaker with whom she identified and that the conflict in her own childhood household might, in fact, have came from a variety of sources. She also began to recognize how her long held grudge against her father had blinded her to his good deeds. When I highlighted her changing response, she went on to describe in detail the various ways her father showed he cared about his family. Recognizing a key shift in my client's attitude, I made the following statement: 'The positive details you just recounted seem so different from your earlier reactions to your father. What do you think accounts for this difference?' My intention in asking such a question was to help her amplify the discoveries she was expressing and to affirm what she herself has done to gain a more mature perspective.

In the couples counseling session referred to earlier where the spouses were given Gibran's poem 'On Marriage' (1971b), the elaboration process can look as follows. Once the husband and wife have identified the image in the poem that they find most personally striking, the facilitator can effectively encourage exploration by asking a number of direct questions, such as the following:

- What is it about this image that specifically speaks to you?

- What related set of images come to mind that help to capture something significant about your marriage?

- Can you describe a time when you felt connected with your partner while you were enjoying two separate activities on your own?

- What does aloneness and togetherness look like in your relationship?

- How do you come together, and how do you create space for yourselves as individuals?

As these questions are being addressed, it is a good idea to invite the spouses to speak directly to each other rather than to the therapist, making eye contact with one another and listening before commenting. Since respectful communication leading to mutual understanding is an underlying goal of most marital therapy work, it is worthwhile to integrate the couple's responses to the poem with communication skill building.

Facilitators, working with a group, family or couple, often deliberately juxtapose the differing or similar responses of various participants and invite them to carefully consider one another's responses, in order to move the therapeutic conversation to a deeper level, while including everyone in the process. The facilitator may highlight two very different responses to the same material or may observe how the responses of several individuals are strikingly similar. The facilitator can also effectively bring together a variety of responses by using such words as the following: 'I've been hearing many similar as well as different definitions of friendship in the last half-hour. Let's explore the set of possibilities that we have generated thus far and see how they fit in our own lives today.'

In a group setting, facilitators may also bring together a variety of participant responses to the same significant behavior present within a poem, in order to deepen everyone's understanding of options that have been suggested in the initial discussion. If, for example, several group members have expressed different opinions regarding the decision of the poem's speaker to stay in an abusive work situation, the facilitator might summarize this array of responses and ask everyone to specify what they would actually say and do if they were in this situation. Role-playing activities at this juncture are very appropriate and can make the exploration come alive in a way that is meaningful for participants.

As facilitators, we must constantly weigh the advantages of offering direction against the benefits of sitting back while participants lead the way. In the present moment, with the energy and welfare of our clients in mind, we also need to assess the value of verbal versus nonverbal interventions and to especially keep in mind the use of productive silence.

Incorporating Writing Activities for Exploration and Self-Application

Introducing a writing activity in response to a poem is one of the most effective ways to encourage exploration. From their writing, participants almost always expand or deepen their emotional, cognitive and visceral responses to meaningful elements of a poem and make the poem, in a sense, their own. Expressive writing both amplifies and complements the therapeutic discussion of a poem, opening the doors to self-awareness.

Writing activities can come in many different forms. For example, in conjunction with Gibran's poetic piece 'On Children' (1971a), previously discussed in Chapter 4, the parents in a couples session can be asked to chose any word, image or phrase from this work and use it as the title and first line of their own written expression. They can each write separately and then share the results or create a poem together. They can also be invited to choose a line, set of lines or image from Gibran's work that reflects a time when they each were adolescents interacting with their parents, and then free write using that line or image as the beginning of their poems. An alternative writing invitation involves the parents addressing Gibran in a letter or monologue, telling him what they want him to know either about themselves as parents or about their child.

At other times, you, as facilitator, may wish to mine evocative metaphors in Gibran's poem, helping parents to 'own' these images in personally meaningful ways. For example, parents may free write on what comes to mind when they imagine themselves as the 'bow' and their children as 'arrows.' Before they begin writing, you might suggest that they identify where they are positioned, who or what is the 'archer' and where the 'arrows' are flying (Gibran 1971a, pp.18–19). Your invitation might involve asking each parent to choose another set of cognate images that even more aptly describes his or her particular relationship with their child or children right now, or the relationship he or she wants to achieve. After they have written, it is important to leave ample time for both to share their separate versions, so that they can clarify the ways their views match or diverge.

There are other richly complex features of this poem that you can invite the parents to contemplate in their writing. For example, you may suggest that they write a reflection on the parents' 'dreams' which Gibran (1971a, p.18) mentions in his poem. If boundary and control issues characterize the parents' interactions with their children, the parents can benefit from writing a two-part poem, with one segment devoted to their own dreams and the other to what they believe are their children's dreams. With their writings in front of them, they have the opportunity to recognize how their dreams resemble or differ from those of their children. They also can take a close look at how their assumptions and expectations regarding their children affect their parenting patterns.

If privacy and secrecy are primary themes that surface when the parents initially discuss Gibran's poem, they can expand their views of these issues by personifying or animating them. When they describe, in their own creative ways, 'privacy' or 'secrecy' as living beings, they have the chance to isolate hitherto unknown dimensions of these often elusive concepts. Creating an acrostic poem with each letter of the word, 'PRIVACY' or 'SECRECY,' placed at the beginning of a separate line, is yet another way to encourage spontaneous and fruitful reflections on these important subjects.

When parents gain insights on how their dreams, expectations and views of privacy influence their current parenting, they are often ready to consider new behavior options. Transforming insight into action can also be facilitated by writing activities at this point. For example, parents can write a monologue addressed to their children, in which they tell them something new that they have discovered, or generate a list of questions they now wish to ask their children, in light of a new awareness they have gained.

The writing process to elaborate responses to a poem can occur in tandem with a schematic or abstract drawing. For instance, when I introduce Robert Frost's 'The Armful' (1979a) to individuals, couples and groups, I almost always follow up a discussion of the poem with an activity that invites participants to draw all the 'parcels' they are trying to carry and 'balance at their breast' (Frost 1979a, pp.266–267). I tell them that their packages can be different sizes and shapes (and even colors if there are markers or pastels available). I then suggest that participants label these packages. When they have completed this first part, I invite them to decide which packages they must continue carrying, which ones they can relinquish altogether, and which ones they can imagine setting down now in the road to retrieve at a later time. After everyone has had a chance to complete this selection process, I usually recommend that they summarize their discoveries, in written form, either as a brief journal entry or as a personalized version of 'The Armful' poem. I have found that when participants take time to name and explore all their roles and responsibilities by completing a graphic and linguistic rendering, they move more deeply from Frost's poem into their own current universe and tackle, in a new way, the challenge of priority-setting. While group members doing this together learn much from one another, I find this activity to be very worthwhile in individual therapy as well.

The writing activity I most frequently introduce in conjunction with many poems, involves asking participants to choose one line, a set of lines or just a phrase from the poem that 'calls' to them in a special way or captures their attention and then to use these words as the starting point for their own poetic creation. I then invite each writer to go further, by choosing the one striking line or phrase from their own response poem and using that as the opening for a second piece. I discovered this technique, while writing along with group members several years ago. I noticed a particularly evocative line in my poem and realized how useful it would be for me to more fully develop that line. I have found that this 'going deeper' technique helps summon up illuminating material that has remained buried for a long time. As I think further about the origin of this technique in my life, I must pay homage to a creative writing specialist at the University of Minnesota, Michael Dennis Browne, who taught a workshop many years ago entitled 'The Poem Behind the Poem.' I recall his emphasis on the notion that the most heartfelt poems within us—the ones that need to get written— often lie hidden just behind the poem that first emerges.

As noted earlier in conjunction with Gibran's 'On Children' (1971a) letters, monologues or direct addresses are another form of writing activity that I present for exploring responses to poems. Letters are useful for clients in individual, couples and group settings. I often suggest writing letters directly addressed to a poem's persona, especially in instances where participants have a strong initial reaction to this speaker. These letters, which may include advice or expressions of approval or disapproval, become a useful vehicle for fleshing out and clarifying participant's immediate responses.

Monologues function in much the same way as letters. The title itself of Levertov's 'Talking to Grief' (2002) suggests a writing activity in which participants speak directly, in a monologue, to grief or any emotion that is currently uppermost for them. After participants have been discussing Levertov's poem, I often introduce this writing activity by asking them to imagine their selected emotion as any live creature of their choosing. I have found that participants appreciate this dramatic technique. They can visualize their significant feeling state and tell it whatever they please. Taking their lead from Levertov's sentiments, they can decide to feed and shelter it or ignore it for a while.

The voice for the participant's monologue can belong to the emotion itself. When participants give words to their emotion, they have the opportunity to hear what this emotion is trying to tell them. They can gain a clearer understanding of the place that this emotion occupies in their lives, in both physical and psychological terms. From listening carefully to what this emotion is expressing, they also may acquire a new perspective or recognize the possibility of untried options. For example, one participant may hear his voice of grief complaining that he is being stuffed with too much food and is growing too large. This striking image can motivate the participant to think about how he is 'overfeeding' his grief and what it would mean if grief went on a 'diet.' Through this activity, the absurdity and wonder of metaphor jolt writers into a world of creative possibilities.

The monologue technique described in the above examples can easily turn into a dialogue in which participants engage in a lively exchange with an emotion of their choice. Whether there is debate or agreement, there is always something new to be learned in this interchange of messages.

The dialoguing technique can be taken even further when two compatible poems are being discussed together. Recently, in a woman's growth group experience in an educational setting, participants shared reactions to Pastan's 'Marks' (1982) and Vodges' 'Snowbound' (1980), which are reprinted in Chapters 2 and 4 respectively. After this initial discussion, I invited group members to create a one to two page conversation between the speakers of these poems. Before the writing began, I asked participants to put themselves into the mindset of the persona of each poem, experiencing fully the tone, the imagery used and the attitude expressed toward the issues presented. In their dialogues, I suggested including each speaker's position, discoveries and feelings. I encouraged participants to go beyond the two texts, to take their dialogue wherever it leads them. To make the dialogue easy to write and read, I suggested using the letter 'M' to designate the 'Marks' persona and the letter 'S' for the 'Snowbound' speaker. After writing, participants were asked to either read their dialogues or share whatever they wish regarding what they learned from doing this activity. When dialogues were presented, I asked if we could have two readers deliver the conversation, so that everyone, including the dialogue's creator, could clearly differentiate the two distinct voices. Once a dialogue was read aloud, participants were invited to respond to one another's words.

I found the results of this activity to be quite illuminating for group members, as their written pieces went beyond the words of the original poems. In giving their own voice to the speaker of 'Marks,' many writers emphasized her frustration and craving for words of love and appreciation from family members. Some focused on the fact that 'M' is probably a perfectionist, busy grading *herself*. Even though the persona in 'Marks' receives passing grades from all family members, some dialogists indentified the grades received as poor, thus magnifying this persona's disappointment, anguish and even sense of betrayal. For example, one writer in the voice of 'M' bemoaned the fact that her 'report card is littered with ugly red marks' and that her 'flaws' are 'so easy to see, so easily pointed out…with that cunning red pen.' Other participants, writing in the voice of 'M,' emphasized how much her husband and children depend on her and raised the question of what would happen if she were not in the picture. Would her family be able to survive without her?

Many dialogue writers using this pair of poems noticed that Vodges' speaker is so much more self-assured than Marks' speaker. Vodges' speaker not only is more ready to take care of herself but also has generated options for this self-care. In some group members' writings, Marks' persona expresses gratitude for the advice of the other, and the two commiserate over their lack of me-time.

When one writer had 'S' tell 'M' that her family members 'cannot see her glow,' her words opened up a fruitful group discussion of how our essential spirit can get buried under our obligations and others' expectations. Several dialogue writers went beyond the self-care options presented by 'S,' adding suggestions to get a massage, take deep breaths, read a book, go for a walk, relax at a cabin retreat in the woods and even take on a new lover. One writer, in the voice of 'S,' poetically encouraged the 'Marks' speaker in these words:

> *Anoint yourself once*
> *again with the*
> *forgiving,*
> *peaceful,*

tranquil,
fresh
breaths of snowy air.

A few participants created spirited dialogues in which 'M' expresses irritation toward 'S's overly confident attitude yet begins to generate her own solutions. There were some writers who had their 'Marks' speaker call the 'Snowbound' speaker 'selfish' because she does not mention any family or loved ones. These writings opened the door to a useful conversation on how we define selfishness, especially in relation to self-nurturing.

Through this dialoguing activity, group members elaborated, in diverse ways, on the 'Marks' speaker's desire to 'drop out.' These words, placed at the end of Pastan's poem, often provoke much commentary. One writer, for example, interpreted these words as a 'new beginning,' while another saw the possibility of abandoning one's responsibilities altogether. In several group members' writings, the 'Snowbound' speaker senses the desperation that the judged woman in 'Marks' feels in her domestic realm and expresses the possibility of balancing the claims of others with self-care, mentioning that 'dropping out' does not have to mean leaving your family forever.

Some dialogue writers intertwined the two poems in ways that led to important explorations. For example, according to one writer, the 'Marks' persona, responding to the words of the 'Snowbound' persona, wonders if she even 'know[s] her own number' to dial and asks the important question, 'what if I dial my own number and nobody answers?' In this same writer's piece, the 'Marks' persona observes that 'this snowbound state of being sounds cold and lonesome.' These statements elicited lively discussion of two important issues: first, how we can balance our need for others with our craving for individual freedom, and second, how we negotiate between our fear of emptiness and our need to relax in solitude.

There was one participant who creatively set the dialogue between the two poems' personae at a 'casting call' for the *Survivor* television show and decided to end her dialogue with a parody of Pastan's poem, after her 'Marks' persona had gained a place in the show. Her creative work, printed below, illustrates how recrafting a poem in your own terms can bring up personally useful material and feed one's sense of playfulness as well:

My husband gets an A
for last night's supper,
an incomplete for washing the dog,
a B plus in bed.
My son thinks I'm awesome,
an awesome mother, and if
I wouldn't mind
his class hopes I'll visit.
My daughter is still embarrassed
about the wardrobe malfunction
but she'll get over it.
I wonder when I should let
them know, I'm meeting 'S'
in Paris.

Providing Closure

Whether you are working with individuals, groups, families or couples, it is important to provide some form of closure at the end of a session, even if it is not very elaborate. You might provide a summary of themes that have emerged during the discussion of the poem and the accompanying writing or creative activity. Or you might ask each individual to capture in one word or sentence what occurred for them during this meeting. If a major issue has surfaced, you may invite participants to reflect or write further on this issue during the interval separating this session from the subsequent one. You might indicate that you will bring another poem related to this issue to the next meeting. If the discussion has been very rich and seems quite incomplete, I often ask participants to bring the same poem to our next meeting.

As a part of the closing, the poem that has been the focus of the current session may be read aloud one more time, with the opportunity for participants to revise their initial reactions or to put forth a one word response that reflects their current thought or feeling. In their book on *Poetry as Experience*, Stageberg and Anderson (1952, p.10) address the fact that 'The individual reader himself changes in the course of time' and thus 'the re-reading of a poem may reveal new perceptions and understandings not previously observed.' With Hynes and Hynes-Berry's term, 'juxtaposition,' in mind, I may ask clients, at the end of a session, to place side by side their two different reactions, so that they can honor their therapeutic journey and recognize significant transformations.

Group poems are a particularly effect way to establish closure and affirm the sense of community within a group. One example of such a poem involves each person contributing a color that captures in some way what they are feeling as the session ends and then naming objects associated with that color. We go around the circle with each participant contributing their line or image as they wish. While most group poems such as these are created aloud, a variant involves passing a paper around as each participant writes their contribution. The final product is then read aloud for all to enjoy. This activity can also be introduced by inviting everyone to think of a color that reflects something they learned about themselves in group today or a mood they are taking with them as they leave.

Closure activities may be predominantly feeling-oriented or theme-oriented. For example, music or a relaxation activity can help participants comfortably re-enter the world outside the poetry therapy space. On the other hand, the facilitator, in closing, may focus on the content that has emerged, perhaps choosing to honor the contributions and the work done during this particular session. If there have been breakthrough insights, the facilitator can invite commitment to put into action, in some small way, what has been learned.

Illustrating the Process—Two Vignettes

The following two vignettes are designed to show how the steps in the poetry therapy process come together from the time the poem is first introduced to the closing of the client session or group meeting. These vignettes highlight the facilitator's intervention choices. They also illustrate the way in which participants' initial identifications with a poem can merge quite seamlessly with in-depth explorations and applications to self. The first example is from an individual session with a client in my psychology practice, while the second is from a growth group. Both show a melding of discussion and writing activities.

The first example involves a poetry therapy session with a woman in her thirties whose primary goals were to improve the quality of her love relationships and enhance her sense of identity as a single woman. In previous weeks, she had been exploring her pattern of passive behavior with controlling male partners. In this session, I presented the following poem by Derek Walcott (1986), 'Love after Love':

> *The time will come*
> *when, with elation,*
> *you will greet yourself arriving*
> *at your own door, in your own mirror,*
> *and each will smile at the other's welcome,*
>
> *and say, sit here. Eat.*
> *You will love again the stranger who was your self.*
> *Give wine. Give bread. Give back your heart*
> *to itself, to the stranger who has loved you*
>
> *all your life, whom you ignored*
> *for another, who knows you by heart.*
> *Take down the love letters from the bookshelf,*
>
> *the photographs, the desperate notes,*
> *peel your own image from the mirror.*
> *Sit. Feast on your life.*

(Walcott 1986, p.328)

Providing a copy for each of us, I asked the client if she were willing to read it aloud, and she readily agreed. Immediately she had two reactions. She said she really liked the poem, and tears welled up in her eyes as she read the line, 'You will love again the stranger who was your self' (Walcott 1986, p.328). When I asked her to stay with this line and to articulate her reactions to it, she focused on how she always became what others wanted her to be. She then expressed a desire to find herself and also to find a partner with whom she genuinely wants to spend time. Without prompting from me, she went on to discuss how she is usually a follower in social situations, yet qualified her remarks as she thought about settings where she 'shines' as a leader. I could see her brighten when she recalled situations where she has taken initiative and has been respected. She then also voiced her desire to stop discounting her needs in relationships.

At this point, I invited her to write for about five minutes, focusing on the above mentioned line that had stirred her so profoundly. When she read her writing aloud, she was particularly struck by an insight embodied in words that went something like this: 'I let go, so others can hold on.' Repeating this line, I asked her to enlarge upon it, and when she did, she articulated that her fear of losing the experience of feeling loved and needed had resulted in habitual self-effacement. She elaborated on this point by recognizing how she frequently obliterates her voice, remaining silent when she has a preference and sometimes not even realizing that she has failed to utter her words aloud. She could also now talk about how being alone has caused her anxiety and how 'feasting' on her 'life' is a foreign yet very appealing notion. In bringing closure to our therapeutic conversation, I invited her to imagine, in written form, what 'wine' and 'bread' she can 'give' herself and to bring these reflections to our next session.

The second example occurred in a time-limited growth group, which met in a community center and consisted of five individuals, four women and one man. The primary goals were to increase self-esteem and attain more satisfying family relationships. This particular meeting, the fifth one in an eight-session group experience, began with the reading of Wellington's 'I Wanted to Be a Cauliflower' (1977), a poem reprinted in Chapter 3. As you may recall, in this poem, an adult woman uses food imagery to describe the difference between her bland personality and the spicy life of her sister who received more attention from their mother. With the passage of time, however, the situation seems to change for all the parties involved.

After I read the poem aloud slowly and with emphasis, I asked if two other participants, each taking a stanza, would volunteer to read the poem aloud, so that we could hear it a second time. During both readings, participants' facial expressions and other nonverbal cues suggested alertness, amusement, surprise, delight and thoughtfulness. With these in mind, I opened discussion by noting the energy in the room and the mischievous look on one group member's face. She referred to her drab hair color which her mother called 'dishwater blond' and distinguished it from the bright hair color of her two sisters. She indicated that she felt stigmatized by this label and had begun coloring her hair in her early twenties. She also recognized how much she currently values vivid colors in many areas of her life.

I used Wellington's word 'verve' in responding to this first speaker, in order to subtly return us to the poem and encourage responses from others. Also, looking around the room I asked if there were specific lines that evoked anything of a personal nature. A second group member, following the lead of the first participant, recounted how she felt 'nondescript' and 'muffled' as a child and had 'verve' only when alone imaginatively playing horses in the field behind the family home. There, 'the boy part' of her could emerge, and she could feel free and 'make noise.' Several in the group, from their nonverbal responses, seemed to resonate with the duality of her life as the 'good little girl' versus the galloping horse-rider. I highlighted this separation between the two worlds of this participant, in order to bring this discussion out into the group. I asked if there were anything about this poem that evoked significant contrasts for anyone else. The one man in the group began to talk about the bland diet he grew up with and the spicy food he presently enjoys. He also differentiated his tastes from those of his 'conservative' father. Intuiting that he had more to say, I reflected the tenor of his meaning with the words: 'You go for the hot chili peppers' and also highlighted the contrast he had suggested between his past and present and between him and his father. A short while later, after others had commented about contrasts and changes in their lives, this man began to discuss another important personal duality between saying what is acceptable versus voicing 'something scandalous' without being 'apologetic.' At this point, I sensed that he had more to say but was not yet ready to do so. Meanwhile, others in the group began to enthusiastically discuss the 'sauce' that they have for themselves these days and how their 'spicy' personalities affect their relationships especially with their husbands. Three of the women in the group began exploring the two sides of 'sauciness' for them—their guilt over being 'bitchy' along with their acceptance of 'feisty' behaviors that add zest to their own and others' lives. My interventions as facilitator were minimal at this point, because group members, in a caring and respectful manner, were asking the probing questions that encouraged others to elaborate on their responses.

As the discussion proceeded and several group members were focusing on the roles and forces that had compelled them to conform, I looked at the man, referred to earlier, sensing, from his physical movements, that he was anxious to speak. Without hesitation, he indicated that he had been 'acting a part' for the first 40 years of his life and, only within the past decade, had come out as a gay man. He also revealed to the group that he had very recently ended a long-term relationship with a man several years younger than him. His revelation was met with support and appreciation. Group members were gratified by his trust in them and felt that they now knew him better. Expressing relief and feeling more fully connected to the other participants, this man could now talk about how he had been identifying with losses that others had earlier discussed. He also recognized how his honesty enabled him to receive support for his current grieving.

The woman who had earlier focused on her jaunts of boyish freedom as a child immediately connected with his revelation, referring to her own sense of gender-related 'imprisonment.' She had felt she could not fully be her female self in a world with so many prescribed rules for feminine behavior. Another participant, who had not said very much but had looked quite attentive throughout the discussion, spoke of her past experience in Alcoholics Anonymous. There she had learned how healing it can be to tell our 'worst secrets' and discover that we are not alone with our stigma. This response led to another group member's sharing of her own 'worst secret'—a deep sense of depression during the early months of her pregnancy many years ago. She described how her shame-filled, isolating experience was eventually relieved and normalized through the support of a community and the reading of others' personal accounts.

At this point, I decided to introduce a writing activity to help participants build upon their insights and to clarify or summarize the ways in which their sense of themselves and their interactions with others have changed over the years. I asked everyone to think of a food they strongly dislike and another they love, and to develop a two-stanza poetic piece using the frame, 'I used to be like (disliked food), but today I am like (loved food) and embellishing each stanza with details of their chosen foods—their flavors, textures, tastes, and appearance. With the 'Cauliflower' poem as their model, group members eagerly put pen to paper.

After about ten minutes of writing, they shared their poems with delight, celebrating the progress they have made in their lives. One chose a 'dried prune' to embody his former non-vital self and a 'juicy plum' for his present self. Another chose for her former self 'liver,' which when cooked has 'an awful color' and for her present self, 'spumoni ice cream,' with its varied flavors and hues. A third, selecting 'booze' for the past identity and 'milk' for the present self, realized that booze 'controls people's opinions' while milk represents 'nurturing.' She also expressed her present desire to work on respecting others more fully without trying to 'jump in to change them.' In concluding the group meeting, I invited everyone to reflect more fully upon what they had written in their food poems before our next session.

While these two vignettes focus on one complete session, the poetry facilitation process usually spans several meetings, whether we are working on a developmental level with community-based groups or on a clinical level with patients. The feelings, themes, and concerns emerging in one session often suggest possible directions for subsequent ones. The choice of poems for these ongoing sessions is thus organically linked to what has previously occurred. Each session builds upon the other with poetic materials to match the areas that are suggested.

Facilitating poetry therapy sessions, as this chapter indicates, involves a series of steps including the introduction of the poetic material, the use of questions and nonverbal behaviours designed to elicit personalized reactions, interventions that encourage in-depth exploration of initial responses and ways to achieve closure that helps highlight newly gained insights and further areas of inquiry that have surfaced.

When we integrate poetry or contemplate integrating poetry into our practice of helping others, we join a long line of our forebears who celebrated the unique personal value of poems for growth and healing. We probably would not embark upon such an endeavour if we did not enjoy poetry ourselves. However, when we introduce poetic materials into our work with clients, patients, workshop participants or students, we go far beyond our own tastes and preferences. In this section, 'Poems: Springboards to Growth and Healing,' we can see how the journey undertaken by the poetry therapist or facilitator involves a series of important steps. The first involves honing our awareness of poetry's therapeutic elements and collecting a sizeable file of poems that have the potential to heal and illuminate. The second step involves making strategic decisions, on a case by case basis, regarding the most appropriate poems to use in specific therapeutic and educational encounters. The third step pertains to the actual facilitation process through which individuals, couples, families or groups are encouraged to actively engage with the materials in ways that will be more beneficial for them.

PART TWO

Stories

Stimuli for Personal Development and Relationship Building

CHAPTER 6

The Role and Personal
Magic of Stories

The Essential Role of Story in Human Civilization

Stories are an integral feature of our human experience and history. They occupy an important place in most people's lives from the time they are very little to the time they grow old. From ancient to present times, stories have had a communal as well as a personal function. Ancient cave drawings suggest that story telling was a significant aspect of very early civilizations and thus has had a time-honored place in human history. Fairy tales, folk tales, fables, parables, and myths have helped provide a record of civilizations, embodying the ethos, exploits and heroic deeds of communities. They have served to explain mysterious natural phenomena, to unite people, to teach moral lessons, to entertain and to touch the soul. Stories of a people are central to one's cultural and ethnic heritage, as Native American author Leslie Marmon Silko (2006) emphasizes in her poem, 'Ceremony.' Here she tells us that stories 'are all we have, …to fight off / illness and death.' For this writer, 'You don't have anything / if you don't have the stories' (Silko 2006, p.2).

Today, readers are entertained and edified by fictional works, including fairy tales, folk tales, literary short stories and nonfictional narratives in the form of memoirs and personal vignettes. While I will be addressing all of these genres in this chapter, I will emphasize the literary short story and its more recent offshoot, the short-short story or what some call 'sudden fiction.' As an educator, workshop facilitator in community settings and clinician, I have found these latter forms to be particularly meaningful for personal growth and relationship enhancement.

While the extended fiction we find in novels or plays can profoundly affect readers and can certainly function as a therapeutic medium, I am not including novels, novellas or plays in this book. My focus on stories ranging from less than one page to 14 pages is due to the fact that these works can be read or heard within the context of a single session. Presenting works in this way provides powerful immediacy, and facilitators can encourage unrehearsed responses from participants, which are then contemplated and developed.

The Personal Value of Story

Many individuals in the fields of mental health, medicine, education and literary study have noticed the therapeutic or edifying quality of stories for the individuals and groups that they have worked with over the years. While formal research studies are lacking, there is abundant anecdotal evidence that stories enrich people's lives, promoting illumination and mental health for individuals of all ages.

In therapy, developmental group and educational settings, stories can be introduced to elicit personally meaningful responses from participants. Through discussion, participants explore their responses to stories, in order to gain new insights and recognize important features within their own lives. In her workshop, entitled 'Palm-of-the-Hand Stories in Bibliotherapy,' Sherry Reiter (1998), one of the leaders of the poetry/ bibliotherapy movement, captured the essence of the story therapy I will be focusing on here, when she noted, 'It is not a bibliotherapy session till the call of the story, with the help of the facilitator, calls forth a parallel or different story of the participants.'

In *Literature as Exploration*, Louise Rosenblatt (1968) eloquently introduces the principles that helped form the foundation of the reader response theory of literary criticism, and her insights are strikingly pertinent to the helper who introduces stories into their therapeutic work. Rosenblatt describes what 'happens in the reading of a literary work' in these terms:

The reader brings to the work personality traits, memories of past events, present needs and preoccupations, a particular mood of the moment, and a particular physical condition. These and many other elements in a never-to-be-duplicated combination determine his response to the peculiar contribution of the text. (Rosenblatt 1968, pp.30–31)

According to Rosenblatt, the reader, like the author, 'is creative' and 'the literary experience must be phrased as a *transaction* between the reader and the text' (Rosenblatt 1968, pp.34–35). Recognizing this active role of the reader primarily in her work with college students, Rosenblatt indicates that they 'valued literature as a means of enlarging their knowledge of the world, because through literature they acquire not so much additional *information* as additional *experience*... Literature provides a *living-through*, not simply *knowledge about*' (Rosenblatt 1968, p.38).

Rosenblatt's view of readers' personal engagement with literature aptly captures what I see as the theory underlying story therapy. She tells us that we as readers, 'participate in imaginary situations, we look on at characters living through crises, we explore ourselves and the world about us, through the medium of literature' (Rosenblatt 1968, p.37). She also even more directly refers to literature's therapeutic effect in these words:

This tendency toward identification will certainly be guided by our preoccupations at the time we read. Our own problems and needs may lead us to focus on those characters and situations through which we may achieve the satisfactions, the balanced vision, or perhaps merely the unequivocal motives unattained in our own lives. (Rosenblatt 1968, p.38)

She adds that another 'personal value of literature' is 'its objective presentation of our own problems. It places them outside ourselves, enables us to see them with a certain detachment and to understand our own situation and motivation more objectively' (Rosenblatt 1968, p.41).

Like Rosenblatt, Sophie Lazarsfeld (1949, p.26) points out that 'While fiction supposedly mirrors life, what is seen in the mirror depends upon the eyesight of the person who looks into it.' Lazarsfeld expresses the essence of story therapy when she makes the following statement:

> After having appraised the utility of 'book discussions' in my collected case histories of twenty years, I am convinced that people who like to read can make strides toward discovery of their real selves by accompanying one trained in psychological techniques upon a few conducted literary tours.' (Lazarsfeld 1949, p.26)

I resonate with this image of 'conducted literary tours' because it suggests the combined presence of a safe, holding place with the self-enhancing adventures of travel. From my own experience, I also agree with Lazarsfeld's observation that 'fictional characters and fictional situations often shorten the road to deeper insight when the usual psychological means do not,' for 'the discussion of fictional situations often flashes light on a critical spot in [a client's] own pattern, illuminating it so effectively that his self-understanding increases' (Lazarsfeld 1949, pp.31, 28). Lazarsfeld speculates that the 'shortcut' provided by fiction may be at least in part due to the fact that the fictional work bypasses the 'resistance' that clients may have to what they perceive as their therapist's 'preconceived' notions. As Lazarsfeld points out, a 'neutral' author's materials 'are offered without any analytical purpose and therefore are easier to accept without reserve' (Lazarsfeld 1949, pp.28, 32).

In her unpublished dissertation on bibliotherapy, Caroline Shrodes (1949) set forth steps in the fiction reader's psychological process that mirror those discussed earlier in the poetry chapter. The steps she delineates involve identification, projection, catharsis and development of insight.

When we first read a story or hear it read aloud, we often identify with a character or experience a personal resonance with some seemingly tangential feature of a story, such as the hero's ruby ring or the pet parrot in a cage. There may be a character in the story that reminds us of ourselves, a parent, a friend or an employer. As with a poem, a particular phrase presented by a story's narrator or voiced by a character may forge an immediate link to some aspect of our personal lives, past or present. This recognition or identification may be quite conscious or may occur on a subconscious level. One major clue that it is taking place is our strong visceral or emotional reaction, whether it be positive or negative.

Projection often occurs in tandem with identification. At times, we incorporate aspects of ourselves into a story, project our own needs, desires and fears onto a fictional character or situation, or simply ignore elements of a story that do not fit or run counter to our world view. In a sense, this projecting constitutes an unconscious creative *misreading* or *rewriting* of the story as presented.

Personal insight in response to a story can occur suddenly like an 'ah ha' response or emerge gradually. We are likely to increase our awareness when we reflect upon the parallels between ourselves and aspects of a particular story. We also tend to experience forward movement when we recognize what helped generate our creative 'revisions' of the original text. This recognition can be facilitated by considering others' contrasting responses to the same material.

Whether we identify with or project onto features of a story, there is always an author behind the scenes shaping the story's experiences. In most stories, there is a sense that the writer's or narrator's guiding voice is an authentic one, speaking to us across time and space. As professor and bibliotherapy expert, Joseph Gold (1988, p.140) points out, 'Since the story-maker or fiction writer is a human, s/he shares the anxieties and hopes of the reader, thus representing and embracing the reader in an organized, coherent story.'

Gold (1988, p.146) addresses the value of fiction as 'therapeutic recreation.' Basing his beliefs on years of his own and others' experiences, he reports being well aware of how readers time and again attest to the personally enhancing and eye-opening nature of the fiction they read. Gold (1988, p.139) points out that reading fiction 'permits role-playing, modeling, socializing experience in a range of situations not available in life experience.' He further notes that 'Reading fiction invites identification, or counter-identification relatively safely by the use of surrogate-selves that can be lived through and then left, an activity which seems to produce insight and self-awareness and thus catharsis.' He also asserts the value of fiction in 'normalizing the private trauma of life-crises' and helping to 'articulate latent feelings' (Gold 1988, pp.139–140).

Based on my experience with students, growth-group participants and psychotherapy clients over the years, I heartily concur with Gold's (1988) statements. When we read or hear stories, we go beyond our personal daily lives, expanding our possibilities, yet also come home to rediscover ourselves in a new way. When we identify with a story's characters, we experience vicariously the triumph and the pain, the laughter and tears, the success and failure, we meet there. Often, we experience a character's frustration and breakthrough in the face of a moral dilemma or particularly challenging choice.

In *Life Guidance through Literature* (1992), Art Lerner, one of the fathers of biblio/poetry therapy, and Ursula Mahlendorf, a literature specialist, point out that when we read fiction about life and reflect on what we read, we:

> have the time and composure to explore in our imagination alternative courses of action and to think through the choices an author attributes to characters. We can agree or disagree with both characters and authors. In fact, precisely because a work of fiction is multidimensional, we can experience and interpret it in many valid ways. (Lerner and Mahlendorf 1992, p.xi)

In *Family Insights through the Short Story*, Rose Somerville (1964) emphasizes literature's potential for increasing sociological as well as psychological awareness. She asserts that imaginative literature can be the most appropriate resource for family life educators. Explaining why fiction is effective in family study, Somerville (1964, p.5) writes: 'Fiction draws him [the reader] into imaginary participation in family situations and interaction. He shares the feelings of the character with whom he identifies and thereby becomes alert to the motivations of other characters in the story.' Somerville (1964, p.6) further asserts that 'Classroom analysis of the story offers the student an opportunity to compare with his classmates the inferences he has made concerning affect and intent of characters and the conclusions he has drawn concerning social pressures operative in the situation.'

In organizing and editing a short story anthology, *Family: Stories from the Interior* (Chavis 1987), I had Somerville's views in mind. For this collection, I chose stories that would enable readers to explore the various dyads within a family: husband-wife, mother-daughter, mother-son, father-daughter, father-son and siblings. The stories contained here invite the reader into the minds and hearts of family members as they face their own ambivalence and the rhythmical movement between intimacy and distance. This collection was designed to provide a forum for readers to better understand the communication patterns, emotions, roles and habits that inform family functioning. It also was designed to be a vehicle for understanding one's own past and present family dynamics. Family life educators who have supplemented their didactic material with these and other short stories report to me that students engage personally with the fictional material in ways that both help them understand their own role in their families of origin and prepare them for their work as family counselors.

Samuel Gladding (1994), a prominent counseling educator, also advocates using fiction to teach family counseling and cites these reasons for doing so: '(a) to increase awareness of affect, (b) to better understand family dynamics, (c) to foster insight, and (d) to promote objective compassion.' He points out that 'Through vicariously experiencing family crises...counselors gain insight into the reasoning that family members go through in creating or resisting change' (Gladding 1994, pp.192–193).

While the previously mentioned individuals all focus on fiction, others have singled out the memoir type story as particularly illuminating. Dean Ornish (1996) celebrates the value of nonfiction stories in his 'Foreword' to Kitchen Table Wisdom, an inspirational collection of vignettes written and compiled by psycho-oncologist, Rachel Naomi Remen. Ornish (1996, p.xvii) attests to the 'healing' power of real life stories when he points out that 'A deep trust of life often emerges when you listen to other people's stories. You realize you're not alone; you're traveling in wonderful company. Ordinary people living ordinary lives are often heroes.' The resonant and evocative parable-like stories collected here demonstrate that creative nonfiction pieces can provide 'surrogate selves' in much the same way as fictional characters do.

In their fictional and nonfictional forms, stories are both socially and psychologically valuable, broadening and deepening our sense of what it means to be human. The authors of stories invite us to vicariously participate in the emotions, relationships and situations of individuals, some of whom resemble us and some of whom are vastly different from us. When we read or listen to stories, we significantly widen our range of cultural realities but also have the chance to revisit personal memories and look more keenly at what constitutes our own current life experience. We have the opportunity to expand our awareness of what to embrace and what to avoid through witnessing and reacting to story characters' internal and external landscapes.

CHAPTER 7

Therapeutic Features of Stories

If you, as a therapist or support group facilitator, wish to use stories for growth and healing, you will probably find it worthwhile to include diverse types of stories in your files. The stories that I consider appropriate for promoting mental health and wellbeing include the following elements: the presence of vividly drawn characters or beings with whom readers can identify; situations or life events that readers can imagine themselves experiencing; relationship dynamics, dilemmas and decisions that evoke personal reflection and response; an engaging style that sustains reader interest; and images that stimulate reader senses and emotions.

Therapeutic stories are also usually characterized by artistic coherence and concisely rendered detailing. Generally, stories, with their carefully chosen words and compact characterizations, organize life's disparate experiences, conflicts and emotions in attention-getting ways.

As with poems, therapeutic stories are universal enough to engage readers on a personal level and also offer some room for hope. If a story takes place in a country and time period foreign to your participants, it makes sense to ask yourself if it is likely to be personally meaningful to them. If a story has mostly tragic elements, it is important that it also contains at least a suggestion of positive possibilities.

As with poems, it is very useful to test stories out on yourself, in order to highlight or pinpoint their therapeutic qualities. As I carefully read each story, I note down key words and phrases that catch my eye and seem personally powerful in some way. I next jot down all the themes or subjects that I associate with these phrases. I also focus particular attention on the characters, their relationships, habits, choices and functional as well as dysfunctional behaviors.

As noted earlier in Chapter 3, Nicolas Mazza (2003, p.149) provides an excellent set of poetry-related questions to be used in training poetry therapy practitioners. Using this list as a basis to build upon, I have developed the following questions to ask when exploring the therapeutic features of stories:

- Is the story engaging, interesting and accessible?

- Does the narrator or point of view character draw me into the story?

- Are there phrases or passages that seem particularly evocative and/or symbolic?

- What are the themes, topics and conflicts brought out in this story?

- Are there characters, situations, behaviors, dilemmas, emotions and images that I can relate to and that others are likely to identify with?

- Are the characters likeable or unlikeable? Do they evoke my compassion, admiration, scorn or anger? If the characters are unsympathetic, do their behaviors and thoughts cause me to assess my own actions and decisions?

- What types of problems or life challenges does this story address?

- Is there a particular group of individuals for whom this story might be helpful (think in terms of age, developmental stage, gender, racial or ethnic background)?

- Is there a part of this story I would like to change? If so, in what way?

- Can I think of any potential harmful effects of using this story with others?

- Does the story have closure or resolution at the end, or does it end in an open, ambiguous way? Does the story's conclusion lend itself to creative elaborations or adaptations?

- Is there any hope or positive possibility in this story? If so, where do I find it?

- Imagine a photograph that captures the essence or a major aspect of this story for you. What exactly would it look like?

Questions such as those contained in the above list help point us toward the therapeutic qualities of stories that are presented at the beginning of this chapter. What these features have in common is their power to engage readers on a personal level, while encouraging forward movement toward life-enhancing attitudes and behaviours.

CHAPTER 8

Choosing Therapeutic Stories for Your Files

Fairy and Folk Tales, Fables, Myths and Children's Storybook Tales

I personally have mixed feelings about using fairy, folk and mythological tales for growth and healing because so many of them are violent and frightening. However, Jungian therapists are particularly at home with the archetypal plots, characters and images found in myth, folk lore and fairy tale. Elements of these works form an integral part of their psychoanalytic therapy with clients and seem to occupy a special place akin to clients' dreams. Both Bruno Bettelheim and Hans Dieckmann have written extensively on the effective use of fairy tales in the treatment of their patients. Bettelheim's work has shown that fairy tales can help children work out their fears in symbolic form. In his 'Foreword' to Hans Dieckmann's book, Bettelheim (1986) points out that 'The fairy tale's obligatory happy ending assures children that despite all their anxieties, they eventually will be victorious' and that 'Such messages help children to manage hardships in their lives, whether real or imagined' (Bettelheim 1986, pp.v–vi). Hans Dieckmann (1986) attests to the therapeutic effectiveness of fairy tales in the following words:

> This language in which fairy tales and myths speak to us out of our own unconscious is one I would miss more than

the cleverest rational theory of science. As an instrument for treating my emotionally ill patients, it has given me endless riches, and not at all infrequently a fairy tale and the insights we have drawn from its deeper significance have become the central element in treatment. (Dieckmann 1986, pp.2–3)

Dieckmann (1986, p.3) further points out that 'It is one of the most profound impressions of my professional experience that the right story at the right place and right time and which precisely grasps the patient's problem can form a bridge between two people.'

From personal experience and ten years of facilitating 'women's gatherings,' the writer and Jungian scholar Gertrud Mueller Nelson (1992, p.43) states the case for the therapeutic value of fairy tales as well as myths in this way: 'How surprised we often were, deeply touched, amazed—but mostly comforted—that the heroic lives described in these stories grappled with the issues we faced in our own lives.' Nelson found that the individual's sense of isolation evaporated in the reading and discussion of these tales, as participants and facilitator both recognized that 'Women everywhere shared our wounds, failed their trials' but 'also were given the means to heal and transform' (Nelson 1992, p.43). Elaborating on her use of the fairy tale, Nelson asserts that in its 'darkness and pain,' it helps us 'engage our own 'stuck' places, the blocks, the wounds, the fears, the passions, the possibilities' and 'We learn that only anguish and a *dis*enchantment can transform us.' She believes that 'In fairy tales the hero is transformed to what he or she was always meant to be—but was unable to become until hard work and heroic deeds had been accomplished' (Nelson 1992, p.48).

In my own work, I believe that a person's most memorable fairy tale can be both a very effective diagnostic and treatment tool. Over the years, I have noticed that 'The Little Mermaid,' 'Hansel and Gretel,' 'Little Red Riding Hood' and 'Rapunzel' are frequently cited by individuals as the ones they recall most vividly. When individuals are invited to recount their special tale as they remember it, the experience is illuminating for both facilitator and participant. I have found that the way in which clients retell this memorable story usually relates to their underlying world view and characteristic behavior patterns. Their act of narration opens up the door to recognizing and revising habitual actions that have outlived their original purpose and are therefore obstructing forward movement. When group members share their remembered versions of the same fairy tale, there is often a rich exchange that is eye-opening. While similar emphases tend to unite group members, participants are often amused and surprised by the differences they notice and usually learn from one another's diverse renderings.

There are times when it is useful to juxtapose the fairy tale as it was originally written with the one narrated from a participant's memory. As clients or growth group members rediscover forgotten elements that appear in the tale's original version, they enter fertile territory to explore. Often they come to recognize previously unacknowledged aspects of self from these newly emerged story features. For example, one client who indicated that Hansel and Gretel by the Brothers Grimm was her most memorable tale, began her retelling by describing the sister and brother getting lost in the forest and coming upon the witch's gingerbread house. She completely omitted the story's entire first portion which recounts a double abandonment. When she had an opportunity to reread the tale as it was written, she was surprised to discover that Gretel had been left to die as a very young child and had been found by the kindly woodcutter, who along with his first wife, raised Gretel as their own. The other detail that surprised this client involved the cruel selfishness of the woodcutter's second wife. This heartless stepmother pressures her husband to abandon the two children in the forest because of the family's poverty.

In focusing on the adventure and adversity the children face in the forest, this client had completely obliterated the elements of the story that reflected her personal core abandonment issues. When she rediscovered these elements of the story as originally written, she had the opportunity to explore, in a personally meaningful and cathartic way, her reactions to Gretel's situation and the stepmother's behavior. She had, in a sense, the chance to confront her own demons through details of the restored story. At the same time, when she explored the heroic and triumphant elements that had been most memorable in her own retold version, she could affirm strengths and values she had cultivated as an adult and thus celebrate who she had become in spite of past adversity.

While I do not usually introduce myths into my healing work, I recognize their symbolic power. Joseph Campbell (1986, p.55) tells us that 'Every myth…whether or not by intention, is *psychologically* symbolic. Its narratives and images are to be read, therefore not literally, but as metaphors.' As a biblio/poetry therapist, I have found the mother-daughter myth of Demeter and Persephone particularly useful because it embodies universal family and identity issues in such a captivating way. In my workshops and therapy groups on women's issues and development, I have noticed that this myth resonates with participants. It reflects the parent's plight of letting go and the push-pull of protecting your child versus accepting your child's maturation. Demeter's transformation from fertile goddess to barren hag when her golden daughter or 'youthful' manifestation disappears also signifies the aging process. Yet despite her aging, when she and her daughter reunite, Demeter experiences a revitalization so potent that it transforms the world. This mother-daughter myth embodies nature's essential rhythm of disintegration and rejuvenation. It is a story of both hope and despair, loss and retrieval, the winter and spring time of life.

Unlike myths and fairy tales, fables usually present non-human creatures who reflect humans and their life situations. These allegorical works can be worthwhile therapeutic tools, providing a safe and often light-hearted space in which to grapple with very real human triumphs and defeats, joys and sorrows. Since fables often teach a lesson, concluding with a moral precept, they can curtail creative, expansive responding on the part of participants, yet a facilitator can invite readers to modify or evaluate in their own personal terms, the simply phrased lesson of the tale. For example, an Aesop fable, 'The Town Mouse and the Country Mouse,' depicts two cousins who visit each others' homes and partake of one another's hospitality. The rural cousin generously offers a simple, wholesome meal, but his sophisticated relative 'doesn't much like this plain country food' (Aesop 2005b, p.82). He also finds the fields and woods to be 'very dull and ordinary' and brags about his 'exciting' and luxurious life in town. In response, the country mouse is enticed into dreaming about 'how wonderful it must be to live in town.' However, when the two cousins travel to town and enjoy a feast consisting of 'scrumptious' delicacies, they are frightened into hiding by a menacing house cat and a 'bounding' dog with a disturbingly loud bark (Aesop 2005b, pp.84, 86, 88). While the city resident, resigned to such harrowing episodes, has no intentions of leaving his home, the country mouse retreats in a hurry. As he does so, he utters these words: 'You may have all the goodies a mouse could ever want in your town house, but I'm going back to the country for the quiet life.' The motto closing this tale is 'BETTER TO BE HAPPY WITH WHAT YOU NEED THAN RISK EVERYTHING FOR MORE' (Aesop 2005b, p.89).

This concluding message and the differing life styles of the two mice can form the basis of much useful discussion in a group context. The story has the potential to lead to a fruitful interchange on how we manage to live in tension-fraught situations and how some of us choose to stay in such an atmosphere while others flourish in a tranquil, unsophisticated environment. The story also raises the question of how much anxiety we are willing to endure, in order to obtain the luxuries or other things we crave.

The even more famous Aesop fable, 'The Hare and the Tortoise' (1912, 2005a, 2006) has the potential to engage a variety of readers as they observe the differing behaviors of the two main characters. Since the original author lived as a slave in BCE times, there exist several versions of this tale that highlight different elements. While all that I have read center on the race between an overconfident hare and an inwardly assured tortoise, some versions emphasize the insults, even bullying of the hare or the verbal assertiveness of the quieter tortoise. Since the tale is very concise, the facilitator may find it useful to introduce two variants to increase the richness of the discussion.

Despite its seemingly simplistic moral, that 'Slow and steady wins the race' (Aesop 1912, 2006) or 'SPEED ISN'T EVERYTHING. THERE ARE OTHER WAYS OF WINNING' (Aesop 2005a), this fable contains many significant and complex themes. There is, first of all, the obvious issue of the diverse ways we tackle a task. The story raises the question of whether slow, steady deliberation or speedy movements and rapid decisions serve us best in various situations. In addition, the story invites readers to react to the hare's cockiness versus the tortoise's more measured approach to reality. In terms of the confidence issue, this story is likely to elicit an exchange of opinions regarding what degree of self-assurance accounts for success. Given the hare's taunts and the tortoise's refusal to be hurt by them, the story also opens up the question of how we characteristically react to bullying or criticisms or how we would like to react. Centering as it does on the theme of competition, Aesop's immortal tale also raises the issue of what constitutes success. Moreover, with its symbolic suggestion of life as a race, the story invites participants to generate other metaphors that they prefer, such as life as a journey or a saunter through a meadow.

An allegorical tale widely circulating on the internet called 'The Cracked Pot' (Anonymous n.d.) substitutes water vessels for people. When a poetry therapy trainee introduced me to this work a few years ago, I knew it would have a permanent place in my collection. Its two main characters are large pots hanging on opposite ends of a pole carried by a water bearer in India. Because one of the pots has a crack in it, the water bearer repeatedly returns home with only one and a half pots of water. 'Ashamed,' the cracked pot experiences 'bitter failure' over his 'imperfection.' However, a turning point occurs in this very brief story when the bearer asks the cracked pot to notice the flowers that have been growing on only its side of the path. This question leads to the upbeat conclusion, in which the bearer tells the imperfect pot that by being himself, he has brought 'beauty to grace the house.' While the individual I was supervising successfully used this story in her work with families of children with a disability, I have found it to have an even broader application. Most adult readers, in my experience, view 'The Cracked Pot' as a story celebrating everyone's unique contributions and inviting acceptance of everyone's flawed self. In addition, because it is so simply and vividly written, it can be used in children's classrooms for a variety of purposes. Children who struggle with disabilities, have been bullied or feel ostracized within their communities are likely to identify with this story.

Besides fairy tales and fables, there are fictional works embodied in the child's storybook. Since the dawn of the bibliotherapy movement in the mid-twentieth century, many works of children's literature have been seen as therapeutic. These fictional pieces are ideal for stimulating adult-child discussions of difficult life issues. These stories also help children feel a common bond with others experiencing a particular problem and can prepare children to cope more confidently with personal challenges. There are classics repeatedly cited as excellent vehicles for helping children express emotions such as anger or grief and cope with transitional events such as the birth of a sibling or going to school for the first time. When children discuss such stories, they can voice their reactions to changing views of self, losses they have suffered, and bullies they have encountered. As they identify with the story's characters, children have an opportunity to vocalize their fears and generate creative solutions to their problems.

Many children's storybooks resemble fables in that the main players are creatures such as bears or rabbits. For instance, each of the books in the 'Berenstain Bears' series depicts a life situation that children are likely to encounter. These situations are developed in an honest and positive way. For example, *The Berenstain Bears and the Trouble with Friends*

(Berenstain and Berenstain 1986) focuses on a friend who is overly bossy yet generous at times. The book provides a platform for discussing how we deal with controlling people and how we accept the imperfections of our friends while asserting ourselves. It also provides a stimulus for discussing loneliness and negotiation of conflict.

Another tale that is a classic in child bibliotherapists' files is *Badger's Parting Gifts* by Susan Varley (1984). This story illustrates a genre of grief narratives appropriate for children but beneficial for adults as well. In this storybook, Badger's death causes overwhelming sadness in his friends, even though he tries to prepare them with a comforting note when he senses his end is near. It is evident that Badger is not afraid to die, and his death, described as a dash through a tunnel and a free fall 'out of his body,' appears painless. In contrast to Badger's sense of peaceful resignation, his friends, consisting of moles, frogs and rabbits, all deeply mourn the loss of Badger who 'had always been there when anyone needed him.' After a dismal winter, the animals gather to reminisce over special times they shared with Badger. Each memory encapsulates some skill that Badger has passed on to them. This story illuminates how healing from grief takes place when loved ones join to affirm the ongoing presence of the deceased in meaningful ways.

There are also many storybooks that depict human characters in various life situations. Ones that have a special place in my therapy files are Maurice Sendak's *Where the Wild Things Are* (1991) and two works written by Judith Viorst, *The Tenth Best Thing about Barney* (1971) and *Alexander and the Terrible, Horrible, No Good, Very Bad Day* (1972).

I began to see the therapeutic possibilities of *Where the Wild Things Are* after one of my clients mentioned that it was her favorite childhood book, the one she returned to in memory time and again. She had grown up with a terminally ill brother and a critical father who both sporadically erupted into rages. With such experiences producing shame, anxiety and deep resentment, she found, in Sendak's work, the embodiment of her struggles with her own childhood 'monsters.'

After this client mentioned Sendak's tale, I began to see this title turning up in discussions of therapy with children. While it is filled with unpleasant images of monsters with their 'terrible' eyes, teeth and claws, this story provides an effective springboard for discussion of ways we deal with our anger and gain some control over our fears. It addresses the monsters inside us as well as the external objects, incidents and live beings that frighten us and is just as useful for adults as for children.

Max, the story's child protagonist, makes 'mischief,' is called a 'WILD THING' and is sent to bed without his supper. A very feisty boy, Max, wearing his 'wolf suit,' even threatens to devour his mother. When he dreams or fantasizes, he enters a forest replete with formidable creatures. Yet he remains undaunted, commanding these monsters to 'BE STILL,' staring directly into their 'yellow eyes,' and even being made 'king' of the 'wild things.' However despite this extraordinary success, his loneliness and desire 'to be where someone loved him best of all' drive him home where a hot supper magically awaits him.

Alexander and the Terrible, Horrible, No Good, Very Bad Day (Viorst 1972) presents the reader with a schoolboy who tells us about all the slights, mishaps and misfortunes that comprise his day. Throughout the story, he feels rejected and criticized by parents, teachers, friends and siblings and fails to receive the comforting he seems to crave. Repeatedly, Alexander claims that he is going to Australia, his way of escaping the reality he currently faces. Lying in bed at the end of this dismal day, he concludes his tale with the words, 'My mom says some days are like that. Even in Australia.'

Alexander is a fitting choice for story therapy because it describes a plethora of irritations and unfortunate occurrences that often distress children in their daily lives. While this book is recommended for children ages five through nine, it can be appropriate for adolescents, teenagers and adults as well. When I have used it with adults, some center on the lack of support or attention the child receives. These participants are often incensed at the seeming indifference of the adults surrounding this young boy. Others responding to Viorst's story reflect on their own 'bad days' when everything seems to go wrong, and they usually end up discussing how they cope with these trying times. Many focus on this tale's suggestion that there are both good and bad days in the cyclical patterns of life. Some take special note of Alexander's tendency to concentrate only on the negatives, such as the pajamas that he hates or the lima beans served for dinner. These same readers often emphasize the fact that the boy's early morning mishaps cause him to assume he will have an awful day. Responses such as these lead to illuminating conversations on how our own negative assumptions can become self-fulfilling prophecies.

Literary Short Stories

Emerging from the epics, fables and tales of previous eras, the modern literary short story genre that became popular in the late nineteenth and early twentieth century typically blends intense psychological realism with evocative symbolic elements. Works of this genre also usually present one or two characters on the brink of discovery or in the throes of a crucial dilemma.

When we read a short story with well-drawn characters, vivid images, striking symbols, and a compelling, believable plot, our mind, heart and gut are engaged. When short story writers portray their characters, they generally move right inside their psyches, revealing to readers the workings of the emotional or psychological self. Through the modern short story, we thus have access to a deep reservoir of material on the interior life of individuals as they confront their demons, affirm their personhood, and interact with others.

As we come to know a fictional person intimately, we can compare and contrast ourselves with that individual, and we may find ourselves relieved to discover we are not alone in harboring feelings of helplessness, shame or anger. Also, from a safe vantage point, we can witness the consequences of risky or unhealthy actions and can mentally try on different ways of coping with challenges resembling our own. Characters that overcome odds or behave in life-enhancing ways may provide roadmaps useful to us personally. Stories presenting a set of values or a life style different from our own may cause us to modify current goals or re-evaluate the direction of our own lives.

Having recognized the therapeutic possibilities of short fiction many years ago in the classroom, I continue to witness its power in clinical and nonclinical settings for individuals of various ages and from diverse cultures. As readers discuss a story in a group setting or one-on-one with a therapist or trained facilitator, they tend to experience a healthy blend of detachment and involvement. Discussing the plight and flawed behavior of fictional characters, they can stand somewhat off to the side and not feel threatened by the possibility that they will expose deeply personal material in an untimely fashion. They may also emotionally identify with the various elements of the story at their own pace or in response to the deft interventions of the helper.

In my files are stories from the late nineteenth century to the present time. While the older ones may be old fashioned in terms of some external details, they are universal enough to arouse personally relevant responses. They contain enough elements to engage readers, in spite of the fact that they may contain obsolete roadsters, gramophones or typewriters. For example, even though Edna Ferber's story 'Sudden Sixties' (1947) was first published in 1922, today's readers find much in common with the 60-year-old grandmother who is trying to maintain control of her life and her time in the face of her adult daughter's demands. Also, while a few readers complain that some details in Ring Lardner's 'Old Folks' Christmas' (1963) are outmoded, they nevertheless usually proceed to discuss the characters and incidents with animation, making personal applications that are very meaningful.

While short stories appropriate for the therapist's files ought to locate the reader in an absorbing specific time and place to enliven the depiction of characters and their actions, these stories should spread a wide enough net to catch the attention of a large number of readers. Even stories taking place in a culture and time foreign to readers can have this broad appeal. For example, many story therapy and growth group participants resonate with the mother-daughter dynamics and identity issues in Amy Tan's 'Two Kinds' (2003) or in Hisaye Yamamoto's 'Seventeen Syllables' (1985), even if they know nothing about Asian family life or have not experienced being the daughter of an immigrant.

In assessing the content of stories for our files, we also need to consider their endings. While some contain definitive endings, the majority are partially or completely open-ended. Those with closure present a clear resolution of the story's central conflict or tension and sometimes present overt moral messages. The open-endedness and ambiguity that is a common, even defining, feature of the modern short story provides a fertile ground for projections and an opportunity for participants to complete the story in their own way.

Although both open and closed endings can be useful in different situations, it is my opinion that stories with didactic conclusions that seem to force their message upon us because of the narrator's tone are usually not desirable in a therapeutic context. These stories leave too little room for the reader's active engagement and can actually militate against free exchange of opinions. However, stories where a serious conflict is resolved through the realistic actions of characters can inspire hope and provide comfort.

While stories lacking closure may trouble some readers, especially those who habitually crave speedy solutions, such nebulous endings can be quite fruitful. For example, if a story focuses on a character whose indecisiveness leaves him or her in limbo, readers may benefit from a discussion of their energetic reactions to this negative role model. Readers, in fact, are often inspired to rewrite such a story in their own more proactive terms, a process that can be very enlightening. Moreover, since our own lives are a dynamic process in which neat closure often does not occur, ambiguously concluded works tend to more closely reflect our own daily experience.

There are short stories that ought not to be included in the therapist's files. These include ones that encourage suicide or violent behavior in general, are filled with gratuitously violent or obscene details, confirm a world view that denigrates a particular group of people or lack even a shred of hope.

Stories that recount traumatic happenings or end tragically need to be used with a great deal of caution. There are two short stories that come to mind here, and while both have a place in my files, as a helper, I introduce them with serious reservations in mind. The first, 'The Widow's Son' (2003) by Irish author Mary Lavin, focuses on a cantankerous widow and her 14-year-old son. The second, 'The Things They Carried' (2010) by U.S. author Tim O'Brien, depicts the experiences of soldiers in the Vietnam War.

In Lavin's story, a poor, hardworking widow centers all her aspirations on her only child named Packy, a clever boy excelling in his studies. While we are told that she 'lived for his sake' and 'wore herself out working for him' (Lavin 2003, p.472), she never shows tenderness toward this adored child, even after the bicycle accident that constitutes the chief dramatic event of this narrative.

As Packy speeds downhill one late afternoon, in his hurry to tell his mother about receiving an important scholarship, he falls off his bicycle when he swerves to avoid hitting his mother's old hen. When he dies from his injuries, the heartbroken mother blames him for causing his own death, asking 'Why did he try to save an old hen that wasn't worth more than six shillings?' For years thereafter, she complains to her neighbors, posing the question, 'Why did he put the price of an old clucking hen above the price of his own life?' (Lavin 2003, pp.474–475). This lasting resentment following her beloved's demise aggravates her grieving process.

Lavin (2003) complicates this tale of grief even further when, in unique fashion, she exercises her prerogative as the story's controlling agent, in order to invent an alternative ending. This new ending corresponds to that which some townspeople may have created as the years pass. In transitioning to this second option, she speculates that some of the widow's neighbors 'must have been stirred to wonder what would have happened had Packy ridden boldly over the clucking hen' (Lavin 2003, p.475). In this revisioning of the scenario, Packy escapes injury but kills the hen instead. Filled with rage, the mother berates her son for his carelessness and even beats him with the hen's bloody, bedraggled carcass. She unjustly accuses him of deliberately killing the hen to avoid going to college because there would then 'be no money in the box when the time comes to pay for books and classes' (Lavin 2003, p.477). When she later finds out about his scholarship, she regrets her reaction and wants to hug her son but is too proud to cuddle him in public. When she looks at her son and what she has done to him, her own shame generates blinding fear and corrosive resentment that eventually drive her son away for good.

While Lavin's story is clearly very sad and does not seem to offer any hope, its dual version format increases its therapeutic potential. The author's juxtaposition of two radically different scenarios not only creates an artistic distance from the morbid details but also presents a powerful message on the tragic wastefulness of bitter recriminations and the ways we can destroy our most important relationships. It also is an effective story for exploring that very powerful yet often hidden experience of shame that drives so much dysfunctional behavior. In her last paragraph, Lavin (2003, p.479) leaves us with much food for thought. She states that 'Perhaps a great many of our actions have this double quality about them, this possibility of alternative' and asserts that 'the tragedy we bring upon ourselves' is worse than even a 'tragic' fortune 'that is destined for us.'

When I introduced 'The Widow's Son' into a growth group about two years ago, a lively and fruitful discussion of the two versions ensued. Participants were particularly struck by the mother's inability to express sorrow in a way that afforded her relief. They also focused on the missed opportunities of loving communication between mother and son, expressing how important it is to voice appreciation for those we love. Some in the group also became more aware of how blaming or shaming behavior keeps people from loving connection with one another.

This group experience with Lavin's work helped me recognize that even a story with such a tragic major event can be quite therapeutic.

I also came to realize how my initial aversive reaction to this story's subject matter related to my own concept of the worst possible thing that can happen to a human being, the loss of one's child. I have had several close friends who have lost a child, and frankly the idea terrifies me. In using stories as therapy, it is important to be aware of our own personal 'demons' and how these determine our acceptance or rejection of particular stories for our therapy files.

The second story, fraught with tragic, discomfiting detail, is 'The Things They Carried' (O'Brien 2010), a frequently anthologized work that I find is surprisingly popular with a wide range of readers. Its powerful imagery and style of narration which resembles the repetitive incantations of a solemn list poem convey the sobering realities of combat in a way few stories do. As readers, we get right inside the soldier's experience, as O'Brien presents a variety of men and their reactions to the ever-present danger they face and the constant physical burdens they bear. The heaviness of the equipment and provisions carried over endless miles of hostile terrain are seamlessly interwoven with the emotional baggage of fear, fatigue, guilt, anger, despair and hope.

The different soldiers cope in their own ways, some turning to drugs, some daydreaming about thoughts of home and significant others left behind and others packing chocolate for survival. While a few totter on the brink of panic, most close off feeling, expressing grim humor and presenting a macho facade to mask inner terror. The main point of view character is a sensitive lieutenant who wants to be a responsible leader of his men. However, he must face his failure to function as an adequate protector, when one member of his platoon dies from a landmine explosion.

It is no surprise that the author of this story is a Vietnam War veteran, for it rings true with every word. When we read, we know O'Brien has been there, but we also see that he possesses consummate skill to bring us there as well. 'The Things We Carried' is an unpleasant story but a necessary one. It serves to sensitize us to the realities of combat situations, so that we better understand what returning soldiers are facing. It is a fitting work for the story therapist's files, because it is a moving and authentic work that can help veterans recount the military experiences they so often keep locked inside. The very existence of this story gives permission to voice one's own unspeakable truths. Affirming the fact that courage and terror can coexist, O'Brien's work provides an effective stimulus for much-needed dialogues on the unseen scars and wounds that soldiers bring home from war zones. Since it is a story that is likely to trigger traumatic memories, it ought to be read in a supportive setting with a skilled facilitator who is equipped to handle severe emotional reactions.

Another story that is filled with travail, but has some ray or hope or positive possibilities is Sandra Cisneros' 'Woman Hollering Creek' (1992b). When I read it for the first time, I recognized its therapeutic potential. First of all, I found myself immediately drawn to the story's protagonist. Early in the story, we are privy to the intense emotional life of Cleofilas, a battered wife and mother who feels helpless to change her situation. We also learn that she is a discerning, sensitive human being with a craving to return to her parents' home across the border in Mexico. The author doesn't dwell on her husband's violence, but shows us the world through Cleofilas' eyes, a world permeated by male dominance and desire. A devoted parent to her young son and pregnant with her second baby, whose health concerns her, Cleofilas visits a clinic for her prenatal exam, despite her husband's objection. At this clinic, her bruises are noticed, and two women helpers are called by the clinic staff to help Cleofilas leave her husband. Although Cleo does not know if she will receive a welcome in her poor home community, her empowerment at the story's end is palpable. This story's conclusion makes it an appropriate choice for women who are and or have been in abusive relationships. Felice, the feisty and independent woman who drives Cleo across the border, is unlike any woman that Cleo has ever met, and her effect on Cleo is profound as these final words in the story suggest:

> Can you imagine, when we crossed the arroyo she just started yelling like a crazy, she would say later to her father and brothers. Just like that. Who would've thought? Who would've? Pain or rage, perhaps, but not a hoot like the one Felice had just let go. Makes you want to holler like Tarzan, Felice had said. Then Felice began laughing again, but it wasn't Felice laughing. It was gurgling out of her own throat, a long ribbon of laughter, like water. (Cisneros 1992b, p.56)

Besides obvious content or thematic features, an author's stylistic choices are important as well when we are evaluating short stories for our therapeutic collection. A story's point of view or narrative mode profoundly affects our reading experience and thus is a factor for the short story facilitator to take into account. In some stories, the narrator speaks in first person, using 'I,' while in others the narrator uses a more objective sounding third person, using 'she' or 'he' or 'it.' In this latter mode, some stories open up to us the mind and heart of only one character, while others allow us to know the inner life of more than one individual. Stories with these varying narrative modes can all be suitable additions to your files as a helper.

Some 'I' stories are told as monologues in which we can imagine a person alone in a room, perhaps facing a mirror, or wandering on a busy street talking to one's self or addressing an absent or listening individual. Since the monologist's voice is usually quite intimate, we can even imagine ourselves at times mouthing the character's words.

There are three monologue stories that I have found very illuminating and therapeutic for my clients and group participants: Sandra Cisneros' 'Eleven' (1992a) and Dorothy Parker's two stories, 'A Telephone Call' (1973a) and 'The Waltz' (1973b). While all of these deal with different subjects, they each contain vivid imagery, a strong sense of voice embodying an authentic personality and struggles that many can recognize in their own lives.

Cisneros' narrator in 'Eleven' engages us immediately with her childlike voice. In a confidential tone, she shares how uncertain and immature she feels on her eleventh birthday. Her state of mind and intimate link with the reader are apparent in these words from the story's second paragraph: 'Like some days you might say something stupid, and that's the part of you that's still ten. Or maybe some days you might need to sit on your mama's lap because you're scared, and that's the part of you that's five' (Cisneros 1992a, p.6). Following her opening remarks, the narrator focuses on a humiliating incident that occurs on this day, laying open to us her struggles with her sense of self as she reacts to peers and teachers and thinks about her parents. Listening to her vivid voice, we are easily lured back in time to our own childhoods. Sitting in her classroom, this young girl is pressured into claiming that she is the owner of a bedraggled red sweater found in the classroom closet, even though it does not belong to her. Small as the matter may seem, it is magnified in her child's mind, as it embodies her embarrassment, frustration and vulnerability as a young person. Repeatedly, the speaker tells us the main thing she has learned, that when you reach a certain age, you can still feel very little.

Upon a first reading, I immediately envisioned this story as a vehicle for discussing formative childhood memories and the ways in which we all may be carrying our eleven or ten or five year old selves within us. In the story's final paragraph, the narrator sums up her perspective with the hyperbole of a distressed child: 'I'm eleven today. I'm eleven, ten, nine, eight, seven, six, five, four, three, two, and one, but I wish I was one hundred and two' (Cisneros 1992a, p.9). This evocative sentence raises the issue of what it means to be a particular numerical age and how this specific number affects our identity. I first discovered this story while preparing for a workshop on the power of words for a poetry therapy conference and used it as a springboard for exploration of the personal connotations we associate with words that designate numbers.

Another monologue, Parker's 'A Telephone Call' (1973a), takes us right inside the interior universe of an adult female speaker as she awaits a lover's phone call. As we read or listen to this monologue, we feel as if we are right there in her home with her, staring at that telephone which she calls a 'damned, ugly, shiny thing' (Parker 1973a, p.120). In a room resounding with silence, her words reflect mounting anxiety, impatience, frustration, anger and sorrow. She traverses through this variety of emotional states, as she negotiates with God, rationalizes her boyfriend's behavior and wishes him dead. Her pain is palpable as she wrestles with her pride, restraining herself from calling the recalcitrant boyfriend and alternating between self-chastisement and rage. This work has wide applicability. It suits anyone who has ever experienced unrequited love or waited helplessly for something they could not attain. It is an ideal springboard for discussing the rejection and betrayal that commonly occur in the courtship arena.

Parker's 'The Waltz' (1973b) is a monologue with a different effect, since it presents the voice of a woman dancing with a clumsy man in a public setting. The speaker's angry, critical thoughts alternate with the polite, accommodating remarks she speaks aloud to her dance partner. The narrator's external and internal voices are clearly differentiated by the author's use of italics for the words spoken aloud. For example, while the narrator opens her story with the words, '*Why, thank you so much. I'd adore to,*' the very next lines are 'I don't want to dance with him. I don't want to dance with anybody. And even if I did, it wouldn't be him. He'd be well down among the last ten. I've seen the way he dances' (Parker 1973b, p.47).

Even though this story may seem dated with its waltz dancing and some of its terminology, the split between one's aggressive/assertive thoughts and one's passive actions is still relevant for a great many people, women and men included. Given its universal themes and emotions, it is ideal for anyone who has trouble saying 'No.' It accomplishes, in entertaining fictional form, what so many assertiveness training books over the years have attempted to convey in a more dry, straightforward manner. Unlike the self-help manual, however, this story leaves us with an unresolved ending that is anything but prescriptive. As the story comes to a close, the monologist, despite her bitterness, sore ankles and fatigue, actually encourages a second dance with this unsavory partner, telling him, '*I'd simply adore to go on waltzing*' (Parker 1973b, p.51). The ending is so extreme that it inevitably surprises and even irritates readers into an energetic conversation on why we agree to tasks and actions that so clearly run counter to our mental and physical wellbeing. As readers, we are called upon to find solutions that Parker's character cannot yet acknowledge or pursue.

Unlike the monologue, most short stories reflect a subtle melding of a third person narrator's perspective with a single character's point of view. While we tend to sympathize with this character whose viewpoint colors the story, we are also affected by an organizing, observing voice above the fray subtly commenting on the character's personality and actions. In this way, we profit from knowledge that the character often lacks. In addition, stories with this single point of view leave a sense of mystery regarding the thoughts, feelings and motives of the other characters. This omission creates a fertile opportunity for the facilitator who introduces a story for growth and healing. The facilitator can ask participants to fill in the omitted details, to flesh out the perspective that is missing. For example, in 'The Widow's Son' (Lavin 2003) discussed earlier, there is a third person narrator, and the point of view character is the mother. If readers retell this story with the son as the point of view character, several new issues are likely to emerge. For instance, participants may find themselves exploring the pressures that the only child of a demanding single parent experiences. In taking on the son's perspective, they may also explore what it feels like to communicate with a parent who is emotionally unavailable and embittered by life's cares.

Carson McCullers' 'A Domestic Dilemma' (1987) provides another good example of third person narration with a single character point of view. This short story recounts one day in the life of Martin Meadows, a young husband and father, who is married to an alcoholic and has a six-year-old son and a daughter of toddler age. His thoughts and emotional intensity dominate the story, as he worries about his children's welfare and cogitates on the measures he has taken to keep his household running while he is away at work. As readers, we are also privy to his ambivalence toward his wife, Emily. His love, tenderness and protectiveness intertwine with intense anger and fear. While trying to understand the genesis of her drinking problem and his responsibility for the present situation, he feels helpless to change his life, in spite of the fact that we see him as quite resourceful.

While Martin's perspective clearly dominates 'A Domestic Dilemma,' the story is strengthened by the presence of the third person narrator who eloquently provides details beyond the immediate range of the protagonist's consciousness. For example, the narrator explicitly names Martin's anxiety, describing how it increases when he recalls past mishaps that endangered the children and resulted from his wife's drinking. Also, after Martin's inebriated wife causes a scene in front of the children, the narrator's word choices emphasize the beleaguered husband's escalating rage. While his conscious self seems to remain calm and in control of his domestic situation, the third person narrator repeatedly drives home the true depth of his anger. For example, after putting the children to bed, Martin is described as 'prowl[ing] about the kitchen making a late meal' (McCullers 1987, p.126). In case we miss the connotation of the verb, 'prowl,' the narrator adds more connotations of savagery in these words: 'But his own anger, repressed and lurking, arose again' and 'With his elbows on the table he ate his food brutishly, untasting.' Even when Martin becomes aware of his feelings, the narrator powerfully conveys the protagonist's emotional state in words Martin would probably not use: 'By bedtime the dull, hard anger was like a weight upon his chest and his feet dragged as he climbed the stairs' (McCullers 1987, p.126).

In this complex story, even this crushing anger dissipates, at least temporarily, when Martin enters the bedroom he and his wife share. Here we are told the following: 'As Martin watched the tranquil slumber of his wife the ghost of his old anger vanished. All thoughts of blame or blemish were distant from him now.' Putting the finishing touch on the story, the narrator gives us one last look inside Martin as he gets into bed with his sleeping wife: 'His hand sought the adjacent flesh and sorrow paralleled desire in the immense complexity of love' (McCullers 1987, p.127). With this conclusion, intimate as it is, readers feel the presence of an observer's voice commenting on Martin's domestic dilemma and are left with an open door to walk through on their own. The story's lack of resolution invites readers to generate problem-solving strategies that make sense to them.

Because this story provides only the inner life of one character, it leaves gaps for readers to fill. For example, we see the wife, Emily and the two young children from only Martin's vantage point and thus never really know their impressions and sensations. Even though the older child, Andy, is only six, it is useful to ask participants in story therapy to develop his point of view out of their imaginations. For many, this activity summons up their own memories of family dysfunction or experiences of living with a parent suffering from an addiction. For those in treatment or recovery programs, it is challenging but ultimately quite helpful to elaborate on the viewpoint of Emily as she vacillates between angry denial, remorse and tearful pleas for forgiveness.

Unlike the single point of view stories, third-person narrated stories with a dual character or multiple character point of view provide us with unique opportunities we never get to have in the real world. We can be privy to the separate hearts and minds of different individuals as they interact. For example, while 'The Things They Carried' (O'Brien 2010) focuses primarily on the lieutenant's inner life, readers are allowed access to the inner life of several other soldiers, as the third person narrator, relentlessly and in starkly objective fashion, recites the litany of objects they shoulder.

'Unlighted Lamps,' an early twentieth-century story by Sherwood Anderson (1987), illustrates the powerful effect of a dual character point of view with a third person narrator. In this story, the father, who suffers from heart disease, and the 19-year-old daughter whom he has raised on his own, have both built an emotional wall that prevents expression of affection and communication on subjects of personal significance. As the story proceeds, the father's and daughter's points of view alternate, so that the reader is privy to the interior universe of both characters. This dual perspective highlights the degree to which the two individuals crave connection despite their external reserve. Each recalls moments when they might have turned the tide of their relationship. However, by the time they both decide they must establish connection, it is too late. The father dies of a heart attack, and the daughter is left to negotiate her passage into womanhood alone. While Anderson's story may seem hopeless with its tragically ironic twist, I find that it often generates discussion of the many obvious and subtle ways in which different individuals show their love. It also elicits conversation on actions we can take to resolve a challenging communication impasse that we face. Some readers find in this story a welcome wake-up call. They recognize that they need to open up communication with a loved one while that person is still living. Many readers also entertain the possibility that the reserved people they know may be submerging deep feelings and a genuine sense of caring beneath a tough exterior.

Short-Short Stories or Sudden Fiction

The short-short story, which Robert Shapard (1986, p.xiii) in his anthology *Sudden Fiction* suggests may be a 'sub-category' of the regular short story form, is a relatively recent phenomenon. Shapard, drawing upon the opinions of many American writers, describes the genre in this way: 'Highly compressed, highly charged, insidious, protean, sudden, alarming, tantalizing, these short-shorts confer form on small corners of chaos, can do in a page what a novel does in two hundred' (Shapard 1986, p.xvi). Author William Peden, quoted in Shapard's book, defines this form in ways suggesting its possibilities as a therapeutic medium: 'a single-episode narrative with a single setting, a brief time span, and a limited number of speaking characters (three or four at the most); a revelation-ephiphany: the click of a camera, the opening or closing of a window, a moment of insight' (William Peden, quoted in Shapard and Layton 1986, p.233). Irene Zahava (1990), an anthologist of women's short-short stories, points out in her 'Preface' that 'There is an energy and immediacy to these pieces that demands attention—secrets to be shared, memories to be uncovered and obsessions to be revealed.'

As the above definitions and descriptions suggest, there are advantages and caveats to consider when deciding which short-short stories are appropriate for growth and healing. Perhaps the most obvious advantage of using the very short story for therapy purposes is that it can be read in just a few minutes. Author Charles Johnson (1986, p.233) likens this form to compact lyric poems when he notes that it 'demands compressions and economy' and given its brevity, it often achieves the lasting wallop carried by Japanese haiku or koans.'

Given its concise quality, the short-short story cannot present characters or plots that are as well developed as those in the traditional short story. Although this lack of detail may diminish the features of psychological realism that help readers identify with fictional works, the fact that so much is left to the reader's imagination can be a plus. Readers have lots of leeway to develop suggestive details according to their own needs and preoccupations.

In my reading of 'sudden fiction,' I have found many works that do startle, leaving readers unsettled in ways that do not seem therapeutic. This is why the facilitator needs to be very discriminating in selecting these short-short stories. Many of these pieces have a postmodern feel to them, with a surrealistic, eerie or shocking quality akin to a Salvidor Dali or Edvard Munch painting. However, there are gems among these works that bring characters and their situations to life with concreteness and immediacy that can be very meaningful in our work as helpers.

One such gem is Pat Schneider's 'Irma' (1990), a one-page story written in the most common third person, single character point of view narrative mode described earlier. 'Irma' depicts a widow who fears her deceased husband's overbearing behavior so much that she virtually imprisons herself in her own home. Obsessing over the smell of her spouse's shoes in their bedroom closet, Irma proceeds to lock up all the rooms in the upper level of her residence, until the only space where she feels safe is her small kitchen. While Irma's visceral and emotional life infuses the story, the third person narrator's commentary provides a perspective that differs from that of Irma herself who clearly is increasingly limited by the choices she is making. For example, at the end of the story after Irma has had every room except the kitchen 'boarded up,' the third person narrator tells us that Irma 'planned the day when she would go lock by lock out into the downstairs hall, up the stairs, into the master bedroom, open the closet and clean it out' (Schneider 1990, p.137). As readers we are skeptical that this plan will materialize especially when in the story's final passage, the narrator conveys Irma's experience in this way: 'the kitchen wasn't so handy with everything in it, but it was a great saving on heat in the winter, she told herself, and the smell of woodsmoke was so full, and rich, and clean' (Schneider 1990, p.137). Irma's self-defeating rationalizations are thus highlighted through the presence of this anonymous third person voice.

Creative Non-Fiction Memoirs, Vignettes and Anecdotes

Memoirs have become very popular since the late 1950s in full-length books and in personal essays and autobiographical vignettes. While some of these shorter pieces are straightforward, literal accounts of special memories, crisis episodes and everyday heroism, others are almost fable-like or allegorical in nature, in their symbolic rendering of the protagonist's narrative.

Years ago when I was a child, my family subscribed to *Reader's Digest*, and I distinctly recall a regular feature involving the most 'unforgettable' character in one's life. In the 1960s and beyond when confessional literature came to be widely recognized, readers turned more and more to creative nonfiction pieces as a source of illumination and entertainment. Today there is even a burgeoning career in memoirist work, where a professional writer with interview or counseling skills is hired to write the story of those who want to capture their life events but do not have the energy, time or expertise to do so without a helper.

The creative nonfiction pieces that have an honored place in my bibliotherapist files are usually one to three pages, are crafted carefully with well-chosen, evocative words, and embody a strong authentic voice. For example, June Jordan's 'Ah, Momma' (1977) reads like a reverent set of letters or monologue in which a daughter directly addresses the mother of her memories. In this mini-memoir, Jordan captures mother's two sides—the mundane worker and the mysterious artistic dreamer. Only in her mother's 'little room' (Jordan 1977, p.37) could this daughter discover the alluring and creative manifestation of her beloved parent. The mother's closet-like space with its 'secrets…costumery, perfumes and photographs' is linked forever to the mother's whispered secret that she wanted to be an artist who could 'just boldly go' to 'watch the setting of the sun.' This magical side of mother that the daughter still seeks to emulate was usually hidden in much the same way as the mother's 'wild and heavy, beautiful hair' was kept covered when she worked in her 'ugly' kitchen or as a nurse or in the hospital that June hated. While the author seems to have grown up resenting the duty-driven parent who relinquished her dreams, she encapsulates her mother's 'life' and 'power' along with her own passion for art, through this written celebration of a sacred repository from her past (Jordan 1977, pp.37–38). With its dense imagery, direct address and hushed tone, Jordan's two-page piece is ideal for evoking memories of loved ones in our own lives. It invites us to confront our ambivalent attitude toward parents, explore our own conflicts between duty and desire, and reflect on the role models toward whom we gravitate.

Another poignant mother-daughter memory vignette, Alison Townsend's 'My Mother's Pastels' (2005), almost seems to form a pair with 'Ah Momma.' From *Kiss Me Goodnight* (O'Fallon and Vaillancourt 2005), a collection devoted to daughters who have lost their mothers at a young age, this vignette focuses on a daughter's special memory of times she sat beside her artist mother trying to imitate her sketching with a whole array of colorful pastels. Even though her mother never kept her sketches, Townsend seems infused with their artistry and still keeps her mother's pastels as a precious reminder of this parent whom she 'will never know' (Townsend 2005, p.173). With its poetic style and tone of tender yearning, 'My Mother's Pastels' invites us to explore the legacy of life's colors we inherit from loved ones. This story is a very appropriate medium for a healing discussion of the ways we honor our predecessors and affirm their current influence in our lives.

Kitchen Table Wisdom: Stories that Heal (1996) by Rachel Naomi Remen provides a source of moving vignettes on the lives of the author, her family members, her colleagues, her friends and her cancer patients. As the subtitle suggests, the stories gathered here are spoken from the heart. The ones that I find particularly useful in my work with others, such as 'I Never Promised You a Rose Garden' (Remen 1996b) or 'A Room with a View' (Remen 1996c) or 'Three Fables on Letting Go' (Remen 1996d), have allegorical elements and powerful endings that are inspirational while not being saccharine. They remind me of Kahlil Gibran's poetry, for they provide wisdom without the self-righteous tone.

In 'I Never Promised You a Rose Garden,' Remen (1996b) presents an important lesson in an engaging, personal manner. In the small meadow behind her California home, the author plants rose bushes and envisions a lush expanse of flowers to gaze upon. However, instead of the expected gift of flowers, she receives daily close-up views of a 'heart-stopping' stag who visits regularly to feast upon her roses. Readers of this vignette can see how Remen possesses the grace and flexibility to deeply appreciate what life hands her even when it runs counter to her original plan. She tells us, 'I thought I was planting rosebushes in order to have roses. It now seems I was actually planting rosebushes in order to have half an hour of silence with the magical animal every morning and every evening' (Remen 1996b, p.176).

'A Room with a View' (Remen 1996c) focuses on a client who has just completed a year of debilitating chemotherapy and is advised by her oncologist not to travel overnight with her husband to San Francisco because she will be 'far too weak to see the sights.' They go, in spite of this advice, and the client is able to have a 'wonderful' (Remen 1996c, p.180) time enjoying every luxury within their hotel room, from the lush towels to the fragrant bubble baths, the love-making with her husband and the view of the city lights. Filled with evocative imagery, the client's story highlights the importance of living life to the fullest and appreciating what is right in front of you. The lens we put on makes all the difference. When I read this story, I could envision its usefulness not only for individuals suffering from serious illness or chronic pain but also for anyone who could benefit from expanding their view of what is pleasurable or meaningful.

In 'Three Fables on Letting Go' Remen (1996d) once again engages the reader with a universal theme. In this piece, she includes three diverse and very brief vignettes, to illustrate how we let go or hold on to things in our lives. In the first, Remen focuses on her father's inability to relinquish a decrepit couch which stands in her parents' living room until her father dies. Even when she selects a new sofa that both her parents love, her father refuses to part with the worn-out item. The second fable-like vignette is my favorite with its image of a cabin that is 'cramped and shabby' when Remen buys it, but becomes a place of light and 'wholeness' when she throws away all the clutter, even staircases and doors. This story complements the first one very well, especially when Remen imagines her father saying, 'Just a minute, that still works, you never know when you'll need one of those' (Remen 1996d, p.183). Presenting these two vignettes together opens up rich possibilities for discussion on how parents' values affect us and on how people differ in their relationship to possessions and their surroundings. Hoarding behavior that results in overwhelming clutter is a subject of concern to many these days, and there are a growing number of individuals joining groups addressing this issue. This pair of stories can act as a springboard to discussion in these settings.

The last in this cluster of three vignettes is quite different from the previous two. It deals with a woman named Jane and her dog of many years, who dies in old age. This story focuses on a letting go that is part of this woman's unique healing process. The lesson Jane learns is that she pays quality attention to so many other dogs now that her special pet is gone. Even though she still misses her devoted canine friend, she gains a perspective that 'all dogs' seem to be 'her dog' now (Remen 1996d, p.184).

While each of the above nonfiction pieces contains a resolution that is heartwarming, they do not present oversimplified or premature solutions to challenging life problems. In my opinion, works are not therapeutic if their simplistic conclusions minimize the pain and dignity of life's struggle. Having said this, I am aware that such stories, like most of those appearing in the popular *Chicken Soup for the Soul* series, do have a temporary comforting effect for many who read them on their own. In 'feel-good' collections such as these, I have occasionally found a story that I use in my practice. One such example is entitled 'Permission to Cry' by Hanoch McCarty (1997) in *A 4th Course of Chicken Soup for the Soul* (Canfield *et al.* 1997). Told in the first person by a recently divorced father with two very young children, this short-short story immediately engages the reader with its evocative, symbolic setting. 'Alone in the wheel of light at the dining room table, surrounded by an otherwise darkened house,' the narrator sits 'in tears' (McCarty 1997, p.125). In a flashback, he recounts his evening for the reader, a time filled with parental and household responsibilities that he now bears alone as the full custodial parent and sole breadwinner. Determined to provide 'as normal and stable a home life as possible' for his children, he 'put[s] on a happy face' for them, and it isn't until he gets them to bed, that he is broadsided by grief. 'Unexpected, convulsive sobs,' we are told, 'overtook' him. Back to the present, this man now sits with his sense of loss, illuminated by the light above him (McCarty 1997, p.126).

The resolution of McCarty's story comes in a form that is evocative and significant. His five-year-old son emerges from his bedroom with 'a sympathetic face' and 'a pair of little arms' to wrap around his father. When, in response to this loving gesture, the father apologizes for his tears, the son wisely utters the story's lesson: 'It's okay Daddy. It's okay to cry, *you're just a person*' (McCarty 1997, p.127). While we might see this ending as overly sentimental, it does focus on a burden several of my recently divorced clients carry. They feel as if they need to repress emotions that might make them look weak or might distress their children. As a result, they give themselves no room to be human in the most trying of times. 'Permission to Cry' presents a message these individuals can benefit from hearing, especially when couched in a fictional scenario with which they are likely to identify.

When collecting therapeutic stories for your files, it is a good idea to include a wide variety of subgenres including fairy tales, folk narratives, myths, fables and children's storybooks. However, my particular focus in this chapter has been on the selection process for the literary short story, which I have found to be a particularly powerful resource in my work as a therapist and educator. When evaluating these narratives for my files, I focus on a variety of salient factors. I pay attention to the narrative mode devised by the author and how this choice affects whose point of view is represented and whose voice is speaking to us. I consider the story's degree of hope and despair along with its degree of universality and its accessibility to audiences in the current day. I also look at how much room readers have to generate their own meaning and activate their own moral judgments in relation to the characters and events they encounter in the world of the story.

CHAPTER 9

Selecting Stories for Specific Participants and Settings

In choosing the types of stories described in Chapter 8 for your therapy files, you probably will be focusing mainly on those that you think are relevant to the clients you usually counsel or the type of population you expect to work with. However, in the actual selection process for a specific client, student or growth group participant, there is a wide array of factors to consider.

Factors to Consider

It is important to pay attention to specific therapeutic goals which involve both the key issues the client is presently addressing and the major areas where growth is indicated. It is crucial to consider the client's present state of mind, primary emotional tone or ego strength and the level of trust that has developed thus far in the therapeutic setting. It is important to keep in mind the individual's significant past events or traumas, present and past family situation, and characteristic style of interacting with others. Additional factors to consider are clients' racial and ethnic background, age, developmental stage, gender issues, sexual orientation, socio-economic background and literacy level. When you evaluate a particular story it is a good idea to ask yourself if the individuals you have in mind are likely to identify with any of the characters, situations, settings, images or symbols in the story.

Matching Stories to Goals

Matching a story to major goals is paramount. For example, if clients are working through the grief of losing someone close to them, I have found 'My Mother's Pastels' (Townsend 2005), a story described in Chapter 8, to be very appropriate. Even though the daughter in this story is recalling a mother she has lost many years before, it is nevertheless a work that I feel comfortable presenting to clients whose loss is much more recent. The author's recounting of a special memory provides an inviting model for grieving clients. Also, the story's reference to capturing the colors of a life supplies a natural segue to a drawing or visualization activity that can help clients honor the person they have lost.

Hanoch McCarty's story, 'Permission to Cry' (1997), was one I selected for a young mother who had just separated from her husband and was parenting two young children almost entirely on her own. She felt the weight of the world and continually focused both on her desire to be the perfect parent and on her attempts to spare her children any pain. She was fatigued and used the word 'overwhelmed' frequently to describe her state of mind. Major goals of our work together consisted of helping her find ways to relax, express her grief, soothe her pain and ease away from her perfectionist standards. She cried in response to this story and began to see how she actually could benefit her children by showing them she was human. The dramatic scenario in the tale seemed to resonate on a more emotional level than my own words on the subject in previous sessions.

When a goal of group members in a school or community setting relates to issues of racial or ethnic identity, Alice Walker's 'A Sudden Trip Home in the Spring' (1975) is a very apt choice. In this story, a young African American woman at a nearly all-white university is struggling to more fully understand and affirm her heritage, as she interacts with people who she assumes cannot comprehend what she is experiencing. The fact that the racism in the story is subtle rather than overt makes it a particularly powerful medium for discussing complicated, nuanced race relations on a college campus or in a work setting. Readers with a bi-racial background or those who feel different from the majority of their peers because of their racial or ethnic background easily relate to the protagonist's role-playing, sense of a divided self and feelings of isolation, even in a crowd.

In making choices for specific populations, I have found that readers tend to identify most fully and become most readily engaged with characters of their own racial background and age group. In contrast, I have perceived that the sex of protagonists seems to play a less crucial role in the identification process, except perhaps in stories dominated by gender identity issues. Yet, even here, I have noticed that many female readers personally relate to stories depicting male gender identity crises, while male readers at times readily relate to the dilemmas and issues experienced by female protagonists.

Matching Stories to Client Issues and Areas of Growth

In selecting stories, I am careful to take into account the presenting problem or focal issue of my clients or growth group members, carefully reflecting on patterns of behavior or mind sets that are preventing forward movement or obstructing wellbeing. For instance, if I am working with clients who are rigid in their thinking or paralyzed in their decision-making by fear of choosing the wrong alternative, I may recommend Rachel Remen's 'I Never Promised You a Rose Garden' (1996b). When I have worked with female or male clients who continually get into unsatisfying love relationships where they submerge their desires and end up feeling controlled, I introduce Dorothy Parker's monologue, 'The Waltz' (1973b). Because this story exaggerates the duality of the inner and outer voice and depicts the almost willful sacrifice of the self to please others, it often acts as a wake-up call, jolting those caught in a frustrating cycle.

When I recently reread several versions of Aesop's 'The Hare and the Tortoise' (1912, 2005a, 2006), exploring its themes and phrases, I thought of a particular client that I had counseled the year before and may work with again in the future. I believe this fable could have enhanced our work together because its core metaphor of life as a competitive race reflects this man's predominant world view and concept of success. In both his work life and family of origin experience, he is the one who plods while others are seen as special. In work situations, he is frequently troubled when he contrasts himself with co-workers whom he labels as 'superstars.' However, he also has come to realize that his view of success has grown more nuanced, that there is a conflict between his desires for a slow-paced, predictable existence and a winner's fast-paced life in the limelight. Aesop's fable could provide him with a fresh metaphor through which to explore his value system and life style issues.

For years I have chosen Ring Lardner's story, 'Old Folks' Christmas' (1963) for clients, growth group members and students whose life stage parallels that of any of the story's four characters—two parents, and their teenage daughter and son. I have mostly used this story with growth groups focusing on family relationships, for it brings forth themes of clashing expectations, intergenerational gaps, and family members' reactions to holiday traditions and gift giving. I also select it for college students who are living on their own for the first time because it elicits fruitful discussions on what they anticipate regarding their return home for their first holiday break. Since the story provides many examples of questionable as well as wise decisions made by the parents, it also is quite an apt choice for parenting groups.

If I am counseling individuals who are enabling family members with an addiction, I often use Carson McCullers' 'A Domestic Dilemma' (1987). For example, I incorporated this story into a counseling session with a 19-year-old woman who was trying to cope with her father's gambling addiction, his denials, and the financial cost to the family. This story served to highlight how burdensome her enabling had become. While my client did not at all resemble Martin Meadows in gender, specific life situation or age, she did immediately identify with him and saw her father in Emily, Martin's chemically dependent wife. She could relate to Martin's anxiety and the delicate dance he continually performs to maintain a sense of order in his household. The most helpful aspect of the story and perhaps the main reason I chose it for her was the permission it gave her to express her anger in our work together. Once she could talk about her anger, she could deal with it out in the open rather than leaving it to fester inside.

The art of choosing the appropriate story for a particular person at a specific time involves calling upon all your knowledge of that person and imagining how a specific story will enhance the therapeutic experience. Louise Rosenblatt (1968), in her exploration of the personal reading process, sheds light on the facilitator's strategic decision-making, when she notes:

> Without an understanding of the reader, one cannot predict
> what particular text may be significant to him, or what may

be the special quality of his [reader] experience. Hence it is important to consider some of the selective factors that may mold the reader's response to literature. (Rosenblatt 1968, p.35)

'Predict' is a key word Rosenblatt uses here. As facilitators of story therapy, we can make only an educated guess regarding the effect of a particular story, but it is a guess based on what we believe will enhance our clients' wellbeing. It may be that a given story falls flat and does not seem very helpful. When this happens, we need to be ready to move on, not force the participant to respond. Many times, the effect of the story is not exactly what we expected or is totally surprising. For example, we may assume a particular client will identify with the wild sister in a story but instead she concentrates on a pair of beat-up black shoes that the family uncovers in the back yard. Our readiness to be in the moment with our clients is what really matters here, and to move with them into areas where their emotional energy centers.

CHAPTER 10

Facilitating the Story
Therapy Experience

When using stories for growth and healing, the practitioner functions in much the same way as he or she does when using poems. After selecting appropriate stories, the facilitator needs to decide how to open the session, introduce the story and foster a therapeutic discussion of its various features. The facilitator works to generate questions and activities designed to amplify and deepen personal connections with the material that lead to life-enhancing insights and behavior changes.

Setting the Tone and Warm-Ups

When I introduce a piece of short fiction to my clients, I usually tell them that I have found a story that may be useful in our work together. I indicate that sometimes stories can generate new ways of looking at our reality. In story growth groups that are time-limited experiences running weekly for a period of six to ten weeks, participants expect to focus on fiction or nonfiction tales as a pathway to personal exploration, so the tone-setting usually involves helping participants relax and center their energies and attention on hearing the current week's narrative. Deep breathing and soft music help participants move into the listening space and become more receptive to what emerges from the story. Occasionally, I bring in an object that reflects some facet of the story that is to be read. For example, I may bring in a gift-wrapped package to set on the table, before we read Ring Lardner's 'Old Folks' Christmas' (1963) to reflect its significant gift-giving theme. Or I may play a piece of music that is congruent with the mood or period of the literary work. The key here is to create a structure and atmosphere for participants that allow for a gradually deepening engagement with the story.

Presenting the Story

In psychotherapy and growth group settings, stories may be conveyed in a variety of ways. These include facilitator readings, joint readings by facilitator and client(s); choral readings of brief pieces, clients' narrations of recalled stories, and professional actors reciting stories on tape.

As the facilitator, you may choose to distribute a written version of the story and read it yourself as expressively as you can. I find that reading aloud, taking on differing tones for various characters and speaking in a clear, easy-to-hear voice, brings the story alive in the room. A monotone reading can deaden the effect of even the most absorbing tale. There are recordings of stories being read by skilled actors that can be quite effective. I have introduced Dorothy Parker's two short dramatic monologues 'A Telephone Call' (1973a) and 'The Waltz' (1973b) in this way. However, since it is desirable to involve participants whenever possible, I usually give out written copies of a story, asking for volunteers to read sections of it aloud in an expressive manner. Since readers vary in their confidence level and ability to project their voice, it is important not to expect someone to read aloud if he or she is not comfortable doing so. On the other hand, in a group setting, there may be more than one person willing and even eager to read. In such a case, I try to ensure that all who want to read have a chance to do so.

I have discovered a very evocative variation of shared reading in a group context. This technique involves converting a story into a dramatic format. Creating 'scripts' from the story, I include all the dialogue of various characters, with the narrator's voice as a separate character. Obviously, stories dominated by dialogue lend themselves more easily to this transformation, but this method of reading has worked well even with stories heavy on narration. Reading a story in this way provides an opportunity to hear a rich variety of voices. Through this dramatic presentation method, participants can more easily distinguish between characters, more vividly experience their interactions and more fully recognize the role played by the commentary of the third person narrator.

I have found that participants who read a character's dialogue tend to become emotionally invested in that character in a way they would not if they did not 'perform' this part aloud. When they express what it was like to speak in this character's voice, they usually learn something new about themselves. The disadvantage of this technique is that it can be distracting for those who read aloud. If they are so preoccupied with playing their part well, they may miss important aspects of the story that could be quite beneficial to them.

Over the years I have repeatedly introduced 'Old Folks' Christmas' (Lardner 1963) in this dramatic format. Usually, given time constraints for group sessions, I do not use the entire story, which runs about ten pages. I sum up the story's opening pages in a few sentences and then distribute written copies of the story's latter portion. This segment contains dialogue of all four characters and the narrator's commentary. Usually I read the narrator's words, while four group members take on the other roles.

In an individual therapy setting, I invite the client to read a story aloud, or I may read it myself, or the two of us alternate the reading. The shared endeavor of this last method creates a particular connection between therapist and client. In the case of a very short story, I may decide that it will be beneficial to invite the client to read silently. While I believe that some of the power of the story will be lost with the silent reading, I make this choice if I sense that it will fit better with my client's temperament. If a story is a short monologue, I sometimes ask my client if the two of us can read it in unison. While this choral reading can be awkward, it tends to result in a resonant, echoing quality that can be quite moving. If a story consists primarily of a two-character dialogue, the dramatic technique described above works particularly well.

As a story facilitator, you will often find it desirable to prepare clients for their listening experience by offering a number of suggestions. For example, you might ask participants to take special note of the characters' communication patterns, or pay special attention to the images in the piece, or tune into their own feelings and visceral reactions summoned up by the story. Specifying in this way helps to bring forth particularly meaningful responses. For example, if you are working with individuals who find it difficult to access emotions and whose goal is to grow more attuned to their feelings and bodily sensations, specific directions of the above nature will be very worthwhile. If your growth group or individual therapy work focuses on communication skills, it is effective to invite attention to patterns of interaction within the story before it is read.

While providing the aforementioned preparatory questions can be advantageous in many situations, these interventions may also limit the possibilities of the therapeutic dialogue that follows a story's reading. For example, if participants focus only on characters' communication patterns, they may ignore a significant personal reaction they have to a particular image or setting, or perhaps assume that their mention of this reaction will not be welcome. They may censor material that might have resulted in very illuminating and therapeutic conversation. For this reason, I usually present preparatory statements or questions that are very general, simply inviting personal connections with the materials about to be heard. In this way, I offer as much room as possible for everyone's idiosyncratic responses to the material.

There are therapeutic contexts in which participants supply the stories. Clients, exploring their own lives, sometimes recall an especially meaningful story they have read recently or long ago. When this occurs, I usually ask clients to narrate aloud or write out the story they remember. This recalled version becomes the pertinent one for our therapeutic conversation. However, there are times when I consider it productive to follow up this discussion with a look at the story in its original form. I will usually ask the client to bring in a copy of the story that they have read so that we can discuss it together. I do this particularly when a client realizes that they may have omitted significant elements in their recalled version.

There are times when I ask clients or growth group members to focus on the fairy tale, folk tale or myth that has been most memorable for them since childhood. Whether clients simply tell or write out their remembered version of this story, these pieces become the texts we explore in either a group or individual setting. While I view the client's version of a memorable story as the crucial one, I usually introduce this story's original written version, after the client has narrated his or her own one from memory. At this point, a fruitful discussion regarding the significance of the differences between the two versions occurs. When doing this activity, it is important to stress that divergences do not represent errors in recall but are rather rich, creative ways in which we have made this story our own. Juxtaposing one's personal re-creation of a story with the original version almost always highlights a client's preoccupations, seminal life themes and meaning-making process in a way that can be quite growth-enhancing.

An example of the above experience occurred with Hans Christian Anderson's fairy tale, 'The Little Mermaid' (1998), which one individual identified as a favorite without knowing why. In her remembered version, she focused on the mermaid's love of a human prince who was out of reach because of their differences. She also vividly recalled the deal that the mermaid struck with an old witch that involved exchanging her fish-like tail for human legs. This client could still feel the agony that the mermaid experienced with every step she took, using the new pair of the legs she gained in order to win the prince's love. When I asked this woman to identify the main theme she garnered from this tale, she emphasized self-sacrifice or the courage to endure great pain in the service of love. Yet, as she reflected further on her telling of this well-known fairy tale, she modified her initial response, focusing on the overly high cost of giving up a part of one's self for another person. She recognized that she had been relinquishing aspects of her 'natural self' in her relationship with a significant other. She also became aware of the push-pull between self-sacrifice and self-affirmation that characterized a great deal of her life. When I invited her to reflect on other aspects of her remembered version of 'The Little Mermaid,' she began focusing on the mermaid's secret-keeping regarding her true identity. She remarked that this deception diminished her relationship with the prince. In response to my question of how this honesty/deception theme fit for her in her current life, she realized that she needed to work on bringing her submerged authentic self more fully into her interactions with her husband and good friends.

When the original form of Anderson's 'The Little Mermaid' (1998) was brought into our work together, it added many significant elements. My client was intrigued by the fact that the protagonist was the youngest of six daughters, described as a 'strange' child, different from the others in the way she decorated her garden and in her intense yearning for the human world. My client immediately resonated with the fact that each sister has to be 15 years old to obtain the 'freedom' to visit the sea's surface. She also was moved by the fact that the youngest mermaid is 'the one who had the longest time to wait' (Anderson 1998, p.38). These details elicited a discussion of how small, inferior and 'strange' my client had felt as the youngest sibling in her own family of female children. She also indicated that 15 was her age to emerge from the family cocoon.

Like the little mermaid, she too was 15 when she began dating and had her first love experience. When she noticed in the original version of Anderson's story that the mermaid saved the beloved prince's life, another forgotten detail, she could see how, even at age 15, she too had been rescuing her 19-year-old boyfriend, acting as his counselor, soothing his worries. She could recognize how she had taken on the caretaker role and had learned to put her own needs aside very early in life.

When my client came to the original story's details involving the tragedy-fraught bargain with the sea witch, she was shocked to learn that the little mermaid agrees to have her tongue cut out, thus relinquishing her power as an alluring singer, in exchange for the human legs that would cause her so much anguish. This unpleasant detail provided the opportunity for my client to discuss the ways in which she too had given up her voice for so many years.

The detail of the original story that proved the most striking for my client was the unromantic, yet spiritual ending, in which the mermaid does not obtain the love of her life. My client was dismayed to find that because the mermaid lacks a voice, she cannot tell the prince that she was the one who saved him, and thus loses her chance to marry him. When the prince marries another, the mermaid knows she is doomed to die and thinks she has also lost the possibility of attaining an immortal soul. However, because she rejects the option of murdering the prince to regain her family home and her mermaid status, she is taken up into a heavenly realm at the story's end by 'the daughters of the air.' Becoming one of them, she can now earn 'an immortal soul' by 'good deeds' performed over a three-hundred-year period (Anderson 1998, p.58). This elaborate final portion of the story elicited a therapeutic dialogue regarding a past love that my client had lost before she married. She focused on how she was still learning to make peace with that loss over the years. She also began to talk about her uncertainty regarding an afterlife and her desire to believe in the soul's immorality. These were subjects she had not discussed earlier in our work together.

The above dialogue with this client was facilitated through respectful listening, careful attention to body language, well-chosen questions raised at strategic moments, and a few writing activities. This combination of techniques, which epitomizes the story therapy process, will be more fully described in the following sections.

Beginning Discussion: Encouraging Personal Engagement with the Story

Whatever stories are chosen and whatever techniques are used to introduce them, the facilitator needs to pay careful attention to clients' spontaneous nonverbal reactions as they take in various aspects of the story or narrate a recalled story. Such responses include loud or suppressed laughter, sighs, gasps, tears or exclamations of surprise, disgust, fear or delight. Clients or growth group members may show facial expressions such as warm smiles, raised eyebrows, smirks or frowns. They may nod their heads, shrug their shoulders, tap their fingers, shift their seating position, or maintain a closed or open body posture.

When therapeutic discussion commences, the first major objective is to address and invite elaboration on the various identifications and projections evoked by elements of the story. Drawing upon participants' nonverbal reactions and opening verbal statements, the facilitator deftly locates and heightens awareness of threads linking participants to the story. I usually respond to the nonverbal signals first, helping others to translate their physiological responses into words that shape meaning. I may comment as follows: 'I heard some laughter just now as I finished reading the story. What do you think or sense this laughter is about?' Or 'I perceive a great deal of energy in the room. What is it about this story that is generating this enthusiasm?' Or 'You look very moved. Would you be willing to share what you are feeling right now?'

When there is a spontaneous verbal response, my first responsibility as facilitator is simply to listen to and affirm these words. If this spoken response occurs in a group setting, I may invite others to speak up as well, by simply looking around the room, remaining silent, or asking if there are any similar or differing reactions. I find that participants' initial verbalizations often reflect approval or disapproval of a particular character's actions. However, it is just as common for participants to immediately express a personal connection to some aspect of the story. For example, one individual might say, 'the overgrown garden in this story reminds me of the place my family used to go in the summers when I was seven years old,' while another might say, 'the woman in this story sounds just like my father-in-law who is always so ready to criticize everything I do.'

Encouraging personal engagement with the story at the beginning of the discussion usually involves open questions designed to create feeling and cognitive bridges between participant and story. General questions beginning with the word, 'what' are very useful. Two very effective openers are the questions, 'What is your reaction to this story?' and 'What were you experiencing as this story unfolded?' You might also ask participants to identify what is familiar or perplexing about this story.

Questions of a more specific nature are also useful springboards to discussion. One example, you might ask, 'What do you feel drawn to say to the grandparents in this story?' or 'How do you feel about the way this story ends?' I also often invite clients to identify the character who particularly grabbed their attention as the story was being read, or the character whose thoughts or actions they want to emulate or would avoid imitating.

When, for a variety of emotional and situational reasons, participants are reluctant to immediately discuss the narrative selection on a personal level, the facilitator may choose to stay focused, for a while, on salient features of the story itself, asking such questions as the following:

- What do you think this character is trying to accomplish throughout the story?

- What do you think is this character's motive?

- What do you notice about the couple's communication pattern in this story?

- How does this character treat his friend, and do you have any idea why he might be treating him this way?

- What do you imagine will happen after the story ends?

- Why do you think the twin sisters in this story are so anxious?

- Why, in your opinion, does the son get so enraged at his mother toward the end of this story?

- Why do you think this character can only relax when surrounded by other people?

Stories that depict striking human behaviors entice readers to call upon their personal knowledge in order to guess the untold motives underlying characters' feelings and actions. Therefore, 'why' questions, such as those listed above, are often received with enthusiasm. Participants can address their views on character motivation without revealing highly personal material, but such questions encourage them to focus on feelings as well as psychological realities and to explore how specific situations elicit particular emotions. Although seemingly impersonal, discussions of this nature can be quite personally illuminating.

While the above questions enable participants to remain in a neutral zone as they explore story elements, the facilitator uses these prompts as vehicles heading toward a more personally engaging conversation. As participants discuss issues raised by these questions, the facilitator needs to stay alert to the emotional tenor of the conversation and the bridges that are forming between self and story. If the facilitator stays too long with questions that encourage critical analysis of the story, the responses will tend to become intellectualized, thus hampering the growth and healing process.

A good example of how a psychological discussion of a fictional character proved useful to readers' self-development occurred with an intense short story by Angelica Gibbs (1987) entitled 'Father Was a Wit.' In it, Helena, the daughter who is the story's point-of-view character, awaits her father's arrival during a graduation awards ceremony. As she thinks about him, readers learn that he is a distant, satirical man who, as a widower, has raised his daughter on his own. Helena's tension crescendos as she imagines her father's negative response to the unsophisticated people at her boarding school who have treated her with special kindness. There are at least two major questions that the story raises but never answers directly. One is, 'Why is Helena so worried about what her father will think of the people at her school?' The second is, 'Why is she both wanting and dreading her father's presence at her graduation?' When I asked these two 'why' questions, participants began exploring the dynamics of this lonely young person's inner life. These explorations led naturally to personal insights involving their own ambivalent feelings toward powerful parents. They also went on to address the ways they have been trying to separate their own world view from that of an influential parent.

As a part of an opening discussion, there are times when you as a facilitator might find it worthwhile to direct participants' attention toward a significant image or symbol within a story that may have resonance for them. For example, in Phyllis Bentley's story 'Mother and Daughter' (1987), clothes signify the battleground upon which the daughter struggles to assert her separate identity. Female readers tend to readily identify with this feature of the story because clothing is a prevalent symbol for many mother-daughter pairs. In Wallace Stegner's 'The Blue-Winged Teal' (1987) the brace of birds that a son brings home from a hunting expedition symbolically highlights his deep ambivalence toward his father. I have found that singling out passages in this story where the bird is prominent evokes meaningful discussions, in which participants identify key symbols that have helped define their own relationships.

Inviting Deeper Exploration and Application to Self

Once the facilitator has helped participants personally engage with features of a story, the next phase of story therapy involves respectfully encouraging exploration of initial cognitive and emotional responses. The transition from the initial personalizing phase to this next one is often seamless. When participants have the opportunity to elaborate upon their personal links to the story, they are often ready to assess current ways of thinking and behaving and entertain changes that contribute to their wellbeing.

'How' and 'what' questions effectively invite elaboration. For example, if a reader reacts angrily to the way a character has handled a situation in a story, you might ask what words or actions of this character specifically provoked this resentment. You might then choose to ask, 'How would you handle the situation differently from this character?' Or 'How would you react if you were in this situation with this character?' Or 'What advice might you give this character, given what you have learned from your own experience?'

'When' questions are also valuable. For example, if clients have identified a feeling or a situation in a story that seems familiar to them, you might invite them to recount one particular time when they felt this way, or ask them when they have found themselves in a similar situation, encouraging them to fully narrate where they were and what was happening. Such a 'when' question was beneficial years ago after I introduced Sherwood Anderson's short story 'Unlighted Lamps' (1987) in a group setting. Many participants identified with either the daughter or the father, who both experience difficulty expressing emotion. In order to deepen the personal links that had emerged thus far, I raised the question, 'When has it been difficult for you to express how you feel with a significant person in your life?' When several responded, I followed up with the question, 'What do you think was making it difficult to open up with this person? Since direct questions such as these tend to elicit sensitive material, the facilitator needs to gauge the trust and comfort level of participants before they are raised.

In the above example, participants arrived at the point where they were actively applying what they had learned to their own current life situations. For example, one group member recognized the possibility that her emotionally unavailable father may feel trapped in his own pattern of reserve. Like the daughter in the story, she too acknowledged some responsibility for the dynamics of her relationship with her father and reflected on how she could begin a heartfelt dialogue with him. Another individual, recognizing some indirect ways in which he and his mother have shown love for each other over the years, was anticipating how he might share these discoveries with her.

In her dissertation on bibliotherapy, Caroline Shrodes (1949) presents a set of questions designed to gauge how personal reactions to reading affect one's present sense of self and life situation. Here are some of the questions she poses:

- What insights did you gain concerning yourself?

- What insights did you gain concerning any of the people close to you?

- What solutions or resolutions were suggested concerning any of the problems confronting you?

- What attitudes toward life were confirmed or modified?
                              (Shrodes 1949, Appendix Form C)

Creative Writing Techniques in Response to Stories

Besides the strategic use of questions to generate therapeutic discussion, helpers who work with stories will find that writing techniques help a story come alive and thus enhance its effect. When clients capture, in writing, links between their personal lives and a story's features, they discover new meanings in a tangible way. The technique I use most frequently involves asking clients to select one sentence or phrase from the story that moves them the most and free write, in poetic or prose form, from these words, allowing themselves to follow wherever their pen leads.

Another technique that I introduce right after a complete story has been read is far more elaborate and has elements of dramatic art. I begin by inviting individuals to retell the story in their own words. This retold version then becomes the basis for an impromptu dramatic re-enactment, in which the client takes the role of the character he or she would like to be. If this is a group setting, other participants can take the other characters' parts to perform the story as it has just been retold. After this re-enactment, a sharing of responses takes place, in order to process what has been learned. In an individual therapy setting, the counselor can perform these other parts for the client, and the discussion to follow will be a dialogue between two.

When participants express an antipathy toward a particular character in a story, they can be asked to rewrite the part of that character to their liking. In this way, they are given control over the story and are more fully able to recognize the specific features that elicited their initial powerful response. Doing this activity can sharpen a participant's awareness of values, preferred patterns of behavior and areas of conflict. Participants may even discover that the aspect of the character they disliked so much resembles a facet of their own personality that they have been struggling to deny or change.

Another technique that can open the door to meaningful features of a story is the invitation to retell it from a different point of view or use a narrator that differs from that which the author has chosen. For example, Helen Perlman's story 'Twelfth Summer' (1987) lends itself to such a technique. The 12-year-old girl who narrates this story watches with envy and chagrin as her 9-year-old brother is set up with a magazine-selling business by their father. The narrator's spectrum of feelings, as her brother enjoys his privileges then fails at his first job, provide a rich mine for a discussion of sibling memories, birth order and gender issues. Asking participants to create written monologues in the voice of the brother enables them to broaden their perspective not only on what is happening in this story but also on what happened in their own lives. For example, if a female reader strongly identifies with the big sister who narrates Perlman's story, she may begin to appreciate the pressures faced by the 'baby' in the family, when she creates the younger brother's monologue. If participants opt to give voice to the mother or father in this story, a whole other set of discoveries can take place. If time is short, the facilitator can suggest that the monologue be brief and based on one segment of the story that participants consider particularly significant.

Meaningful writing activities can also be focused on symbols found in stories. A significant symbol in Marsha Portnoy's 'Loving Strangers' (1987) easily lays the foundation for a personal writing activity. The story's narrator, Marianne, is a young woman with a new baby who visits her mother for lunch one afternoon. It is clear from the outset that Marianne has grown up viewing her mother as thoroughly in control. Preoccupied with her own shortcomings as wife and mother, Marianne resents her nearly perfect parent and fears her judgment, until she is asked to look at 'a little chest of drawers' that her mother had 'fixed up' for her before she was born (Portnoy 1987, p.99). When the protagonist notices it is a 'homely piece of furniture' that has been covered with 'glossy white paint and the tiny flowers stenciled on the drawers' that 'distract from the ugliness,' she realizes that 'It is a perfect example of the triumph of style over substance.' She recognizes that this simple piece of furniture is 'emblematic of Mother's entire married existence,' which has in fact involved 'disappointments' and 'failed dreams.' This moment of discovery helps Marianne connect in a new way with a mother who now seems much less a 'stranger.' The piece of furniture takes on even more significance when Marianne wonders if 'in 20 or 30 years' from now, 'that little fragile construction of wood and glue, paint and hope, may still be usable for [her] own grandchildren' (Portnoy 1987, pp.99–100). Thus we see how this object represents not only the turning point in a relationship but also the power of legacy and family continuity.

The piece of furniture that forms the centerpiece of this story provides an ideal springboard for written explorations of personal family objects that have taken on symbolic value. After leading a brief discussion of this item in Marianne and her mother's life, I usually invite participants to select a specific object in their own families that has acquired special significance over the years, an object that links them in some way to their mother, father, grandmother or grandfather. I suggest going back in memory to conjure up the sensory details of this object before free writing. Since these creative pieces are often quite substantive, I try to allot ample time for participants to share and process the meaning of their writings before the session is over.

Having the opportunity to write an informal, honest letter that is directly addressed to a particularly admired or disliked character in a story is effective in developing personal reactions to that character's specific behaviors, choices and values. Providing time for such letter-writing enables participants to organize their thoughts and more fully recognize the underlying reasons for their immediate emotional or visceral reactions to evocative characters. If there isn't adequate time remaining for the letter-writing, a sentence completion activity can be effective as well. You might suggest, for example, that participants complete the following sentence stem:

> If I were [the chosen character's name], I would… or I would not…

When clients fill in the blanks here, they can bring into focus their own values, preferences and needs.

Since so many modern short fictional works end in mid-air without resolution, I often ask participants to supply their own written conclusion in an extra paragraph or two. This invitation provides an opportunity for readers to develop their personal reactions to protagonists' patterns of behavior and to generate solutions to challenging problems. Participants are usually eager to step into the story, to travel beyond its limits, and, in effect, make it their own.

In a women's therapy group focusing on interpersonal relationships, I introduced this writing activity in conjunction with Pat Schneider's 'Irma' (1990). As indicated in Chapter 8, this short-short story focuses on a widow so intimidated by her deceased husband's shoes that she gradually closes herself off from nearly every room in her home. After the individuals in this group had a chance to share their initial reactions to the story, I asked them to create a paragraph or two that they imagine would follow the author's closing words regarding the small kitchen space Irma now occupies. After writing for about ten minutes, all group members were eager to share what they had created, and their story closings were intriguing and varied. This diversity led to a lively and enlightening exchange. A few members devised an ending in which friendly neighbors stopped by to visit Irma and more or less rescue her. Others portrayed a decisive and proactive Irma who finally released herself from habits that had constricted her life space. One person meticulously detailed Irma's systematic recollection of every combination lock as she reopened her rooms. Another emphasized how the protagonist destroyed and thus demystified her deceased husband's dreaded shoes. There were two members who described Irma dying in her chair and never escaping the kitchen that had become her self-made prison. One who created such an ending did so with glee because she was so frustrated with this woman's self-defeating behavior.

As participants created and juxtaposed their varied written responses, they gained new awareness. Those who identified with Irma's fears and sense of helplessness tended to opt for the happy ending, recognizing that in fact there are always choices one can make. The group member who had angrily killed off 'Irma' indicated that this character reminded her of some friends presently struggling in their relationships. After acknowledging her impatience with these individuals, she admitted that her insensitive responses to them grew out of her own past experience of victimization that she had worked so hard to overcome. During this group meeting, she became increasingly committed to behaving in a more compassionate manner. As I watched this group's process unfold, it was clear to me that gaining written control over the story's outcome helped participants see new ways to view current habits and envision the possibility of overcoming their fears.

With Ring Lardner's short story, 'Old Folks' Christmas' (1963), I invite readers, at times, to imagine the dialogue between family members that could possibly occur the morning after the story concludes. I find this is a useful writing activity because so many participants are frustrated by the communication pattern in the family. This story follows the experience of a middle-aged, nouveau riche couple who expect to preserve their Christmas traditions and eagerly await the arrival of their late adolescent son and daughter who have been away at school. When son and daughter return home, they are obviously more interested in socializing with their friends than enjoying the full array of holiday customs they experienced as children. When the parents shower them with expensive gifts, the children are less than enthused and ask to exchange them for others more to their liking. Disappointed repeatedly, the mother and father react in a passive manner, never communicating the extent of their anger or disappointment. Reluctantly, they decide to enjoy a night out together as a couple, yet return home to find the house in a shambles from a party that takes place there while they are gone. During their evening out, they avoid talking about their children and never discuss the mess they find when they return home. They also do not mention any plan to speak with their son and daughter about what has occurred. Instead, Tom leads his wife to the music room where the couple exchange their Christmas presents and agree that they need a good night's sleep.

When participants have the opportunity to write beyond the story's ambiguous ending, creating their own 'morning conversation' between the parents and their teenage children, they often bring up themes of respect, appreciation and assertive boundary setting. In these creative dialogues, some writers have the children apologizing for their selfishness and the parents honestly expressing their feelings. Others focus on the expensive gift-giving and the contradictory expectations of the two generations. Some of the most fruitful dialogues involve frank discussions of how one's own tastes dictate the gifts given and interchanges on ways to respectfully accept or reject gifts. Through this writing activity, participants often find themselves practicing an effective communication style that they can use to resolve conflict and build bridges with their children and/or parents.

Ellen Hunnicutt's short-short story 'Blackberries' (1992) also provides a model of dysfunctional communication, this time with the focus on a young couple experiencing a camping trip. Rather than writing beyond the ending, with this story, I invite participants to redo the dialogue as it is written, so that the story is more satisfying. Since this work of 'sudden fiction' is heavy on dialogue, it easily lends itself to a dramatic reading with three voices: the husband's, the wife's and the narrator's. It is important to hear the dialogue in order to experience the gaps within it. The communication pattern between the spouses is so quirky and indirect that the effect is almost amusing, and most readers are quite eager to revise the interchange. While they can readily cite the flaws in this couple's ineffective verbal interactions, they also recognize that there are times when they may have come close to such a pattern in their own lives. When participants rewrite the couple's dialogue, they have the opportunity to experiment with ways to negotiate differences and to stay true to self while hearing another person's opinions.

Once clients have experienced the satisfaction of rewriting the dialogue in 'Blackberries,' it is a good idea to request that they identify the useful ways of communicating they have generated in their version. The facilitator can provide effective closure to the session by asking clients how they might put into practice what they have discovered. The facilitator might also invite clients to observe during the ensuing week how their practice of effective communication affects their relationship with others.

Providing Closure

Bringing story therapy sessions to a close often involves summarizing the themes that have surfaced. Since many complex stories can summon up a discussion of several significant subjects, there may not be sufficient time within one meeting to do them all justice. For example, during a recent growth group session in which 'Old Folks' Christmas' was discussed, participants spent most of the time focusing on gift giving, yet had brought up serious concerns regarding how parents discipline children and teach them values. When it was time to end the meeting, I asked the group if they wanted to consider these unexplored themes next time. Since they were very ready to do so, I asked them to bring their copies of the story to our subsequent meeting and made a mental note to have some extra copies on hand in case some participants forgot to bring theirs. To help wrap up our discussion, I invited everyone to mention one insight or thought about our explorations that they were taking with them. In other story therapy sessions, I help provide closure by inviting everyone to provide a one-line reaction to anything in the story that comes to mind, and we join everyone's statements to form one composite that I read aloud. A variation of this closure activity that is effective in individual therapy sessions is the creation of a one-line message addressed to the story's characters that reflects in some way the personal insights that have emerged.

The process of facilitating story therapy begins from the moment a story is introduced and continues through a series of verbal and nonverbal interventions that encourage participants to interweave their own emotional reactions and narratives with the stories they read, discuss and write about. Most of us have a natural affinity for stories and storytelling from the time we are very young to the last days of our old age. Very few of us can resist opening our ears when a good story is shared. Literary short stories, in particular, tend to catapult readers into a world where a small cast of characters experience intense relationships and negotiate their way through a dramatic event or two that affects them in profound ways. Like the lyric poems discussed in the previous chapter, stories derive particular therapeutic value from both their vivid detailing and the compactness of their forms. While the details that are present invite personalized reading, that which is left untold or mysterious invites readers to use their imaginations, to bring themselves even more fully into the fictional experience.

PART THREE

Creative Writing for Life Enhancement

CHAPTER 11

The Power of Self-Expression

Building Self-Esteem and Affirming Creativity

The very act of putting words on paper can foster self-esteem and affirm the viability of one's truth. I have seen time and again how individuals, who do not define themselves as writers or as artistic individuals, create a piece that sounds and looks delightful to them. They are surprised that pleasing and meaningful word combinations have poured out on their paper, and more often than not, they are excited to share with others what they have written.

As helpers, we can encourage written creative expressions, through the use of many different non literary stimuli. These written pieces may take the form of poems, stories or journal entries. The materials presented here are based on my observations and belief that growth and healing occur not only within the creative process itself but also during the reflection and discussion that focuses on the written piece in a one-on-one therapy setting or group context. The ideas contained here have come from many years of facilitating poetry therapy sessions with clients, students and growth group participants and attending expressive arts therapy and creative writing workshops.

In 1974, when I was teaching humanities at a medical center in New York State, a guest speaker at a workshop series sponsored by the psychiatry department presented unedited transcripts of clients' words uttered during times of major emotional upheaval. As I listened spellbound, I was struck by the fact that these individuals had unwittingly created real 'poems' while in session—heartfelt and rhythmical expressions that had crystallized into well-wrought poetic compositions. This experience left me with the strong belief that we are all poets when the true self finds its voice. Hearing these transcripts had a tremendous impact on me and was at least partially responsible for my discovery of the poetry therapy field soon thereafter.

Rose Solari (1996) points out that:

> More and more people are coming to see that poetry *can* matter—in their daily lives, in their jobs, and in how they understand themselves and their own spiritual yearnings. Whether or not one considers oneself a 'poet,' the human impulse to give voice to thoughts and form to feelings lies within all of us. (Solari 1996, p.32)

While some individuals are more comfortable with prose writing in journal or story form than with poetry, I have found that most individuals can be encouraged to write what I call 'creative expressions.' Since freedom to explore one's authentic self is a key aspect of the writing process for growth and healing, my definition of a poem remains very broad. I conceive of poetry as an open form, a free-associative set of words through which writers can spontaneously generate lines of any length, defy laws of grammar and discover unique linguistic combinations and striking sound effects. Given the flexibility of this form, writers are likely to access unconscious material and gain significant insight.

Providing Opportunities for Growth and Healing

I have found writing to be helpful because it provides opportunities to:

- safely express heartfelt emotions, dilemmas and desires
- describe suppressed or elusive feelings in concrete form to increase understanding of how feelings impact behavior
- increase empathy toward significant others, by imagining what it is like to be 'in someone else's shoes'
- work through the grieving process for a loved one
- be ourselves without critical put-downs

- recognize what we want or need after years of habitually accommodating to others and effacing the self in response to others' demands

- make significant connections between present problems and past experiences

- make sense of a puzzling, complicated life situation

- recognize and celebrate positive traits that we can build upon, instead of focusing on negatives that drain self-esteem

- differentiate from others in enmeshed family situations, as we sort out ways we resemble and differ from these family members

- increase our understanding of the self-defeating patterns that have resulted in anxiety, loneliness, shame and/or helplessness

- discover a new, illuminating way to view a past (often painful) memory, situation or relationship

- generate options in situations where we feel trapped

- sharpen awareness of specific ways we have grown over the years

- envision a healthier future life style

- creatively structure life review material

- affirm our heroic moments, our acts of everyday courage

- increase enjoyment and sensory awareness of the world around us.

While the above list suggests how purposeful writing can be in a variety of situations, writing for growth and healing basically points in two major directions: the first, to fully realize the self, affirming the heroic aspect of one's own life journey, and the second, to find relief from suffering due to loss, trauma or the shame of a dark secret.

Florida Scott-Maxwell (1975), an artist and Jungian psychologist, illuminates the triumph inherent in realizing one's heroic self. Even though she focuses on women, her words fit men as well. She tells us that 'you need only claim the events of your life to make yourself' your own hero and that 'When you truly possess all you have been and done, which may take some time, you are fierce with reality' (Scott-Maxwell

1975, p.363). These words suggest courageous confrontation with even the most difficult aspects of one's experience.

Grappling with Pain: Writing as Catharsis and Meaning-Making

Putting in writing what lays dormant inside can be cathartic and liberating. In her poem, 'From the Threshold,' Jane Butkin Roth (2002) eloquently asserts the necessity of embodying our feelings in language when she urges readers to 'Give Sorrow a song' and 'Hand Loss a microphone / especially when she's voiceless' (Roth 2002, p.21).

In *Bird by Bird*, Annie Lamott (1994) tells us:

> Your anger and damage and grief are the way to the truth. We don't have much truth to express unless we have gone into those rooms and closets and woods and abysses that we were told not to go in to. When we have gone in and looked around for a long while, just breathing and finally taking it in—then we will be able to speak in our own voice and to stay in the present moment. And that moment is home. (Lamott 1994, p.201)

While release of emotions from a troubled past can provide relief, simply expressing raw emotion or spilling out details of a traumatic experience on the page can be alarming and distressing. In a therapeutic or growth group context, there needs to be the opportunity to write reflectively, to shape memories and the abundance of disorganized sensory details, in a way that forges meaning for oneself. In our work as expressive writing facilitators, it is crucial for us not only to provide a safe space where writers share their work with compassionate listeners, but also to recognize that individuals suffering from trauma need to proceed at their own pace.

Virginia Woolf's observations on painful personal material highlight both the therapeutic aspect of writing and the importance of timing. In an autobiographical essay 'A Sketch of the Past,' Woolf (1976) refers to 'exceptional moments' that bring 'with them a peculiar horror and a physical collapse' and leave us feeling 'passive.' Yet, she goes on to point out that 'as one gets older one has a greater power through reason to provide an explanation' which 'blunts the sledge-hammer force of the blow.' Instead of being the 'dominant' force, the painful memory can now even be seen as 'welcome' and 'valuable.' The initial experience that left the child reeling now becomes 'a revelation of some order,' and Woolf can 'make it real by putting it into words.' Woolf celebrates how writing, shaping and meaning-making processes go hand in hand to liberate the self from past demons: 'It is only by putting it into words that I make it whole; this wholeness means that it has lost its power to hurt me; it gives me,...a great delight to put the severed parts together' (Woolf 1976, p.72).

Much has been written on the emotional and physical benefits that follow from opportunities to complete writing that not only links feelings with events, but also helps integrate painful experiences into one's sense of self and one's life journey. The research psychologist, James W. Pennebaker (1997), and others such as Stephen Lepore and Joshua Smyth (2002) have presented the results of research studies showing the efficacy of structured writing about one's most distressing life events. Results of these studies suggest that purposeful writing strengthens the immune system, alleviating a wide range of illnesses from arthritis to respiratory diseases.

In *Opening Up: The Healing Power of Expressing Emotions*, Pennebaker (1997) points out that whether we focus on our 'most traumatic experience' or 'the issues' we 'are currently living with,' it is essential 'to explore both the objective experience (i.e. what happened) and your feelings about it.' He advises his readers in these terms: 'Really let go and write about your very deepest emotions. *What* do you feel about it and *why* do you feel that way' (Pennebaker 1997, pp.40–41). According to Pennebaker (1997, pp.194–196), writing is good for your health if it is 'self-reflective' rather than safely impersonal or filled only with 'uncensored complaining' or unexplored expressions of anger.

In line with Pennebaker's conclusions, Louise DeSalvo (2001, p.49) points out that we have a better chance of deriving mental health benefits from writing that is 'detailed, organized, compelling, vivid and lucid' rather than simply 'dumping thoughts onto the page.' In the same vein, Linda Myers (2003), psychologist and creative writing specialist, indicates that autobiographical writing heals when we reflect upon memories.

Sherry Reiter's book, *Writing Away the Demons: Stories of Creative Coping through Transformative Writing* (2009), is 'a primer of transformative writing, a collection of stories to illustrate the benefits of writing for psychological health and well-being.' Reiter (2009) indicates that 'Writing is a form of empowerment,' when 'we have the courage to identify the demons, externalize them onto the page, and view them from a different perspective.' She further points out that 'When we write, our natural creativity finds new ways to view ourselves and the world. We renew ourselves, and in some sense, we are born again' (Reiter 2009, pp.1, 5, 14).

The Freedom Writers project, pioneered in California by teacher Erin Gruwell and providing the model for other programs across the United States, attests to the fact that bringing one's stories out into the light of day to be read with interest by others is helping to improve the quality of life for teenagers who were considered 'unteachable' and 'at risk' (Draper 2009).

Writing in the Group Setting

While the writing process and product help to heal and enlighten the writer, an individual's creative expression can be therapeutic to others within a group setting. When the facilitator creates an atmosphere that enables expressing an authentic voice in writing, all participants benefit. Although Anne Lamott (1994) is focusing here on writers' groups in general, her words are distinctly apropos for writing in a therapeutic context:

> Becoming a writer is about becoming conscious. When you're conscious and writing from a place of insight and simplicity and real caring about the truth, you have the ability to throw the lights on for your reader. He or she will recognize his or her life and truth in what you say, in the pictures you have painted, and this decreases the terrible sense of isolation that we have all had too much of… If something inside you is real, we will probably find it interesting, and it will probably be universal. So you must risk placing real emotion at the center of your work. Write straight into the emotional center of things. Write toward vulnerability. (Lamott 1994, pp.225–226)

Free Writing and Creative Process

Like Lamott, creative writing educator, Natalie Goldberg (1986) describes the writing process in terms that are also very pertinent to writing for therapeutic purposes. In her widely used handbook, *Writing Down the Bones*, Goldberg emphasizes some rules to help get the pen moving and the creative juices flowing. She tells readers to keep their writer's hand moving, to 'lose control' and not to 'cross out' or 'worry about spelling, punctuation, grammar,' or 'get logical.' Perhaps most important of all, she urges readers to 'dive right into' the first thoughts or images that come up, even if these are 'scary or naked.' She points out that 'First thoughts have tremendous energy' representing 'freshness and inspiration,' but our 'internal censor usually squelches them, so we live in the realm of the second and third thoughts,...twice and three times removed from the direct connection to the first fresh flash' (Goldberg 1986, pp.8–10). Basically she is telling writers to trust their free association process and risk bypassing their censor when they write.

The writing process that we facilitate for others can begin in a straightforward, simple way. As Molly Peacock (1999, p.166) notes, 'When you can't make sense of the world in any other way, merely to describe what you see before you leads to understanding. That is the lesson of the watching way of life.' In these words, there is an important link between self-awareness and writing that is sensory and richly detailed. Lamott (1994) too focuses on how we need to pay attention to the word around us, if we are going to be writers: 'If you start to look around, you will start to see. When what we see catches us off guard, and when we write it as realistically and openly as possible, it offers hope' (Lamott 1994, p.101).

The organic nature of poetic expression that enhances us personally is suggested by Robert Frost in his essay, 'The Figure a Poem Makes' (1972). He describes the joy of spontaneous word play as well as the forging of meaning that emerges from this freedom to experiment with language:

> For me, the initial delight is in the surprise of remembering something I didn't know I knew. I am in a place, in a situation as if I had materialized from cloud or risen out of the ground. There is a glad recognition of the long lost and the rest follows. Step by step the wonder of unexpected supply keeps growing. (Frost 1972, pp.440–441)

As this chapter suggests, writing is not just for the Robert Frosts of the world or for professional writers who see themselves as artists. We all can be writers capturing the truth of our own lives, with their pain, joys, grittiness and heroism, if we give ourselves a chance to trust our voice. Expressive writing can serve a wide variety of life-enhancing purposes. Fundamentally, when we put pen to paper, we have the opportunity to celebrate who we are and create a tangible product that surprises us with welcome new meanings and links.

CHAPTER 12

Setting the Atmosphere for Writing

Creating a Safe, Supportive Space for Authentic Expression

The counselor or educator who invites writing for growth and healing needs to establish an ethos of trust, supportiveness and spontaneity. Even though Brenda Ueland (1987) focuses on the writer's experience in general, she eloquently sets forth, in *If You Want to Write*, core beliefs for writing in a therapeutic context. As facilitators, it is important for us to believe, as does Ueland that 'Everybody is talented because everybody who is human has something to express' and that 'creative power and imagination is in everyone' along with the 'need to express it' and 'share it with others' (Ueland 1987, pp.4–5). Another essential observation made by Ueland is that 'Everybody is original, if he tells the truth, if he speaks from himself. But it must be from his *true* self and not from the self he thinks he *should* be' (Ueland 1987, p.4).

When we facilitate the expressive writing process for growth and healing, we need to gently encourage others to write from their authentic self and help them distinguish between what they assume they are expected to write and what is genuinely real for them. As we motivate others with sensitivity, we need to have walked this road of authentic writing ourselves, so that we really know how challenging, but ultimately rewarding, it can be. Gillie Bolton (2006), therapeutic writing specialist, has described her 'work' as 'rooted in [her] experience' and conveys the following important message: 'If we are to ask our patients and clients to go on these journeys fraught with dragons and demons, and enlightened by angels, we need to have travelled the path before them, and be aware of some of the dangers' (Bolton 2006, p.4). Addressing those who facilitate others' therapeutic writing, Bolton emphasizes a similar message in her book, *The Therapeutic Potential of Creative Writing*: 'Trying out the methods and processes before you suggest them to others is an essential part of the process' (Bolton 1999, p.12).

Brenda Ueland (1987) drives home yet another point that is useful for helpers who facilitate writing experiences. She indicates that the 'joyful, imaginative, impassioned energy' of our self-expression 'dies in us very young' not only because we have 'dry obligations' that 'take its place' but also 'because we don't respect it in ourselves and keep it alive by using it' and 'don't keep it alive in others by *listening* to them' (Ueland 1987, p.6).

As facilitators of therapeutic writing in a group, individual or family setting, we need to be aware of barriers to creativity and active listening. Many of the people we serve come to us with messages that make creating and sharing of their personal writings a daunting and risky business. Some may have been taught that creative writing is a frivolous enterprise, or have been acculturated to write only polished prose or poetic lines. Many expect others to judge or turn a deaf ear to what they write. Given these factors that militate against free expression, it is essential to create a safe space where fun and serious reflection are welcomed and where compassionate response and respect for everyone's contribution are the norm. We can lay this groundwork by our own modeling along with clearly stated guidelines.

When I engage others in a process of writing for growth and healing, I overtly communicate that this place and time is not about improving writing skills. This is not a writing class. I also clarify that while writing and sharing are significant healing ingredients of our process, reading one's written work aloud is always voluntary. I almost always ask clients, students or support group members, after a writing experience, if they are willing to share the whole or a part of what they have written or even just relate what it has been like for them to do this writing. Providing choices such as these helps sustain the open, caring atmosphere that promotes spontaneity and trust.

Facilitators Writing Along With Participants

In describing her own writing journey, Gillie Bolton (2006, p.4) tells the reader that as writing therapists, we 'need to write alongside' the individuals we are trying to help. I personally adhere to this practice for a few reasons. I believe that it is respectful to write along with others, doing what I am asking them to do. I also sharpen my awareness of what my clients are experiencing and am thus in a better position to generate subsequent writing invitations that are likely to be fruitful. There are, however, some colleagues in the field of biblio/poetry therapy who do not espouse writing along with clients. These practitioners are concerned that facilitators will become overly absorbed in their own material and will therefore miss opportunities to observe clients' reactions during the writing time. I personally believe that many facilitators can write and also stay attuned to the energy and progress of participants. Being aware of the pro and con side of this issue can help us make our own informed decision based on what we know about ourselves and what we need to do to provide the best service to others.

Those who write along with their clients or growth group participants may be asked to share what they have written. I have found that this request actually occurs quite rarely. While I am not sure why this is so, I have noticed that clients get so involved in their own writing and sharing processes that it does not occur to them to ask me. If they do ask, I choose to read at least a portion of what I have written, in order to model the willingness to share. However, I direct the focus back toward others, as soon as possible, to avoid detracting from their therapeutic experience.

The therapeutic writing process depends on creating an atmosphere where everyone can feel free to express their authentic self in a spontaneous manner. Since many individuals have learned to approach writing situations with trepidation, allowing their inner critics to take over, facilitators need to consciously provide a space that is as nurturing and respectful as possible. Armed with the belief that everyone is capable of creativity and has a voice worth hearing, facilitators need to establish norms that ensure support and give participants room to share as much or as little of their written work as they wish. Facilitators gain valuable knowledge about what constitutes an optimally safe setting, when they themselves experience the writing activities they are encouraging others to pursue.

CHAPTER 13

The Therapeutic Process of Telling Our Stories

We *Are* Our Stories

Our lives are a patchwork quilt of varied stories and we are, by nature, storytellers. We tell one another stories to record our personal life journeys, revealing aspects of ourselves and our social settings and inviting others into our inner world. We are born into our father's and mother's stories and into our family's sagas or legends, which involve success and failure, feuds, abandonments, and acts of courage. In our childhood years, we live in our parents' story, encountering the roles we are expected to play and the labels applied to us. In adolescence and early adulthood, we become a more deliberate author of our own narrative. If we marry or enter a long-term relationship, we begin to live in our partner's story and to meld two sets of narratives into one. As we grow older, with the decades lining up behind us, awareness of our life's trajectory and repeated motifs grows more acute.

Rachel Remen (1996a) advocates for the telling of our own stories as a necessary healing and spiritual practice. I strongly resonate with her statement that 'Everybody is a story' and has stories within them worth telling, yet these 'real' stories of people's own lives take 'pausing time, reflecting time, wondering time' (Remen 1996a, p.xxv). It is the expressive writing facilitator's role to help provide the necessary interval for recording the events that make us who we are.

Capturing the Essence: Mini-Autobiographies

Within the first few sessions of a group experience or during an intake with a new client, the writing of a 'five minute autobiography' can be an effective way to tap into a record of significant life-changing events. When we are given an absurdly limited amount of time in which to capture our life story, we often discover some fundamental truths regarding our major choices, behavior patterns and constructed meanings. As facilitators, we can more fully appreciate how illuminating the mini-autobiography can be, if we write some of these ourselves.

When I facilitate an 'Oasis for Helpers,' which is designed to encourage self-care and personal understanding through creative expression, I often invite participants to write five to ten minute 'autobiographies.' In these groups, we explore how the helper's life and view of the caretaking role affect her or his experience with clients. When helpers capture the essence of their life transitions and journeys in this mini-autobiography, they often forge edifying links between their own narrative and the reactions or expectations they have when they work with specific clients.

'Spots of Time': Recapturing the Moment

Most of our stories do not cover our entire life span and often simply embody 'spots of time,' to use Wordsworth's memorable phrase (1965e, p.345). His words here model a worthwhile writing invitation. He describes those significant segments in our 'existence' that 'are scattered everywhere, taking their date / From our first childhood.' These are experiences 'That with distinct pre-eminence retain / A renovating virtue' and help 'our minds' be 'nourished and invisibly repaired' when we are 'depressed' by the troubles and trivialities of daily life (Wordsworth 1965e, p.345). Like Wordsworth, we and the people we serve can reclaim our own reparative moments through our written recollections.

Natalie Goldberg (1986) provides opportunities for her students to share special personal tales. She affirms the power of what she calls a 'story-telling circle' in which individuals share a personal tale, as they sit in a circle with a candle burning in the middle 'to create a sense of magic.' As facilitator, Goldberg suggests the subject of these stories with such requests as 'Tell us about a place you really love or a time you were really down' or 'Give us a magic moment that you remember from last week' (Goldberg 1986, p.147). After all the group members have a chance to verbalize their stories, she invites them to capture these narratives on their own, using their 'talking voice' to help them get started (1986, p.149). This last part could take place within the group setting itself, if there is time to write and share some choice phrases or passages that participants have generated.

When I facilitate 'creative counter transference' groups for therapists and other helpers, I invite participants to focus on their experience with particular clients, using writing as a medium for exploration. I recognize that helpers usually counsel clients who bring pleasure and others who bring pain. With this fact in mind, I invite participants to go back in memory to a specific time interval, so that they may bring sensory components into their writing. I ask them to close their eyes and imagine that there are five to ten minutes remaining before the arrival of a particular client who usually elicits either a blatantly positive or strongly negative reaction. This may be a client whom the therapist dreads seeing or has been worrying about, or may be one whose appearance the therapist enthusiastically awaits. I begin this imagining process by inviting group members to place themselves in their office or therapy space. I ask them to 'look' at their clocks or watches and other details within this room. I invite them to imagine what they are sensing in various parts of their body—their neck, arms, stomach, back, shoulder and hands. I encourage them to summon up the specific thoughts and feelings they have during this waiting time and to actually feel, on a physical level, what they are anticipating or fearing.

After these moments of deep concentration, participants are invited to free write for approximately five minutes, after which time I ask them to choose a 'gift' they most want to give to this client. This gift may be something abstract such as courage or a concrete object such as a lantern with a bright light. At this point in the process, I invite everyone to share features of both their reflections and their writing experiences. In closing the session, I encourage participants to verbalize insights they have gained from doing this activity. I often also propose that we generate a group list of ways to reduce the stress that we feel as we await the arrival of challenging clients.

Retelling and Reframing the Story

When individuals seek our help in times of trouble or at times when they desire to enhance the quality of their lives, they often recount an important life event using the exact language they have employed many times before. If these individuals feel stuck in particular past life scenarios that are counterproductive to present wellbeing, they can benefit greatly from the chance to write about features of these scenarios that have affirmed rather than diminished them. By integrating such positive elements into a past narrative, they can bring new meaning into an old self-defeating story.

As clients or growth group participants elaborate in writing on a significant narrative from their lives, they often bring forth fragments from beyond consciousness that have begun to clamor for attention. At this juncture, they can incorporate these submerged or forgotten elements into their stories. While some details may be troubling or traumatic, others may be joyful memories that counterbalance the one-sided dreariness of a current narrative. Whether old or new ways of telling one's story predominate, individuals, who have the opportunity to embody their narratives in written form, produce a concrete product that is available to explore and reframe.

Our repeatedly told stories of memorable experiences not only help constitute who we are but also provide a record of how we have grown. Dorothy Canfield Fisher's 'Sex Education' (1997) provides a dramatic model of how this process works. The narrator recounts three versions of the same basic story told by her aunt over a period of many years. The aunt first relates the story when she is 30 years old, then retells it at ages 55 and 80. This story involves her experience as a teenager getting lost in a cornfield and encountering a minister she knows. This man, unmarried and ten years older than her, is a respected person in her community, yet has an unfortunate disfigurement on his otherwise handsome face. The teller of this tale has obviously been affected by previous vague warnings regarding dangerous men. She therefore panics when she believes she is lost and, in her initial version of this occurrence, interprets the minister's behavior as sexually suggestive. In her second telling of the story, she recognizes that her own unconscious sexual desire may have colored her interpretation of the minister's actions. By the third version, the teller of the tale focuses on her empathic awareness of how her horror as a teenager must have hurt the lonely minister. She is filled with remorse as she recognizes the man's normal desire for connection and his pain at a deformity that has kept him from the joys of a loving marriage. The niece, narrating Fisher's short story, learns how her aunt's faulty 'sex education' fed her fears and distorted her perceptions. Privy to three very different versions of her aunt's experience, the narrator and we as readers recognize how the passage of time and increased wisdom can help reframe troubling events from our past.

The act of 're-storying' as an empowering process is deftly captured in Michael Blumenthal's poem, 'The New Story of Your Life' (2006). Employing subtle imagery of Odysseus' epic journey, Blumenthal adds resonance and heroism to the struggles we all experience. Addressing us directly, the speaker notes that 'you finally invented a new story / of your life.' Instead of recording 'defeat,' this new story is the one you win through your 'large thrust / into the difficult life' and with 'a plentitude / entirely your own' (Blumenthal 2006, p.83). It is clear that the seeds of this authentic story lie fallow and come to fruition when we are ready.

As writing facilitators we can foster growth by encouraging experimentation with various perspectives on a personally significant, perhaps life-changing past experience. For example, we can invite clients to tell a particularly memorable childhood story in three different ways. They might begin in first person with a child-like voice, then switch to first person with an adult perspective; and finally move to third person with the view of an outsider looking at the situation. If there is an identified protagonist and antagonist, the story might be told in the voice of the antagonist, to extend the possibilities of new recognitions even further.

The technique of retelling one's story can also involve first narrating the tale as it is usually told and then creating an idealized version, in which the client, as main character, recounts only the most positive outcomes and reactions from others. This 'life as it should be' story is often quite empowering, as clients are given the opportunity to realize their deepest desires on paper and to exert their imaginations to conceive the kind of life they crave and deserve. I have found this writing activity particularly energizing for clients who are trapped in a particular past story, the one that has left them feeling damaged, shameful, afraid or inadequate, or evokes tears every time they tell it. While they cannot change the actual events that have occurred, imagining their past in idealized terms helps highlight choices they are already making in their present life or can make in the future.

Healing From Abuse: Empowering the Voice of the Survivor

The healing process in relation to past abuse can also be facilitated by writing activities. According to psychologist and story therapist, Lani Peterson (2005), 'The abuse victim is stuck in the secret of the abuser's story,' and having the chance to write her or his own story helps to 'free it,' so that the abuse survivor 'can own it, rage and grieve over it, feel strength, or bury it in a special place.' In addition to privileging one's own voice over the self-serving lies of one's perpetrator, the client can be invited to write a series of letters. Directly addressing one's abuser in a letter that is written in a safe and nurturing space can help transform feelings of vulnerability into a sense of self-assurance. Also, I have found letter-writing in the voice of one's child self to an imaginary and much needed protective parent to be powerfully healing. Inviting clients to respond in the voice of this ideal parent figure is a particularly effective next step. When clients create, develop and affirm their own self-soothing parent voice in their letter-writing, they gain a valuable resource to carry within themselves during times of distress.

Since clients with past trauma often come to therapy when they begin to have recurring disturbing dreams, it can be quite therapeutic to introduce writing to help access dream messages and empower the dreamer. Several years ago, I worked with a young woman who was distressed by terrifying dreams that occurred quite frequently. In these dreams, the perpetrator of past abuse appeared as a beast-like creature chasing and menacing her. After describing these dreams and her visceral reaction to them during one of our sessions, she was asked to write the words she wanted to tell this creature and to vividly imagine what she wanted to do in this dream. She read what she had written several times, and I asked her to reread these powerful words when she returned home, and particularly before going to sleep. She reported at the subsequent session that she had actually incorporated these words and actions in her next dream and had successfully warded off her pursuer. She experienced the exhilaration of fighting back against her own terror, and her nightmares diminished at this time. While I am not suggesting that this is a quick fix for past abuse, this experience does highlight the power of using one's voice and imagination to confront even the most challenging past experiences.

Employing an Heroic Paradigm for Personal Narratives

When we invite others to write their significant and most difficult stories, we can suggest a heroic paradigm for their narratives. Events in their lives can be framed as mythic sagas involving journeys, quests, adversaries and honored guides. We can encourage tellers of personal stories to highlight their heroic acts of courage and take a close look at the internal and external 'dragons' they have had to slay or may need to defeat in the future as they seek their own 'holy grail.'

Besides reconfiguring their own life trajectory into archetypal hero tales, clients and group members can be invited to name heroes from stories they remember that they wish to emulate or heroes they seem to resemble most closely in their present lives. These characters may be from folk or fairy tales or mythic stories, or may be from especially memorable nonfiction accounts. The way in which individuals choose to tell or modify an admired hero's story provides a doorway to personal discovery.

Reversing Roles for a New Perspective

While the act of writing down our stories affirms our own capabilities in a fundamental way, there are times when listening to another's written distillation of our own story can be particularly meaningful. A few years ago, I participated in a group in which everyone met in pairs to tell each other a set of stories about his or her first name. As we each told these name tales, our listener gave us full attention, jotting down salient details. After the first narrator concluded, the roles were reversed. When the telling and listening processes were finished for both partners, we each created a poetic expression designed to embody the other person's name. The results for me and for most others in the group were astounding. The person who had acted as my compassionate listener not only captured the very heart of my name story as it had played out over a period of many years, but also expressed it in words that symbolically celebrated the essence of my life's journey and meaning. Since she had used my details, I could own what she had written, yet being an outsider, she brought a perspective to the task that I did not have at that time. The combination of objectivity and caring and the sense of mutuality and respect engendered during this activity proved very effective for growth and healing.

We have so many different sorts of stories to narrate, and the prompts that invite a therapeutic writing process can be as simple as telling someone about your name or as complex as distilling your whole life into a five-minute autobiography. The writing activities discussed in this chapter are designed to encourage participants not only to recapture their stories in specific, sensory terms but also to reframe past stories. By adding fresh elements to past personal tales or experimenting with varying points of view, new perspectives can emerge, allowing for forward movement and increased wellbeing.

CHAPTER 14

Developing Personal Waking and Dream Metaphors and Symbols

Using the Metaphor-Elaboration Process

When I began doing long-term psychotherapy many years ago, I became aware of the way in which I was especially attuned to hearing and honoring my client's metaphors, which probably related to my literary background. In my work, I encourage clients to enrich their sensory and cognitive awareness of the metaphors that emerge during our sessions together. As this oral metaphor-elaboration process unfolds, I invite clients to write, or at times I perform the role of scribe, writing down poetic phrases and passages that clients are voicing as they develop their metaphors. I choose the latter method in situations where clients are not ready or able to express themselves through writing.

Through the years, clients have spontaneously compared themselves to a chameleon, a tornado, a whirling dervish, a packhorse, a waif passing through time, a ghost-husband whose self is parked outside the door, and a small VW Beetle automobile stuck behind a huge truck on a superhighway. Clients using metaphor have described their lives as a cave of despair, a blank page, a car race, and a penthouse apartment in a swaying skyscraper. They have spoken of self-censoring to avoid setting a relationship 'aflame' or of having to 'shave off' who they were when interacting with others. One young woman, who had been sexually abused by her stepfather and emotionally abused by her mother, referred several times to her fear that others would take 'a piece' of her away or that her mother still had 'pieces' of her that she 'can't get back.' These fragments of her identity constituted precious entities for us to explore and honor in our work together. Even the cliché metaphors, such as 'walking on egg shells' or 'getting the short end of the stick' or 'wearing a mask,' are worth pursuing with clients, if you believe, as I do, that our spontaneously generated metaphors are integrally linked to our emotional core.

While Richard Kopp's (1995) exploration of 'metaphor therapy' involves more verbal communication than writing, his work provides worthwhile suggestions for the expressive writing facilitator who engages in metaphor exploration with clients. Kopp delineates a process involving 'deeper immersion into one's metaphoric imagination.' By asking a series of open or 'nonleading' questions, the counselor 'invites the client to explore the metaphor *as a sensory image*' (Kopp 1995, p.7) and encourages the client to elaborate on the situation or story elements surrounding the metaphor. The therapist then 'invites the client to describe his/her feelings and experience associated with the metaphoric image' (Kopp 1995, pp.6–8).

Kopp goes even further in his presentation of metaphor therapy by focusing on the ways therapists can invite clients 'to transform the metaphor' that emerges in a session or that dominates a significant memory. To increase insight after the client has modified his original image, the therapist may ask the following question: 'How might the way you changed the image apply to your current situation?' (Kopp 1995, pp.9, 11). Asking clients to juxtapose their initial and transformed metaphors in written form can be a powerful tool to add to Kopp's model here. This contrasting that he describes can be an effective way to highlight new possibilities in the face of entrenched behavior patterns. For example, a client recently described his upbringing as 'suffocating,' envisioning himself as an indoor plant without the sun or oxygen he needed to thrive. When I asked him to explore in writing his vision of a thriving outdoor plant, his transformed metaphor consisted of trees, for which he felt a great affinity, breathing in the open air with their sense of purpose intact. As he focused on this new image, he was able to imagine experiencing the benefits of increased nutrients and the physical sensation of an improved oxygen supply. He was also ready to articulate what specific features he would try to incorporate more fully into his daily life, the most important one being a sense of playfulness.

When I invite individuals to explore their metaphors in writing, I often simply repeat the phrase or sentence containing the figurative language. Before the writing begins, I, like Kopp, provide guided imaging questions that ask what is seen, heard, smelled and tasted, and what is felt inside in connection with the metaphor. As the client elaborates, I repeat aloud their images, so that they are heard in the room and their presence is reinforced for the client. At this point, the writing invitation involves jotting down words already spoken aloud and elaborating for five to ten minutes upon anything these words suggest. At times, I provide some extra structure, inviting participants to insert their metaphor into a sentence frame such as 'My life is like _____' or 'I am like a _____.' Another technique consists of placing the word 'my' before the crucial image and making this word-set the title and opener for the client's writing. When inviting others to free write whatever comes to mind, I rarely use the word 'poem' because many view poetic endeavor as a daunting task. However, I have found that the resulting written piece is almost always a powerful poetic expression that provides the writer with a great sense of satisfaction. Thus written work encompassing a client's personal metaphor not only raises self-esteem but also functions as a fertile base from which to explore a significant image's meanings and connections to present life situations.

When metaphors emerge during clients' narratives, I recognize that we often are sitting at the crossroads of past and present. A seminal past experience is couched in imagery that embodies significant meaning and emotion in the present moment. Elaborating upon this imagery through writing provides an opportunity to clarify meaning embedded in key memories and to re-vision unresolved conflicts from the past.

Exploring Clients' Imagery: Clinical Vignettes

The following example from my practice highlights how free writing enhances the moment when the past and present meet through a client's choice of imagery. A woman in her early twenties had come to see me because of extreme anxiety over being late for work and social engagements. As she focused on her image of watches and clocks, she suddenly saw her mother's round face lined with worry. When I asked her to stay with latter image and free write whatever memories, feelings and events came to mind, she recounted her mother's extreme helplessness and frustration as she waited every Sunday for her large family to get ready for church service. As this client fleshed out her mother's story, she recounted her own past defiance of her mother's compulsive need to be on time, along with her deep guilt at complicating her mother's difficult life. Through her written exploration, she recognized her ambivalence regarding both tardiness and punctuality. She also realized how her chronic lateness and the distress it continued to cause her were integrally linked to both her avoidance of and her identification with her mother's life script.

Years ago, when I was working with a couple, the husband, an aloof and somewhat domineering man, likened himself and his life to a penthouse apartment in a high-rise building. When I encouraged him to describe this apartment, he indicated that it had all the comforts of a luxurious residence but was hard to reach. As he more fully imagined this space and the physical effort it took to reach the top, he viscerally experienced the profound loneliness that was so much a part of his daily existence with his wife and two teenage daughters, who were both repeatedly aligned with their mother against him. While everyone in the family viewed him as the 'head' of their domestic world, he could talk more fully than ever before about how desolate that position on the 'top' was for him. Through elaborating upon the inaccessible quality of this penthouse unit, he allowed his emotions to show and could begin to recognize chronic behaviors that were making him 'unreachable.' This exploration took place with me functioning as scribe and his wife participating as an active listener. When I read aloud the piece that had been generated by the husband's words, the couple began to dialogue on what these words meant to them. The tenor of this dialogue was favorably affected by the emotion he had shown and by his wife's new awareness of her husband's previously hidden side.

Another example of metaphor exploration involves a man in his early twenties who had recently graduated from college. He was focusing on his failures and revealing his tendency to contrast himself with friends and peers whom he viewed as exceptionally successful. In the early phase of therapy, he repeatedly described himself as chasing a wagon that was moving too fast for him. Every time he would catch up to it and was just about to hang on, he felt he was losing his grip. As he embellished this dynamic metaphor, he saw the wagon filled with his 'superior' friends whose achievements he wished to emulate, and experienced the breathlessness and anxiety that had become so familiar to him. His visceral re-enactment helped him better understand why he felt so tired and overwhelmed in his current life. After he developed his metaphor, I invited him to create in writing an alternative but cognate image that would feel more manageable and less fatiguing. He wrote about a similar wagon parked at his door with only one friend who was waiting patiently for him to climb in for a leisurely ride. He identified this friend as the relaxed part of himself that was capable of waiting for his own creativity and life direction to emerge. Through generating this image of tranquility, he was able to view his unrealistic deadlines and expectations more objectively.

In a later phase of therapy with the same client, he related a vivid dream with a powerful set of metaphors. In his dream he was up to bat in a baseball game which his parents and siblings were watching. He was mortified to discover that instead of a bat in his hand, he was clutching a stone sculptor's mallet. Just as he was feeling frustrated at his inability to hit the ball and was about to make his third strike, he awoke, suffused with sadness and a sense of failure. When he shared this dream, I thought of what he had been telling me about his role as the 'oddball' in his family. As an adopted son in a family of three siblings, he was the only artistic person in a group of business-oriented, mathematically minded individuals who were pressuring him to choose a 'practical' career. I also knew that my client had aspirations to become a stone sculptor. With these details in mind, I asked him to focus on the sensation of holding that dream mallet and to address it directly in his writing, including whatever he wanted and needed to say. As he wrote, his joy was palpable, and he realized just how right he felt holding that artist's tool, even though it handicapped him in the game of baseball. Despite his sadness that he could not hit the ball, he expressed confidence that he was holding something he really knew how to use. When he read aloud what he had written, he affirmed what had been a steadily growing and underlying desire to pursue his art. He now could see his direction clearly despite others' dissenting voices. Tracking his dream analogy and its accompanying affect, I used these words, 'I know how frustrating it has been for you to try playing in other people's games, but this dream seems to have helped you recognize what your true game is.' Resonating with these words, the client left my office energized. Within the next two sessions, he had put into effect plans to enter a graduate fine arts degree in sculpting and was able to address his parents with a newly acquired assurance. He reported feeling far less susceptible to their opinions than he had previously been. Through elaborating in speaking and writing on a dream he had recognized as crucial, he found the energy and determination to gain control of his future.

Metaphor exploration that links past and present, conscious and subconscious levels, as well as spoken and written words is again apparent in this next example. I counseled a young woman struggling to find her voice, to capture what she came to call her 'woman wisdom.' She was terrified of being inarticulate and viewed her communication skills as inadequate. She was very apprehensive about written expression but, as therapy progressed, was becoming more and more comfortable expressing herself aloud in our sessions.

Midway through our work together, she voiced a desire to capture some of what she was saying and discovering in therapy, and when I gave her some writing and drawing options to pursue outside of therapy, she welcomed them but still reported that she could not bring herself to write. Since she was attuned to her body, being a gymnast, dancer and massage therapist, I very consciously highlighted her physical self to help nurture her speaker's and writer's voice, while also honoring the silences as well.

In one session, she clearly articulated her experience growing up as the only child of an overburdened single mother. She recalled walking 'silently' like a 'cat' with 'wisdom,' moving around on 'soundless feet' chiefly because she feared adding to her mother's distress. Having summoned up this image, she immediately stated that she wanted to be a 'lioness with a roar.' As she developed aloud these two contrasting images, I proceeded, in a very unobtrusive way, to write what she was relating. When I read aloud her words, she was a bit embarrassed but was primarily amazed and exhilarated. While she feared she would later judge these written words, she did want to bring them home, and at the next session, she indicated that she had finally been able to do some writing. She had developed her cat image, getting to her core of grief. She also began to understand why she was still walking on 'tiptoes' in her present apartment. She spoke of how she is currently learning in her dance class to walk 'flat' on the ground and even 'roar' a bit without feeling guilty. Through her metaphor work involving both vocalizing and writing, she could begin to separate her mother's pain and lot in life from her own anxieties and self-image. She could also accept that she had her own way with words and that writing and speaking her truth did not have to be foreign territory.

Metaphor, Symbol and Writing as Ritual

Personal symbols and images are often tied to rituals that can be healing and growth-enhancing. In the vignette described in the previous paragraph, the client, through vocalization and writing, deepened her appreciation for the timid cat and roaring tiger imagery in her present and past life and had consciously linked these dual images to her sure-footed, expressive dancing. When she participated in an open air performance as the culminating activity of her dance class, she was experiencing a ritual that embodied her improved self-image.

There are particularly meaningful rituals in the form of writing that constitute crucial symbolic actions in people's lives. In describing the 'expressive/creative component' of poetry therapy, which pertains to clients' writing activities, Nicholas Mazza (2003) speaks to the power of working with clients' own metaphors and symbols and providing opportunities to enact meaningful rituals that have symbolic function. He points out that 'Rituals, for example, are helpful in endings (e.g., death, divorce) by allowing a person to recognize the past, let go, and move on' (Mazza 2003, p.22). He provides examples of rituals involving creative expression, such as writing a eulogy or 'writing—and then burning—a letter to someone unavailable regarding unfinished business' or creating a prayer (Mazza 2003, pp.22, 40).

We can greatly enhance our effectiveness as writing facilitators by staying attuned to the metaphors, images and symbols that emerge from those with whom we are working. It can also be very worthwhile to stay aware of how rituals in written and nonverbal form, can help to encapsulate key symbolic meanings for individuals. When clients express their self-image and life scenarios in figurative language, I employ a metaphor-elaboration process that interweaves oral and written exploration. While at times, I act as scribe, noting down what clients say aloud, at other times, clients do most of the writing themselves. The degree of writing that takes place depends upon the client's current comfort with putting words on paper and on the particular therapeutic context.

CHAPTER 15

Word Play and Creating with Linguistic Structures

Inviting clients or group participants to play with words and use linguistic structures is an important aspect of expressive writing in a therapeutic context. Participants can be asked to write in relation to specific words that carry emotional loadings for them, or to use linguistic structures such as word stems or acrostics that provide a writing situation in which an optimal blend of freedom and form is present.

Focusing on a Choice Word

I have conducted various workshops on word power in which participants have had the opportunity to explore in personal terms, first, an everyday, widely known word; second, a word that captures their notion of beauty; third, a word capturing a quality they greatly admire; and fourth, an invented or largely unknown word that reflects their idiosyncratic experience within their family or their family's ethnic background. All these word ventures have led to self-discoveries and have provided opportunities for people to communicate important information about themselves with others. For example, it has been very enlightening for group members to recognize the varied connotations that ordinary words, such as 'selfishness,' 'wig' or 'lock' have for them. In terms of words capturing beauty, participants have been able to savor the images conjured up by one another's words and can appreciate others' differing aesthetic sensibilities. When participants share their written reflections on ethnic words or family-generated words, they open the doorway to exploring their identity and educating others about who they are. When the group focus is on our ethnic heritage, I often introduce Ray Gonzalez's poem, 'Praise the Tortilla, Praise the Menudo, Praise the Chorizo' (1994) as a model for group members to emulate. His repeating linguistic structure for each of three stanzas is 'I praise ____' (Gonzalez 1994, pp.347–348). These words usually summon up energy, encouraging individuals to express pride and to detail positive features of their uniqueness.

A fruitful way to explore a special word is to complete a word tree, word wheel or cluster. In this diagram, the focal word is centered on a blank page, with spokes or branches radiating from it to other related words and images that the participant generates. The word's significance then radiates in all its dimensions in an appealing visual form. I recall selecting this writing technique for a group of female cancer survivors. At the opening meeting, I asked everyone present to think of one word that describes her life situation right now and then to complete the above sort of diagram. There were 19 participants, and the rich array of diverse words with their associations was astounding. The resulting set of word clusters reflected a wide spectrum of issues faced by cancer patients and became the ideal platform from which to begin our healing work together.

The implications of a key word can be creatively explored through written dramatic monologues and dialogues. When such a word surfaces, clients can be encouraged to personify it and give it a voice. For example, after a client used the word 'frazzled' to describe her present state of mind, I asked her to allow 'Frazzled' to speak to her, conveying whatever needed to be said. Before she began writing the words of 'Frazzled,' I invited her to create a portrait of this being, in order to add energy and authenticity to the experience. I asked her if 'Frazzled' was female or male, what clothes he or she was wearing, and what was his or her voice tone, body language, body size, and attitude. I also invited my client to imagine the physical position of 'Frazzled' at the present moment. Was he or she sitting, standing, or dashing about? Once the palpable presence of this being was established, I asked my client to simply listen and watch as she generated her monologue. After she read this piece, I asked her to respond in her own voice to the message that 'Frazzled' had sent. Through this activity, my client obtained a clearer understanding of the multilayered role that her frenetic state of mind had been playing in her life. She also reported feeling more in charge of her own choices when she had the opportunity to reply to the words of 'Frazzled.'

A word that frequently surfaces when I am counseling individuals is 'disappointment.' Clients repeatedly indicate how disappointed they are with themselves or with their lives. At times, I ask these individuals to create a persona named 'Disappointment,' listen to what this persona has to say and then reply with whatever words come to mind. When clients write this kind of dialogue, they tend to hear and see their own punitive voice with refreshing clarity. When 'Disappointment' speaks, clients hear phrases like 'You should know better' or 'never make that mistake again.' When clients reply, they often feel quite empowered, writing words such as 'Stop following me around!' or 'Let me make mistakes, that's how I learn' or 'Let me be at peace with myself.' These latter phrases can actually function as significant mantras to draw upon when internal critical voices return to create their usual havoc. In one case, a client who created a dialogue with 'Disappointment' was surprised at how frequently she said she was sorry. She recognized how often she apologizes for trivial mistakes and even for problems she does not cause. She pinpointed this behavior as one she wished to change, for it diminished her sense of self and failed to win others' respect.

Using the Acrostic

Personally meaningful facets of a chosen word can be generated in an acrostic poem. In this poetic structure, the letters of a word are written vertically to provide the opening letter for each line. For example, the word, 'FAMILY' would be written as follows:

F

A

M

I

L

Y

While the acrostic is ideal as an opening and closing activity, it also provides a useful way to meld structure and spontaneity at any point in the therapeutic process. For example, during one particular session, a client enthusiastically expressed her reverence for elephants, so I joined with her to explore this creature. Together, we completed an acrostic with the letters of the word 'ELEPHANT.' In a spontaneous fashion, we developed a poem, which began with the line, 'Elegant in its heavy stillness.' I acted as the scribe, writing the client's words and supplying a few lines or images from time to time which I intuitively sensed matched her sentiments. She was very pleased with the results, for they illuminated the symbolic dimensions of this animal in her present life. While it is unusual for me to compose a poem with a client, there are times when a team effort is both affirming and healing.

Writing From Sentence Stems

Sentence completions or sentence stems also provide a set of words that usually evoke fresh, authentic responses. Providing a creative combination of direction and freedom, the sentence stem helps clients not only to focus their thoughts but also to generate new insights. Nicholas Mazza (2003, p.165) suggests a variety of engaging and promising sentence stems, such as 'Today, I am…,' 'Tomorrow, I…,' and 'If you knew me…'

In counseling sessions with couples, I keep handy a set of six sentence stems, which I usually introduce within our first three meetings. Useful for both diagnostic and treatment purposes, these sentence stems are as follows:

> I get angry when…
>
> I feel hurt when…
>
> I feel safest when…
>
> I feel loved when…
>
> I feel discounted when…
>
> I get scared when…

I developed these after years of working with couples and discovering that the very apparent anger, along with the hurt and sadness lurking just beneath this anger, were prime forces bringing couples to therapy. My choice of these stems is also based on my belief regarding the basic goals of couples counseling: to create safety and mutual respect that enables open communication and to restore the love that has been buried under a mountain of pain, blame, fear and habitual rejection.

After giving each partner a copy of the six stems, I ask them to complete each statement in writing with the first words that come to mind. I then ask each to read one at a time, so that they can juxtapose their responses to the same stem. As this sharing unfolds, the two partners are invited to elaborate on what they have written and what they are hearing from one another. It is important to leave ample time to complete this entire process, so that the couple can fully absorb what the other has expressed and at least begin to contemplate the similarities and differences that surface.

What has been striking for me about this activity are the parallels between partners' responses, even when the two individuals seem to be so much at odds with one another. This commonality both surprises and pleases the couple, often bringing them closer. For example, one wife wrote that she gets 'angry' when she is 'not heard' and her husband wrote that he feels 'hurt' when his wife doesn't 'listen.'

This sentence stem activity for couples also evokes illuminating distinctions that open the door to new awareness. A couple's ability to recognize and accept their differences serves as a useful prognosis of their capacity for healthy functioning. For example, in one case, the wife indicated that she feels loved when her husband tells her he loves her and hugs her, while the husband wrote that he feels loved when his wife acknowledges his moods and acts concerned with how he feels. When both partners discussed their responses, they recognized two very important truths. First, they acknowledged that they tended to show their love in ways that matched what they wanted from their partner. Second, they came to realize that they needed to honor diverse ways of expressing love.

Completing the above sentence stems together as a couple can also reveal new information that has been repressed. For example, when two spouses discussed their completions of the last stem, 'I get scared when...,' the husband indicated that the only words he could generate were 'when loved ones argue.' However, when I asked him what he immediately thought of when he saw this sentence stem, he reluctantly admitted that he feels scared when his wife gets 'advice from her parents.' This information turned out to be very valuable in our work together, which involved the central role of parents in the couple's conflicts.

There are times when I use a reverse of the above sentence stems with couples, individuals and groups. These go as follows:

When I am happy, I...

When I am sad, I...

When I am worried or feel anxious, I...

When I feel hurt, I...

When I am angry, I...

When I feel respected, I...

Completing these structures helps individuals link their feelings to their habitual behaviors. They become more aware of how their emotions drive their actions and are then in a position to explore options that are more satisfying or less self-defeating.

I introduce a wide variety of sentence stems that develop from significant material that is emerging in the present moment. For example, recently when a young woman I was counseling was focusing on blame in her relationships, I asked her to complete the following pair of sentence stems: 'When I blame others...' and 'When I blame myself...' In an elaborated prose paragraph for each, she was able to clarify important cycles of habitual behavior that were not serving her well, causing much anger, sadness, physical tension and extreme reactions. On her own, she added a third paragraph which opened with the words, 'If I do not blame you or me.' In it, she listed options that promote healthy and soothing ways for her to interact and cooperate with her spouse. Through her writing, she was empowered to move beyond destructive patterns.

Another example of a spontaneously generated sentence stem occurred when I was working with a man in his mid-thirties who was focusing on his role as a husband and was experiencing a great deal of ambivalence regarding his marriage. In an effort to help him make meaning of his plight and clarify the pros and cons of staying married, I asked him to write a two-stanza piece. The first stanza began with the words, 'When I am a husband,' and the second with the words, 'If I were not a husband.' The ten-line poem he created helped him see how he was following the track laid out by all the passive men in his family. He also recognized how he was craving the freedom to enjoy some solitude and the opportunity to explore his true identity without guilt. His written words laid the foundation for subsequent sessions in which he explored how he could stay married without feeling suffocated.

Generating List Poems

Often, but not always, sentence stems set the stage for list poems that clients can be invited to write during an individual therapy session or group meeting. For example, during one session, when a client was troubled about an upcoming trip with her partner of many years, I asked her to complete a list poem using the frame, 'When we are together during this trip, I want to…' Through generating this list, she was able to focus on what she needed and could enjoy while vacationing with this man. She also became aware of how her relationship with him had been moving in a positive direction, and she recognized that as a couple they could coexist in a meaningful way despite their differences and the disappointments she had experienced.

List poems are useful in a wide variety of therapeutic and growth group situations. By their very nature, they foster a generous outpouring of creative alternatives. In a way, these list poems resemble a journal writing activity that Kathleen Adams (1990) calls a 'List of 100,' which can focus on any aspect of your life that you wish to explore, such as '100 Things I Want to Do Before I Die' or '100 Decisions Others Have Made for Me' (Adams 1990, pp.135–136). When I facilitate self-care groups for helpers, I introduce a writing activity that functions like a list of 100. I invite participants to quickly jot down two lists, one about what saps their energy and the other about what revitalizes them. These lists, when juxtaposed, can be quite illuminating. For example, there are times when the same activity appears on both lists, and the writer has the opportunity to look at how that is so. In one instance, a participant indicated that 'walking' both drains and adds energy and was able to realize that overdoing even a healthful activity can be self-defeating. When I bring this activity into my work with therapists who are exploring their counter-transference reactions, they have the opportunity to recognize what features of particular clients fatigue or energize them and can then take steps to prevent burnout and foster their own wellbeing.

The 'I prefer' list poem writing activity works very well with individuals who have learned to submerge or ignore their own desires within their families of origin or within their current relationships. It is a playful way to begin an intense getting-acquainted-with-self exploration for those who are consumed with living up to others' expectations, have lost sight of what they want and sense a void where their identity is supposed to be. It also is useful for those in transition who are trying to find their vocation, their passion in the work world. I sometimes initiate an 'I prefer' list poem writing experience by reading the first eight lines from Henry Bobotek's poem 'Reflections' (2003) to suggest to clients how they might proceed. Repeating the sentence frame, 'I prefer,' Bobotek mixes objects with actions, the concrete with the abstract to present a rich and, at times, contradictory array of tastes, desires and values.

Using the sentence stem, 'I am a woman (man) who…' or 'I am the woman (man) with…' also helps writers explore dimensions of their identity. When individuals free write within this framework, quickly pouring out on paper their 'definitions' of self, they generate ample material to explore. In reading over their list, invariably, there is a particular facet of self that stands out for one reason or another. The line conveying this facet can then become the opener for a more fully developed poetic piece. For example, one respondent resonated to her line, 'I am a woman who carries out other people's garbage.' As bizarre as this line initially seemed to her, when she developed it in writing, she was able to identify a few incidents which helped make sense of these words and had the opportunity to recognize feelings evoked by these incidents.

The above writing frame also helps individuals in a group setting get to know each other better. It can be varied depending on the context. For example, in a growth group facilitated at a work site, the stem for this list poem can be, 'I am a worker who…' In a family therapy setting, the parents can write a list poem, using the words, 'I am a mother/father who…,' while the children complete the line, 'I am a son/daughter who…' Spouses in couples counseling can also benefit from this activity, creating innovative list poems from the sentence stem, 'I am the wife/husband who…' The initiative, playfulness and freedom involved in this writing invitation help to set a positive, creative tone in therapeutic situations that are often fraught with anxiety. Furthermore, when spouses or family members generate these list poems and share what they have written, they take responsibility for who they are, summon up new images to explore and have the chance to gain a fresh perspective on their roles and behaviors.

Another variant of this 'I am' sentence stem list poem emerged recently when a client counseled by one of my poetry therapy trainees modified the 'I am the man who' framework to suit his preference. He chose to begin with the stem, 'To some, I am…,' and then shifted to 'I am…,' alternating these two as he created his poem. This individual's writing, coming at an early stage in his therapy, contained very useful information, especially regarding differences between his public and private self.

Suggesting a Metaphor or Image Motif

Besides providing frameworks, the writing facilitator can suggest a category of metaphor for clients or group participants to use when they are describing themselves, their relationships or their life challenges. This category of metaphors may grow out of the therapeutic discussion itself. For example, in a couples group, one spouse referred to his wife as the saucer and himself as the cup. Following an energetic response to this metaphor, I decided to invite all the couples to select domestic imagery of their own, drawing upon perhaps items of furniture or household objects, in order to capture their own marriage in some way. In other groups when the focus has been on the natural world, I have suggested likening one's self to a specific species of tree or plant. When I invite clients to write a two-stanza poem using the framework, 'I used to be… Now I am…,' I often suggest a category of metaphor such as moving vehicles, places of residence, foods or colors. For example, one might choose to begin the first stanza with 'I used to be a horse-drawn carriage' and the second stanza with 'Now I am an express train.' The journey of discovery takes place when these stanzas are then developed in a freely expressed way.

I frequently introduce the metaphor of color because it is ordinary with extraordinary possibilities. Almost everyone can relate to colors and the associations that arise in conjunction with specific hues. Many years ago, a very eye-opening experience occurred when I introduced a simple writing activity within a long-term psychotherapy group for men and women suffering from anxiety and depression. I began one session with an invitation to write from the prompt, 'Today, I feel (supply a color of your choice)' and add anything associated with that color. As I wrote along with the group, realizing that having a choice of two colors might enrich the experience, I suggested the option of adding a second color. The results for one participant actually constituted a turning point for her. When first asked to choose a color, she selected 'blue' and began developing a written piece consistent with her habitually somber mood. For over two years since the death of her husband, she had remained embroiled in her grief, consistently viewing the world as a gloomy place. Responding immediately to my second color option, she chose yellow and proceeded to introduce sunshine and warmth into her writing. The light in her face as she read her 'yellow' lines was palpable, representing a real change from the apathy that had defined her for so long. When she discussed her creative response, along with her surprise over the bright tones that had emerged, she admitted to the group that she had recently experienced a few joyous moments. She also acknowledged her guilt over the pleasure she felt. At this point, both her honesty and impulse toward renewal were compassionately supported by the two co-therapists as well as other participants.

Animal metaphors, like color images, are engaging and accessible for most people. When I facilitate 'Oasis for Therapists' groups, where self-care and self-understanding are the focus, I invite participants to describe their 'therapist-self' as an animal of any type, using a sentence stem such as 'When I am doing therapy, I am like a swan or a tiger.' I invite group members to use all their senses—sight, touch, sound, smell, and taste—to identify what this animal looks like, what it eats, how it moves, how it expresses itself, where it lives, where it hides and what it wants. Through expanding upon their analogies in writing and discussing them with group members, participants almost always gain insight regarding their therapeutic style. This activity highlights both the strengths of helpers and the challenges they face.

Playing with Paradox: Exploring the Polarities

Word combinations to stimulate therapeutic writing can also come in the form of paradoxical expressions. As an educator discovering paradox and irony in literary texts over the years, I have always appreciated the quirkiness and suggestiveness of oxymoron, those word-pairs that so compactly embody a paradox, such as 'calm storm' or 'loud silence' or 'muscular fragility.' Perhaps the power of paradox to stimulate insight comes from its very nature. Stageberg and Anderson (1952, p.184) define it as a 'statement which seems to be self-contradictory or opposed to common sense, but which may be essentially true.' The truth unveiled through paradox often provides illumination that is personally affirming and useful in one's life. As Stageberg and Anderson (1952, p.186) indicate, 'The effect of the paradox—juxtaposing in a playful way…is a mental exhilaration that is an integral part of the poetic experience.'

The Romantic poets, in particular, recognized paradox as a vehicle toward a deepened understanding of the human condition. Wordsworth (1965a, p.106) celebrates 'wise passiveness' in his poem, 'Expostulation and Reply,' while Blake (1968, p.36), in 'Proverbs of Hell,' describes 'Shame' as 'Pride's cloke' and tells his readers that 'Excess of sorrow laughs. Excess of joy weeps.' Keats (1990b, p.370) affirms a concept he calls 'Negative Capability' in a letter to his brothers, and for Emily Dickinson (1961a, p.101), 'Much Madness is Divinest Sense.'

The melding of opposites that characterizes paradox can expand our sense of life's possibilities. Because we are human, sun and rain, compassion and anger, pleasure and pain, and life and death go hand in hand. As helpers, we so often experience together with our clients the following enriching paradoxes:

- growth and an expanded appreciation for joy often emerge from traumatic events

- sometimes we have to go backwards to move ahead

- gain and loss often occur simultaneously

- we sometimes feel like laughing during a funeral and crying at a wedding

- our enemies can teach us more than our friends

- the people who enrage us the most are the ones we love most deeply.

Paradox is a powerful tool for self-growth because embracing opposites frees us from black-white thinking. When I recently reread 'The Use of Fiction in Psychotherapy' by Sophie Lazarsfeld (1949), I came across a striking example of paradox when the author discusses a perfectionist client who was invited to read Helen Howe's novel, *The Whole Heart*, in which a psychiatrist advises his patients to acquire 'the courage of imperfection.' This phrase was one of the most memorable elements of the book for this client. She even regarded it as a 'formula' to help her (Lazarsfeld 1949, p.30).

Mental health and maturity are characterized by the ability to appreciate complexity, humor and irony, to encompass opposites, and to reframe the pain of the past, assimilating it into a healthy sense of self. Paradox or oxymoron as a poetry therapy technique can help transform painful past memories and one's view of loss. The merging of starkly contrasting words can thus jolt us into new awareness and contribute to our revisioning process.

The oxymoron writing activity, that I have found works well with both groups and individuals in therapy and community settings, once again reflects the combination of structure and spontaneity that fosters growth-enhancing writing. I first supply a list of nouns like the following:

INNOCENCE	GENEROSITY	QUARREL
GIFT	FUN	CONFIDENCE
SMILE	ANGER	GROWTH
TEARS	HUNGER	SUCCESS
HELPLESSNESS	AGGRESSION	DARKNESS
TRUST	HATRED	HEAT
PRAISE	CHARITY	FORGIVENESS
PUT-DOWN	LOVE	GIRL
COMPASSION	GUIDANCE	BOY
JOY	SATISFACTION	CHILD
SORROW	TRUTH	PUNISHMENT
LOSS	FAILURE	LONELINESS
LAUGHTER	ESCAPE	EVIL
FEAR	LISTENER	FRUITFULNESS
SCOLDING	VOICE	ACCIDENT
INDEPENDENCE	PATIENCE	TRANQUILLITY
WOMAN	WISDOM	IGNORANCE
SLAVERY	MANLINESS	REWARD
JOURNEY	CHAOS	EXCITEMENT
DANGER	FREEDOM	SADNESS
BULLY	SCAR	STORM
MASTER	LIES	APOLOGY
STINGINESS	VALLEY	POWER
TYRANT	HOPE	SAFETY
GREED	SHAME	FACADE
FULLNESS	FOOLISHNESS	MASK

I then ask participants to choose five of these nouns and combine each with a descriptive word or adjective that carries an opposite connotation. So, for example, if one of my noun choices is 'safety,' I might choose to link it to the word 'dangerous,' thus creating an oxymoron such as 'dangerous safety.' After creating five such two-word units, each participant then selects the one that seems most striking personally in relation to a past or present experience or life challenge. This oxymoron then functions as the title and first words of a poetic piece that I invite participants to write. I suggest that they develop their two-word expression with any images, scenes, feelings, and/or beliefs that come to mind.

The following example of an oxymoron poem that I created will suggest the ways in which this activity can open the door to discovery. It was written shortly after I returned from a three-week teaching trip to Ireland and Cornwall, during which time my husband had remained in the United States.

United Aloneness
For my husband Ken

United aloneness—
We are here together
Rowing this boat
Hearing the loons cry.

But we are two people
Alone in our individual
Set of memories.

For you, hammer, drill, tile cutter,
Views of this luscious lake and
Its cool breezes brushing your skin
Dominate.

For me, lilting Irish tunes,
Cornish pasties and
Warm, profound
Cross-cultural conversations
Prevail.

How to bridge the gap—
Can we tell each other

Enough,
Paint the images in detail,
So that you see
My inner world
And I see yours?

Some gap will always exist,
But let us purposefully
Form a bridge
Like the one you so
Skillfully are laying
Over the little marsh
We own together.

The magic of this process is that if I had not chosen a word from the above list along with a contrasting descriptor, I would never have generated the images and insights that emerged in my poem. A deliciously loaded paradox, condensed into a provocative two-word set propels us as writers toward an unexpected creative journey. When we embark on such a voyage, we can recognize more fully important present issues waiting to be addressed.

We can discover the possibilities of our chosen oxymoron in other ways than the above. There are two variant forms that I have found particularly useful. One is to invent a very short story centered on this paradox, starting with the words, 'Once upon a time, there was' (insert your oxymoron here). The second is to write in a form called a cinquain, a five-line poem with the following structure:

Line 1: Title (your oxymoron—two words)

Line 2: Word or two to describe the title

Line 3: Action words or phrases about the title (Going, Running, Laughing)

Line 4: A feeling about the title

Line 5: Refers to the title

Using 'Deliberate Accident' as the paradoxical two-word unit, a resulting cinquain might look as follows:

Deliberate accident
What a mystery
Biking, hiking, swimming
Proud of my risk-taking
Courting the unknown.

What I call the 'paradox poem' can also be quite appropriate for reframing family members' single-minded, perhaps exaggerated views of one another, either in family or couples therapy. Spouses or family members, for example, can be invited to select a trait or habit about which they have been complaining and then to pair it with a descriptor that is opposite in meaning. For example, if a father is frustrated by his child's stubbornness, he may come up with the term, 'open-minded stubbornness.' If a wife is fuming over her husband's 'selfishness,' she may generate the term, 'empathic selfishness.' Exploring in writing the implications of such seemingly strange word combinations can lead to more even-handed perceptions of the other person and a more forgiving attitude.

From Proverb to Personal Discovery

Like paradox, proverbs, even cliché ones, can open up the door to personal discoveries, when introduced as springboards to writing in a variety of growth group and therapy settings. Participants may, for example, suggest proverbs such as 'haste makes waste,' 'all roads lead to Rome,' or 'birds of a feather flock together.' Even more evocative are the sayings generated within one's family. We can invite participants to recall family proverbs or those 'admonitions' we 'carry' in our 'pockets' that Patricia Fargnoli (1999, p.10) mentions in her poem 'Going.' These usually carry special resonance for us and influence our behavior in one way or another. In my own family, for example, there was a saying, 'I worry about you because I love you.' Out of this family truism, I wrote a poem that I found very personally illuminating many years ago. Entitled 'Worry is the Way,' this poem helped to encapsulate for me the feeling tone and value system permeating my family of origin. This piece of writing also motivated me to explore how this saying has colored my present way of living and my views of my husband, daughter and friends.

Family-generated sayings can be useful for groups serving therapists and other helpers. When these individuals free write from their chosen saying, they have the opportunity to recognize how their most readily recalled 'wisdom message' impacts their work with others. For example if one participant's significant proverb is 'If at first, you don't succeed, try, try again,' her most prominent modus operandi might be perseverance when encountering a client's continuing resistance. Or if another participant's most memorable parental 'admonition' is 'Don't put off until tomorrow what you can do today,' he may tend to press clients to move forward before they are ready because of his own sense of urgency.

As this chapter suggests, a basic principle underlying writing experiences for personal development and healing involves the melding of structure with freedom to invent and experiment with words. The structure provides the holding place or jumping-off point for thoughts, images, feelings, and memories, while the open-ended aspect of the writing invitation allows for discovery of insights or uncovering of material lying beneath the surface. Writing from personally meaningful words, quirky word combinations, sentence stems and free associative listings can be quite therapeutic when the facilitator thoughtfully matches the suggested prompt to participants' present issues, emotional state and goals.

CHAPTER 16

Creatively Working with Objects

Creatively engaging with objects is akin to the metaphor work described in Chapter 14. The difference is that the presented or selected object embodies the metaphor or symbol that clients or group participants are invited to embellish in terms of their personal life and identity.

Analogy of Your Life Activity

The power of working with objects was driven home to me in the early years of my involvement with the poetry therapy movement in the United States. I attended a workshop in which participants were asked to choose an object from among those that the facilitator had placed on a large table. These included everyday items such as umbrellas, scarves, necklaces, pens and vases. After we had ample time to explore the physical properties of our selected object, we were asked to write, using either one of two prompts: 'This object is like me,' or 'This object is like my life.' Since our heads were filled with sense images gathered from our careful study of our chosen items, we were able to call upon this fund as we set forth into this uncharted territory. Even though this experience took place many years ago, I still recall that my own and others' written pieces were evocative, surprising and personal in an extraordinarily meaningful way. Since that time, I have continued to experience, in my facilitation work, the power of this 'analogy' activity.

Now when I introduce this writing experience, I provide a wide array of natural and manufactured objects with varied textures, shapes and hues. When participants develop their analogy of themselves or their lives in a way that points in a negative direction, I make a special effort to mention some shading in their language that leaves room for a positive slant.

As I have used this very fruitful writing activity with groups, I have evolved a variant which adds a second part to the activity if there is time. After all group members have selected an object, studied it and written about it, they are asked to pass it along to the person sitting on their right hand side. The new object now held by each individual then becomes the focal point for a second writing. After the two written pieces are completed, participants are encouraged to share words, phrases or lines that they have generated and to relate anything that has been learned from these writings. Since the first object was one that 'called' personally to the individual, each participant's process with it often differs from that involving the one given to them. Yet, there can be significant learning and illuminating surprises with either object. An interesting phenomenon occurs quite frequently when individuals are asked to pass their originally chosen item to their neighbor. They discover how emotionally invested they have become in this item and often state that they were reluctant to give it to someone else.

The object providing the vehicle for one's life analogy can be an imagined one as well. 'Your Tree of Life' creative writing exercise, described by Stephanie Dowrick (1993, pp.64–66), centers on an imagined object. It involves a combination of free, uncensored drawing and written reflection focusing on any kind of tree, in any season and in any setting, as an analogy of the self in the present. While some workshop participants may find themselves creating fruit trees with birds, others may draw and write about oaks or maples shedding leaves in fall, or redwoods with especially large, intricate roots. The possibilities are limited only by one's creative impulses. In the cancer survivor groups that I have facilitated, this activity has helped build a healing community, as individuals learned much about themselves and one another.

Exploring Others Through a Special Object

Written elaboration on a special object of a significant person is another very powerful experience. This expressive writing activity is quite appropriate if the goal is to explore intimate relationships, to increase understanding of another's role in your life or to reminisce as a part of the grieving process. If, for example, a client chooses as his special object his brother's old baseball mitt, he is asked to really 'look' at this object in his mind's eye, seeing its creases and color gradations, feeling its rough and smooth textures and recalling its smell. Then he is invited to reflect on the mitt in relation to its owner—when and how he used it, how he looked with it, what it seemed to mean to him. At this point, beginning with the prompt, 'My brother's baseball mitt,' the client is encouraged to free write for about ten minutes from these words to see where this creative excursion will take him.

Possessions of significant others as topics for writing can be extended to include parts of that person's anatomy that carry special meaning or that simply draw our attention at the moment. For example, in recent years, I have written two poems that have helped me honor and affirm important people in my life, one entitled 'My Father's Eyes' and the other called 'My Sister's Right Knee.' The first one is included below to show how a spontaneously written exploration of this sort can go:

My Father's Eyes

Pale rimmed glasses glinting light
are removed ever so slowly
for a moment's reflection,
revealing eyes much larger than
I ever imagined.

Reluctant you are
to enter this temporary world of near blindness,
but for me this sight is welcome:
eyes soft like the brown velvet pile of cattails in a virgin marshland,
a ridge of high check bones roughened slightly
with stubble left from your morning shave.

I see
almond-shaped eyes just like mine,
red ruts where the eyeglass frame
bridges your nose.

I see
veined eyes that have viewed
graffiti, the grime of subway walls and
the green insides of self-service elevators

that look like padded cells
for the criminally insane.

I see
a salesman's expectant eyes greeting
the smeared orange smile
of the new receptionist whose voice rasps
with the smoke of unfiltered cigarettes,
a woman who doesn't even know your name.
when she tells you
the buyer you have come across town to see
is not in today.

Mercilessly,
her lashes flicker upwards for a moment
to catch your so tired gaze.

I chose my father's eyes as a starting point because I was struck one day by the beauty and sadness of his face when he removed the glasses worn during virtually his every waking hour. While I consciously selected my initial title and subject, I had no idea that my words would lead me into the burdensome work history of my earnest and generous breadwinning parent.

Our Special or Ordinary Objects as Vehicles to Discovery

Poetically exploring our own objects also usually leads to personally significant insights. As writing facilitators, we can ask our clients or group members to bring a particularly meaningful item to an upcoming session in preparation for this writing, or this invitation can be issued spontaneously, with individuals choosing some object that they are wearing or carrying with them. Experiencing this object on a sensory level from all angles can generate symbolic resonances that shed light on one's identity or current life situation.

There are times when we as facilitators may want to be even more specific regarding the choice of possession. For example, a few years ago, when I was working with a group that was discussing the road they were traveling in their lives and how they 'walked' in the world, I decided to ask everyone to write about the shoes or sandals they were wearing at the time. First, they studied these items of foot ware very closely from their buckles to their soles, noting their condition and reflecting upon the terrain they had traversed. Then starting with the words, 'My shoes,' everyone began to write.

When I have counseled individuals or group members whose goal is to improve their self-esteem or body image in particular, I find it very useful to introduce a writing activity that focuses on their physical being. I ask individuals to think of a body part or physical feature that they can celebrate and then to write, using the same sort of framework as above. So, for example, if I wish to celebrate my cheekbones, I would study and reflect upon its characteristics and then begin writing, using the words, 'My cheekbones.' A more challenging but worthwhile variant of this activity is choosing a body part that causes distress and affirming whatever good you can discover about it. A powerful way to explore this subject involves creating a written dialogue in which you and that unlovable body part converse until you arrive at some form of agreement.

Imagining Your Life's Book Cover

Another writing invitation involving objects requires active imagining. We could call this activity the 'Symbol of Your Life.' Participants are asked to create the book cover of their life story. Doing this activity helps to highlight key turning points and salient life themes. After the book cover is conceived in the mind's eye and in some cases drawn in abstract form, participants have the opportunity to write from the picture or set of symbols they have generated, in order to discover what their book cover has to tell them.

Finding Natural Objects in Outdoor Surroundings

Going out into the natural world to write about objects we find there can be a rejuvenating and personally enlightening experience. Such sources of contemplation might include ones we can hold in our hands, such as rocks, shells, feathers or pine cones, or those we observe while we are outside, such as birds, trees or bubbling brooks. When I accompany individuals into a natural landscape on a temperate day and invite them to settle down in one place to pay loving attention to some aspect there,

I find that calming effects are nearly universal. As we imbibe the beauty of what we observe and write about it, we nourish our psyches as well as our souls.

The previous object-writing examples all suggest how the ordinary can become extraordinary, when we take the time to sense, reflect and shape our reality with words. As facilitators, it is almost as if we are giving our clients microscopes or spotlights within the context of a space where time stands still. During these dense moments, our clients generate sense impressions and cognitive associations that when written down in some sort of order supply new information or emphasize something suspected all along.

Objects that become the focal point for personal writing can take a variety of forms and be garnered from many different sources. They may be real or imagined, natural or manufactured. They may be items that already retain symbolic value or simply everyday objects one happens to have with them at the time of writing. These items can belong to the writer or to someone else whom he or she knows. They may even be physical features of self or other. They may also be a random set of objects that the facilitator supplies to provide illuminating surprises for participants.

CHAPTER 17

Nature Writing and Healing

As the years have gone by, I have become more and more convinced of the healing powers of nature and have increasingly incorporated nature walking and contemplation segments into my expressive writing workshops and growth groups. I have also used many of the techniques described below with individual clients, especially those suffering from burnout at their jobs and those seeking more balance amidst overwhelming responsibilities.

Fostering Passionate Attention and a Habit of Contemplation

The 'nature movement' that emerged in the 1960s continues to flourish nowadays. It incorporates Native American teachings, seems profoundly influenced by Zen meditation and Asian philosophy but also harks back to the nature worship of the British Romantic poets. In *The Soul Unearthed: Celebrating Wildness and Personal Renewal through Nature*, editor Cass Adams (1996) captures the spirit of this 'nature movement' in these words:

> The opportunity offered in the sanctuary of nature is one of turning inward to the source, of seeing beyond surface appearances. This plunge is a plunge into the peace and joy of being. Nothing else is needed. Removing ourselves from the business of our lives and meeting the depths of presence and

beingness found in the outdoors is a gift we can give ourselves
at any time. (Adams 1996, p.26)

In Adams' collection, Anngwyn St. Just, a therapist specializing in trauma
education and recovery, writes that 'Nature offers a mirror of wholeness
in the often shattering aftermath of overwhelming life events' (Adams
1996, p.74). St. Just also refers to 'acts of attention' and tells us, 'If we
relax our minds, open our hearts and enter into quiet dialogue with the
landscape that stands before us, our understanding will silently deepen
of its own accord. Insight and clarity come naturally' (Adams 1996,
p.130).

I employ three ways to bring the natural world to others. One of
these ways is to actually go on a nature walk, stop by a natural object or
scene that grabs our attention and savor what we perceive before putting
pen to paper. The second way, if weather or location do not allow for the
first alternative, is to imaginatively enter alluring photographs of natural
settings. The photos I supply all contain some sort of path or vista, so
that onlookers can readily 'position' themselves within the visual space.
I bring an ample supply of these photos, so that every group member
can find one that is particularly appealing, one that will 'call' to them
in some way. The third alternative is to invite participants to recall a
special, honored place where they have found peace or joy. I often ask
them to imagine a natural scene that has taken their breath away with
its beauty, or a healing place that they wish to retain as a restorative
memory. These last two alternatives expand our ways of engaging with
the world of nature, even when we find ourselves cooped up in dreary
indoor environments or caught up in the stressful daily round of energy-
sapping tasks.

The nature-centered workshops that I conduct are appropriate for
individuals of all ages who are receiving outpatient treatment at health
care or mental health facilities or are attending support groups or
enrichment seminars at community centers. They are also particularly
useful for caregivers who need to replenish their own physical, mental
and spiritual energy. These workshops are built on the premise that
there is something inherent in the human spirit that craves beauty, is
soothed by natural settings, and needs to be in contact with these. When
participants capture in writing their responses to phenomena from the
world of nature, they almost always create pieces that provide solace
and contentment. In fact, many wish to keep these written expressions

close by during trying times. They recognize that, through their own resources, they have the power to self-soothe even during periods of great adversity.

The healing nature activities that I facilitate begin with a call to immerse ourselves in the natural world. To do this, I offer the words of writers who so aptly convey the power of paying passionate attention. Writer and visual artist, Kirsten Savitri Bergh (1997), in her prose poem, 'Beginning Barefoot,' conveys the wisdom of 'going barefoot' to metaphorically convey full empathetic connection with nature's elements. For example, in her craving to be 'the tree's interpreter,' she poses the following heartfelt question: 'Why can't I stretch like the trees until my skin cracks like theirs and my fingers explode into bursts of green leaf joy?' (Bergh 1997, p.70). Words such as these model for other writers a form of interaction with the natural world that helps them discover authentic language for their own awakened sensibilities.

At times, I help foster a reflective, tranquil mood by quoting Wordsworth's reminder (1965a, p.106) that 'we can feed this mind of ours / In a "wise passiveness"' or by mentioning Keats' term (1990c, p.378), 'delicious diligent indolence.' At other times, I introduce Wordsworth's description of 'Nature' as a wise 'Teacher' who provides 'Spontaneous wisdom breathed by health' if only we 'Come forth and bring with [us] a heart / That watches and receives' (Wordsworth 1965f, p.107). These words from Whitman's 'Song of Myself' (1993, p.33) also work well as a tone-setter: 'I loafe and invite my soul,/ I lean and loafe at my ease observing a spear of summer grass.'

Walking and Writing in Natural Settings

Walking and writing in a natural setting is an activity I introduce chiefly in my stress-reduction workshops and in groups that I call 'Oasis for Therapists and Other Helpers.' This activity is also well suited to grief groups and groups of individuals recovering from trauma and serious illnesses. If there is a garden, meadow, country road or waterfront close to where these groups are being held, I include an outdoor mini-excursion, weather permitting.

The act of walking itself has been linked to poetic expression. Seasoned poet and creative writing professor, Michael Dennis Browne (1998), in 'Poetry and Walking,' explores the inspirational possibilities of walking. Linking the rhythms of walking, heartbeat and breathing,

Browne believes that the excursions we take on foot bring the body to 'a pitch of rhythmical intelligence, and in this condition the improvisations are sometimes known to begin' (Browne 1998, p.612).

Like Browne, Helen Boden (2006) describes herself as a 'walking writer.' She tells us that when she walks, she gets 'ideas for workshops, beginnings of poems and creative solutions to both creative and personal problems' (Boden 2006, p.8). Bringing together her passions, she has facilitated groups that alternate between writing and guided walking tours in the Scottish countryside. Introducing word games while the group walks, the facilitator asks participants to 'pay attention to changing underfoot sensations and textures' and to the ways these 'might affect their writing.' She also invites them, during the writing process, to call upon 'sounds recorded on the walk,' in order to further integrate the walking and writing experiences.

Henry David Thoreau (1975) insists on the importance of existing in the present moment with nature and links this experience to both walking and creating authentic poems. In his essay, 'Walking,' Thoreau asserts: 'In my walks I would fain return to my senses. What business have I in the woods, if I am thinking of something out of the woods?' Thoreau exhorts his readers to constantly discover the newness of even the most familiar places and conveys his opinion that the true poet of nature would be able to 'transplant' words to his page 'with earth adhering to their roots' (Thoreau 1975, pp.661–676).

Entering Nature Photos and Recalled Scenes

When participants *imagine* walking into their chosen nature photos or vividly *recall* a special natural scene from their lives, I invite them to 'Be there now' before introducing the writing time. I encourage them to luxuriate in the scene's various features—its colors, shadows, shapes and movements. I ask them to listen, with their inner ear, to the silences and the sounds, loud and soft; to feel the temperature of the air and its movements on the skin; and even to register their internal sensations. I also invite them to range freely within the scene, halting or sitting at a place of their choosing that offers particular comfort or an enticing vantage point.

Haiku Writing From Sensory Impressions

For me, haiku writing goes hand in hand with all three types of nature writing activities I have been describing. After participants have listed their images or free written their sensory impressions, I will usually present a variety of haiku by such masters of this form as Basho, Issa and Buson. These time-honored gem-like combinations of words provide vital links between the natural world and universal truths of human existence. We read these aloud several times, to repeatedly hear their rhythms and savor their purity, simplicity and reverential tone. We have a chance to hear their sounds as well as their silences and to exist within their unadorned mysticism. If anyone wishes to spontaneously react to any of these haiku, they are encouraged to do so. However, my primary purpose is to subliminally suggest a writing form that participants can use to embody the images that they have generated in their nature walks or indoor contemplation activities. Therefore, immediately after these haiku are heard and seen, I invite participants to return to their images and to generate as many of their own 'haiku-like' creations as they may wish to write. I emphasize that the number of syllables per line ought not to concern them. I tell them to simply stay with the impression of the haiku's tempo and tone. With the rhythms of the haiku models in their head and their own ready supply of personal imagery, participants usually experience ease and pleasure in creating their own haiku at this point and are eager to share their writings. This sharing helps foster group trust and coherence, as those present have the opportunity to exchange cherished material.

Natural Objects as Sources of Renewal and Insight

Whether participants walk outdoors, imaginatively place themselves within enticing photos, or recall a special place, they can be encouraged to focus on a specific object within that setting, one they wish they could take home in order to better remember this scene. Essentially, the chosen item functions as a transitional object embodying the restorative experience.

While walking outdoors, participants may find alluring objects that are symbolic of some facet they wish to obtain or restore in their lives. An excerpt from Anne Morrow Lindbergh's (1955) *Gift from the Sea* provides an apt model for workshop participants engaged in such an enterprise.

The carefully explored shell of a whelk becomes an emblem of the unadorned, authentic life Lindbergh craves. When she must leave her primitive hut by the sea to return to her busy world, this shell functions as a talisman for her spirit's renewal.

When we work indoors with photographic or recalled nature scenes, I ask participants to identify and lovingly reflect upon a choice object in the scene. It may be something like a cloud in a sunset sky, an alpine lake or a solitary rowboat resting against a weeping willow tree. I invite participants to hold this object in their imaginations, sensing its roundness or sharp edges, its roughness or smoothness, its fragrance or taste, its weight, color and shape. I also invite reflection on what associations this object evokes. Once participants have come to really know this object, I suggest they write using such sentence stems as:

I see... I hear... I touch... I smell... I taste... I feel...

An even more intensely personal way to engage with an object in your real or imagined natural setting is to 'become' that object, and then, speaking in its voice, write using the same sentence stems included above. For example, if I assume the voice of the solitary rowboat, I may write that I smell mossy bark and dewy grass or that I feel nurtured within the shady circle of that flourishing willow against which I nestle. It can be especially illuminating to generate a message that the chosen object wishes to convey to its observer. For example, as the rowboat, I may directly address the participant who has chosen me in words such as these: 'Why don't you simply rest for a while without worrying about your weathered appearance or solitary condition?' When I invite participants to take on the persona of their selected object, I encourage them to enter this world of pretense by putting their censor aside and allowing the object to express what it needs to say. Since this activity goes beyond the reasoning, practical mindset, it can open doors to truths waiting to be heard.

Whether we imagine ourselves into a hallowed natural place of retreat or actually feel the soft mash of autumn leaves beneath our feet on a misty morning, the world of nature is, I believe, inherently restorative and enlivening for our minds, spirits and bodies. When, in our role as helpers, we provide opportunities for writing, in a sensory and contemplative way, about the grandeur and simple beauty to be found on a remote country road or within an urban rooftop garden, we harness a powerful resource for growth and healing.

CHAPTER 18

Writing in Response to Visual Stimuli

Visual stimuli constitute rich sources of inspiration for writing that is growth enhancing and therapeutic. I use a variety of such visual materials. These include the above mentioned scenic photos, relationship postcards, pleasant and unpleasant picture collections, personal photos, collages and museum art pieces.

Relationship Postcards

I have amassed a collection of postcards depicting or suggesting relationships between people of all ages. A few of these feature animals in human-like poses and scenarios. Clients and growth group members are asked to choose one postcard that particularly 'calls' to them and to 'become' one figure that they see there. The writing activity involves conveying the words of this figure as he or she addresses another individual or feature within the postcard. The picture on the postcard functions as illuminating projective material, and participants' core relational issues usually emerge in their writing.

Pleasant and Unpleasant Picture Collections

Pleasant and unpleasant picture collections are chiefly photos drawn from magazines and calendars. While some are overtly beautiful and tranquil, others depict what would usually be termed unpleasant images. In this latter category, I never include those with violent or extremely anxiety-provoking images. When I spread out this medley of photos, I invite group members to select the one they find either the most pleasant or the most unpleasant, or I invite them to choose one in each category. As with the relationship postcards, I encourage an intuitive selection process, asking participants to choose a picture or two pictures that are demanding their attention at this particular moment. The writing invitation involves spontaneous expression of reactions—emotional, cognitive, sensory and/or spiritual. I encourage writers to engage with their picture(s) in an honest, open way. While I most often combine the two categories of pictures, some facilitators may choose to introduce only the pleasant or only the unpleasant ones, depending upon a variety of factors such as the specific goals, the clients' particular background or the trust level within a given group.

Collages

The collages that I use are comprised of about four or five diverse photographic images. Writers responding to these are asked to bring two or more of these images together in a free associative way. I became an advocate of this visual writing prompt when I first encountered it in a growth group at a poetry therapy conference. In the collage I chose, there was a large hand and a piano and probably a few other images as well. When I wrote, I found myself on an unexpected journey. My love of music and desire to begin learning how to play the piano were at the forefront, but the large hand became the chief catalyst for my self-awareness. Through my writing, the imposing hand morphed into the forces prohibiting my dream to play this instrument, and I was able to recognize how I had created my own barriers. This recognition actually led to the commencement of my first piano lessons and the purchase of a piano a short time later.

Personal Photos

I, like many other helping professionals, utilize personal photos to enrich the therapeutic process. Clients exploring identity issues benefit from studying and writing about photos of themselves that epitomize for them a specific stage or seminal event within their lives. In the context of our work together and taking into account the particular therapy goals, I often ask clients to bring a significant personal photograph taken at a time of joy and one taken at a time of sorrow. When they bring together these opposing photos, interesting juxtapositions take place.

Family photos tend to evoke writings that illuminate clients' sense of their own roles and labels in relation to parents, siblings and other family members. Paying close attention to an old family photo can lead to reframing of long-held, unproductive assumptions about one's self within the family constellation.

When I have facilitated women's growth groups focusing on mother-daughter relationships, I ask each participant to bring a photo of her mother as a young girl or very young woman. The adult women in these groups are there to primarily explore patterns of interaction with their mothers and the differences and similarities between themselves and their mothers. Given these goals, their chosen photo provides an opportunity for a fresh look at their female parent. When working with these mother photos, I invite participants to speak in the voice of the parent they see before them, or to write a letter to the woman depicted in their photo. Through their writing in relation to these photos, participants have the opportunity to more fully understand the factors that helped mold their gender identity and can envision a new mother-daughter story from which to view the self.

Museum Art Pieces

Writing facilitators can also utilize museum art pieces as catalysts for enlightening personal expression. There are two ways to introduce such pieces. One is to bring a copy of paintings with evocative scenes containing human figures, such as Pierre-Auguste Renoir's *Luncheon of the Boating Party* (1881) or William-Adolphe Bouguereau's *Temptation* (1880). The second way, if you are working with a growth group in the community, is to take a field trip to a museum which has a substantial collection of the above type of paintings. For example, in the Museum of Russian Art in Minneapolis, Minnesota, there is an abundant collection of richly rendered 'genre' artworks which each seem to tell a fascinating story about its human figures. The original Tate Gallery in London is another repository of this kind of inviting people-centered artwork, and one can undoubtedly find such collections in every city. When I accompany groups to museums, I locate the appropriate section and then invite participants to roam freely there before selecting for special study one painting that compels their attention. I then ask participants to write whatever comes to mind regarding the characters, situation and setting they see there. To engage them even further in a self-exploration process, I encourage them to write a monologue in the voice of one of the characters they see in this painting, including anything that comes to mind at the moment. The sharing of responses takes place either in a private space located at the museum or back in our group room after we leave the museum.

Comic Strip Sequences

With their combination of attention-getting pictures and words, comic strip sequences can also stimulate meaningful personal writing. The kind of comic strips that seem to lend themselves to therapy settings involve realistic life situations such as those found in 'Sally Forth' by Greg Howard, 'For Better or for Worse' by Lynn Johnston, 'Feiffer' by Jules Feiffer and the 'Peanuts' cartoon series by Charles Schultz. Comics such as these deal with common psychological realities in a non-threatening way that merges serious content with levity of tone and wit. Humor is known to be a stress-reducer, and laughter often increases our sense of mental and physical wellbeing. When we write in response to these pieces, we can savor their humor while exploring the personal ramifications of their messages.

For example, in one 'Sally Forth' cartoon sequence (Howard 1990) that I have used many times in a therapeutic context, Sally leaves her office and returns to find a huge stack of memos on her desk. When her secretary asks her if she had a good lunch break, Sally responds by saying she 'didn't have time to eat.' When she encounters this heavy load of challenging phone messages, she seems burdened, indicating to her secretary that she would love to return to 'an absolutely clean desk' with 'not a single crisis in sight.' Knowing Sally better than she knows herself, her secretary does not believe this wish is genuine, and Sally reluctantly agrees. When alone in her office, she fully admits to herself, 'It's so nice to feel needed' (Howard 1990, p.7).

The paradox embodied in this sequence and its punch line is graphically conveyed in the cartoon's last frame. Here, Sally sits looking with contentment at the daunting piles of paperwork before her. I introduce this cartoon to help clients in individual and group therapy settings recognize how we create our own overloading at times and respond to a payoff that perpetuates overly responsible behavior. I often use this cartoon after clients have explored Robert Frost's 'The Armful' (1979a) discussed earlier in Chapter 4. I find two writing prompts particularly worthwhile in conjunction with this cartoon. One is to respond in writing to the question, 'What is your immediate reaction to Sally in this cartoon?' The second is to write a letter of advice to Sally, in which you communicate with candor and compassion. While both prompts allow writers to act as observers assessing Sally's situation, I find that they open the door to explorations of a more personal nature, since so many see themselves in Sally or know someone who strongly resembles her.

Since most individuals are immediately stimulated by visual images, these provide appropriate catalysts for writing that can bypass one's censor and open the door to new insights. As this chapter shows, these visual pieces come in a variety of forms and are drawn from different types of sources. They may be comic or serious in nature. They may contain a solitary image or a pastiche of disparate images. They may be unearthed from an old family album, found in magazines or viewed during a museum visit. As with the objects and natural scenes discussed in the last two chapters, the facilitator encourages full engagement with these visual pieces before the writing begins. By closely attending to and even at times 'entering' these pictures in a visceral way, participants can bring more personally meaningful detail into their written pieces. They can generate meanings and forge new links from their visual journeys.

CHAPTER 19

Writing in Response to Film

Active Viewing of Evocative Films

Films, one of the dominant storytelling vehicles of our time, profoundly affect viewers. They combine linguistic elements with an array of evocative visual and auditory stimuli, sequenced in powerful and meaningful ways. Jay Gould Boyum (1985) in *Double Exposure: Fiction into Film* suggests that the film image may be 'much richer in connotative possibility than the word' because in film, there's 'the combination of image with word with music' (Boyum 1985, p.26). He also points out that 'We are anything but passive in watching a film: we are involved in a complex process of evocation,' for what we see 'depends not only on [our] own situation and sensibility but on what is given up there on the screen' (p.45). John Hesley and Jan Hesley (1998) in *Rent Two Films and Let's Talk in the Morning* point out that films can act as therapeutic metaphors, the metaphors that therapists use to broach sensitive areas and go beyond the conscious material that clients have identified in therapeutic conversations (Hesley and Hesley 1998, p.9). The authors also indicate that films involve surprise that disrupts habitual responses and present rich images that invite clients to supply personal content in order to construct meanings that are relevant (p.9). When:

> clients watch films, they have internal conversations with the characters of a film; they reflect on the relationships they are viewing and think of actions they might take (similar to or

different from the characters on the screen) to solve their own problems. (Hesley and Hesley 1998, p.12)

Basically, their 'approach to films in therapy is to encourage clients to examine films for what is life affirming and reject what is not' (Hesley and Hesley 1998, p.28).

Caveats for Film Use in the Therapeutic Context

Since films' dramatic effects have a potent immediacy, Hesley and Hesley (1998) provide the following wise cautionary statement emphasizing the responsible use of this medium:

> Clients will most likely get more from a film than was intended, and clinicians must be able to manage whatever emerges. Clients should be psychologically strong enough to handle dramatic material, and that determination can only be made by a therapist based on a specific client's strengths and vulnerabilities. (Hesley and Hesley 1998, p.39)

Choosing Short Film Pieces to Stimulate Written Response

While movie therapy experts such as Hesley and Hesley (1998), Boyum (1985) and Solomon (1995) focus on full-length feature films that clients view on their own, I am highlighting the use of selected film clips or film shorts as stimuli for personal written expression. Within a particular session, I show film pieces that usually run from 5 minutes to less than 20 minutes and introduce the writing invitation immediately thereafter. When we as facilitators work in this way, we can encourage an unrehearsed response. The spontaneous outpouring of words can then be contemplated, discussed with others, and more fully developed in subsequent writings.

When choosing film shorts or excerpts, I look for engaging characters facing real life situations, challenges and decisions. I also look for film pieces that are thought provoking, suggest possibilities for change and offer some degree of hope. Some of the suggestions that I present to stimulate journaling activity are as follows:

- Write about one particular character in this film clip that attracts or repels you, and explore what features are involved in your reaction.

- Free associate on the part of this film short or clip that left the strongest impression on you? What was it about this part that moved you?

- Write about a moment in your life that this movie scene reminds you of.

- Write a letter to the father, mother, teenager, etc. in this scene, saying whatever you really want to say to him or her.

- Write one word that sums up your reaction to this film clip, and create a clustering of associated thoughts, feelings and related words.

- Take one line or phrase you recall from this film clip that is particularly striking or moving for you, and write whatever it suggests.

Encouraging Purposeful Viewing

The writing experience in response to a film clip can be enhanced if you encourage participants to engage in purposeful viewing. For example, before the film begins, you might say, please be aware of your feelings and any changes in feelings as you watch this piece, or stay alert for words, phrases or sentences that are particularly striking or memorable, and keep your paper and pen handy to jot these down for later reference. I also prepare for the viewing process by asking clients or group members to focus on the behavior of one character that elicits a strong reaction as they are watching. On Birgit Wolz's website (Wolz 2009), there are helpful hints for 'Watching Movies with Conscious Awareness.' Some of these hints involve paying attention to 'how the movie images, ideas, conversations and characters affect your breath' and identifying if 'your breathing change[s]' as you view the clip.

The Animated Short Film as Productive Writing Prompt

Among the cinematic materials that I find particularly appropriate for growth and healing purposes is an animated short of under 5 minutes entitled *Boundin'* (2003), created by Bud Luckey of Pixar Animation Studios and included as one of the headers for the full-length animated hit, *The Incredibles*. It contains engaging human-like talking animals, cleverly rhyming lines and catchy music. In a uniquely creative way, it raises important issues on how we get through crises and accept life's vicissitudes. In it, the main character, a lamb, begins in innocence, preening over his soft, snowy-white coat and energizing his friends with his jaunty dance steps. When suddenly one day, he is hauled off to be sheared for the first time and dumped back to his home base, he is devastated by the trauma. He is ashamed of his new naked and pink look and mortified by the snickering of his gopher friends. He is immobilized by grief, until a 'Jackalope' comes upon the scene, asking him, 'Why the mope?' In a no-nonsense and compassionate tone, this helper proceeds to tell the downtrodden lamb that he has a 'pink kink in his think' and ought to focus on his strengths and 'get a leg up.' He even picks up the little lamb's leg, until he is able to stand on his own two feet and restore his verve. Dancing with renewed energy and winning once again the admiring attention of his companions, he is pleased to discover his coat has re-emerged. Thus, when he encounters the shearing ordeal a second time, he philosophically bows to necessity without a murmur, now confident of his own resilience. As the video ends, viewers hear the words, 'In this world of ups and downs, it's so nice to know there are Jackalopes around.'

Recently I introduced this film short with a writing activity at the Minnesota Poetry Therapy Network, an informal growth group in which participants gather for four hours to focus on a specific theme every other month. This particular group experience centered on the theme of resilience, rebounding and cultivating our strengths; about 15 people attended. Before we began viewing the film, I asked group members to be aware of their visceral, emotional and cognitive reactions and to note parts that were particularly striking to them. After viewing, I invited everyone to write a direct address to one of the characters—the lamb protagonist, his gopher friends, or the Jackalope-wisdom figure. I also presented two alternatives. One was to write about a significant moment in the film, and the other was to focus on a choice phrase heard in the film, such as a 'pink kink in your think' or 'getting a leg up.' Whatever alternative they selected, all participants were asked to free write in either poetic or prose form.

The immediate response to the video was applause, laughter and a general expression of emotional release. The writings, some prose but mostly poetry, were rich and varied. They encompassed themes uppermost in the minds of the writers and blended the playfulness inherent in the film's rhymed language with serious exploration of core issues. When various writings were shared, the ensuing discussion lasted for over an hour.

When group members wrote, some took on the voice of the helper-figure while others took on the voice of the lamb. Several group members focused on the plight and feelings of the lamb, recalling times in their own lives or in the lives of significant others when hardship prevailed. A few individuals chose to zero in on the moment when the lamb, with his hind leg raised, signaled his readiness for a second shearing. Individuals who had experienced periods of depression first hand and others who had experienced the depression of loved ones initiated a discussion of what forms of help from others are desirable, possible, respectful or necessary. The basic issue around which these participants juxtaposed their varying and similar responses was whether the person with depression needs to find ways out of their doldrums or whether others ought to spur them to action. The group discussion involved accepting versus rejecting help from others; negative versus positive self-talk; coping with recurring unpleasant realities; people laughing at us; true versus false friends; intrusive versus healing helpers; ways to rebound from troubles; and faith in our survival powers. Many read their written work aloud, while others chose not to do so, yet engaged in the lively conversation, responding to others' creativity and insights.

Another short animated Oscar-award-winning film that is of a very different nature but also appropriate as a writing prompt for therapeutic purposes is entitled *Father and Daughter* (2000), written and directed by Michael Dudok de Wit. This film, available on YouTube in its entirety, consists of simple drawings that poignantly evoke a daughter's lifelong yearning for the father who disappeared when she was a little girl. Told with evocative music and no words, this film lasting 8½ minutes seems designed to draw forth the viewer's own language and personal connections. Because of this film's sensitive subject matter and subtle yet intense drama, it should be chosen with care and used with clients or growth group members who are ready to explore serious loss in their lives.

Choosing Clips From Full-Length Feature Films

While clips from full-length films can be very useful, the facilitator needs to be creative in selecting a segment that constitutes a coherent unit, with a beginning, middle and end of its own. Also, you will probably need to provide enough background information for the clip to be meaningful to viewers.

For example, I have introduced a clip from Mark Rydell's film *On Golden Pond* (1981, based on a play by Ernest Thompson) several times in my work with others. It is a realistic and superbly well-acted movie focused on the relationship between a middle-aged daughter and her aging parents. The clip I have chosen to show over the years involves the daughter Chelsea's attempt to connect with Norman, her distant, critical father. The clip begins with a dialogue in which the daughter and her mother Ethel discuss the father. Although these women usually enjoy a very compatible relationship, they argue over the daughter's enduring bitterness toward a father who is clearly at a stage where his health is failing. Spurred on by her mother's words, Chelsea, with much trepidation, attempts to communicate with her father in a new way. In spite of being rebuffed by his characteristic armor of gruffness, she persists. The two eventually connect when the daughter attempts to successfully execute the back flip dive she could not manage when she was a girl. The breakthrough moment is clear yet not overstated or sentimentalized. I choose this clip as a stimulus for therapeutic writing because it raises significant issues regarding self-esteem, forgiveness, and family communication patterns.

Before the viewing of the above clip takes place, I request that participants pay attention to the character that most draws them into the action and stay aware of their own feelings. After the clip ends, I invite participants to write a letter to any of the three characters that they most feel drawn to address. This could be the father, mother or daughter. As participants express their admiration, anger and/or impatience at the various characters, they have a chance to work through challenging issues within their own family systems and to conceptualize these issues in a new way. One of the most fruitful questions that repeatedly surfaces as a result of writing about this film clip is what are the healthiest ways for us to deal with our lingering resentments?

Participants viewing *On Golden Pond* might find it interesting to discover that Jane and Henry Fonda, who play the roles of father and daughter, actually experienced conflicts that parallel those depicted in the film and that 'Jane Fonda purchased the rights to the play specifically for her father...to play the role of the cantankerous Norman Thayer' (Fonda 2010). However, as a film therapy facilitator I would choose to share this information after participants have had the chance to discuss and write about the struggles these characters face. Knowing this background information could detract from the participants' spontaneous and idiosyncratic reactions to the way this relationship unfolds.

When I am working with groups of helpers who are training to provide services for elderly people, I often introduce two different clips from Paul Mazursky's *Harry and Tonto* (1974), starring Art Carney. Developing the experiences of an aging widower, named Harry Coombs, this film, in an energizing and moving way, highlights an abundance of issues not only facing senior citizens but also pertaining to life transitions in general. I often use a 17-minute clip that begins with the film's opening establishing shot of Harry's urban neighborhood and ends with his trip to his son Burt's home after he has been forcibly removed from a soon-to-be-demolished apartment building. After having protested this change of residence with every fiber of his being, Harry now faces a new living arrangement with his eldest son, daughter-in-law and teenage grandsons. With all his belongings stuffed in the vehicle, Harry says to his son: 'When an old man loses his home, he's just a wanderer.' When the clip ends, I usually ask viewers to write one word or phrase that sums up their reaction and to create a clustering of free associations on what this word suggests. This writing activity provides an effective entry into viewers' personal links to the cinematic material. At times, I ask participants to write specifically about Harry: how they feel about him, his relationship with his cat, Tonto, what his neighborhood means to him and/or his reaction to his eviction. I also often invite viewers to write a scenario beyond the end of the clip—to imagine what will happen to Harry after he moves in with his son's family.

There is another segment from *Harry and Tonto* (1974) that I have also prepared. It occurs after Harry has decided it is time for him to move out of Burt's home and visit his single daughter in Chicago and unmarried son in Los Angeles. This segment begins when Harry arrives at the airport with his cat and begins to encounter a series of obstacles because of the pet accompanying him. He ends up not being able to board the plane and is forced to take a bus that leaves him behind during a rest break when Tonto gets lost. Once he finds his cherished pet, Harry hitches a ride, purchases a used car and picks up a young hitchhiker to drive it for him because his driver's license has expired. While these experiences are comical, they show not only Harry's distress but also his remarkable resilience.

After I show this clip, I often ask viewers to put themselves in Harry's shoes when he is left stranded and searching for his cat. I invite viewers to write from that moment, imagining how they would be feeling inside and what they would do in his circumstances. I then ask them to create the ideal scenario, imagining how they would want themselves to react. I also often suggest that viewers recall and narrate in writing a time when the unexpected happened to them and they were forced to improvise. I encourage them to flesh out their story with details of the setting, their circumstances and their various reactions.

The clip I have selected from Carl Franklin's film, *One True Thing* (1998, based on a novel by Anna Quindlen), centers on a crucial decision that the main character, Ellen, must make. From the visuals and words in this segment, it is obvious that Ellen, a very ambitious young journalist, has always idealized and emulated her professor father while discounting her nurturing housewife mother. In the clip I use, a major dramatic situation occurs. Ellen receives her father's request that she come home to take care of her mother, who she is told requires cancer treatments. Assaulted by her father's guilt-inducing words and adamant call for help, Ellen is left to make a decision of whether or not to put her New York life on hold for an indefinite period of time. In one shocking moment, she experiences grief over her mother's illness, encounters her father's self-absorption and faces the potential dismantling of her self-concept and entire life style. In conjunction with this film clip, I usually ask viewers to write two letters, one to the father and the other to Ellen, articulating whatever they are moved to say in the moment. If they wish, they may choose to write a letter of advice to either one of these characters. At other times, I have asked viewers to write about a time in their lives that this scene resembles or to address the specific ways in which Ellen's dilemma reminds them of a situation in their own lives.

In addition to the above films, I have introduced writing prompts in response to selected clips from Stephen Daldry's *Billy Elliot* (2000),

Robert Benton's *Kramer vs. Kramer* (1979), Ron Howard's *Parenthood* (1989), Wayne Wang's *The Joy Luck Club* (1993), Jon Avnet's *Fried Green Tomatoes* (1991), David Frankel's *The Devil Wears Prada* (2006), Peter Cattaneo's *The Full Monty* (1997), Michael Lehmann's *The Truth about Cats and Dogs* (1996), and Gus Van Sant's *Good Will Hunting* (1998). This is obviously a short list, since there is an abundance of powerful cinematic material that is continually being generated.

Writing Responses to Films Viewed Outside of Session

There are times when writing to a film stimulus does not involve the actual showing of a clip in the session or group meeting. When clients reveal an obvious interest in cinema, I usually ask them to identify a film that has been particularly important to them and to directly address in writing the character in that film with whom they most strongly identify. One example from my practice involves Ron Howard's film, *Parenthood* (1989), starring Steve Martin. While comic, it also contains substantive material regarding the dynamics of family life. The client who resonated to this film identified with the protagonist, and, in his writing, focused on this character's place in the family as the oldest, responsible brother who felt basically ignored by his father. Not surprisingly, this family situation closely mirrored the client's own. Through addressing the protagonist of *Parenthood*, he highlighted significant experiences within his family of origin and their effects on his present relationships.

One of my poetry therapy trainees was counseling a woman who had been sexually and physically abused. During one of their sessions, this woman mentioned that many years before she had very much enjoyed seeing Steven Spielberg's film, *The Color Purple* (1985, based on Alice Walker's novel). He asked if she would be willing to view it again during the upcoming week, and she agreed to do so. When the therapist requested in the next session that she free write her reactions to the film, she centered her energies on a particular scene in which the female hero confronts her abusive husband for the first time and begins to take control of her destiny. This client's vivid recollection of and profound appreciation for this scene were solidified through the writing that she produced. In this writing, she could fully capture, in the present, the strength and renewed hope that this favored scene had engendered.

Films can be especially potent stimuli for personal writing experiences. Right before our eyes, they animate characters, relationship dynamics, symbols and events in living color and form. They also introduce riveting features of sound to amplify the effects of the visual material. Because films generate an immediate impact, they need to be chosen with particular care when used in therapeutic and growth group settings.

An ideal scenario for tapping unrehearsed reactions to film material occurs when participants can view a short film or clip of a full-length feature film within a single session or group meeting and then have the opportunity to write immediately following their film-viewing. It is also effective for facilitators to invite writing in response to full-length films that clients consider particularly meaningful and/or memorable. The writing prompts suggested in this chapter resemble those introduced earlier, particularly in relation to story therapy, since films are fundamentally vehicles for narrative.

CHAPTER 20

Melding Art, Music and Movement with Creative Expression

Writing in Response to Free Style Drawing, Collage-Making and Clay Sculpting

Combining writing with spontaneous drawing using markers, crayons or pastels is quite a common practice for those who facilitate creative writing workshops or growth groups for therapeutic purposes. Such an activity can also be effective when counseling couples and families, as well as children and adults in individual therapy settings. As with writing, when adults do artwork, they usually need encouragement to dispel their inner critic's influence and simply allow their hands and imaginations to take over. Therefore, to allow movement toward the joy of free expression, it is important for the writing facilitator to create a relaxing atmosphere where judging voices are kept at bay.

It can be edifying and rejuvenating for couples, families and groups to work on a collaborative freestyle drawing, where everyone spontaneously adds their own touches to the composition and then writes what comes to mind as they gaze upon their joint venture. Engaging in this cooperative activity usually brings individuals together in a way that diminishes tension and promotes cohesion. Moreover, when they have the opportunity to convey in language both the experience of doing this activity and their responses to the visual product, they often more fully understand their roles and feelings in relation to others.

Collage or montage-making is also quite effective in conjunction with expressive writing in all of the above therapeutic contexts, especially in groups. Both collages and montages resemble a quilt, in which heterogeneous images are arranged or blended in an artistic composition that is meant to suggest a total idea or impression. The images that clients or workshop participants collect for their compositions are usually drawn from magazine and newspaper pictures and personal photos but may also include drawings, words and/or objects such as feathers and buttons. When collage-makers write a poem, journal entry or story to reflect the essence of these creations, they have the opportunity to explore in depth the meanings and links they inadvertently forge when they first assemble their diverse materials. Asking collage-makers to title their visual pieces before they begin writing reflections or narratives can help galvanize or structure their response even more fully.

It is desirable for the general subject of a collage or montage to reflect major goals and focal issues of the individuals or groups you are serving. For example, in a life or career transitions group, participants may be invited to assemble a set of images representing key segments of their life journey or capturing the future ventures they envision. Clients can also acquire perspective and recognize important patterns in their lives when they build a montage juxtaposing images of losses and gains they have experienced or assemble images denoting places they have lived. In my experience, elderly individuals who are engaging in life review or young individuals exploring their identity usually welcome the creative opportunity to design the 'book cover' of their hypothetical 'autobiography.' They find it beneficial to position images and words in a configuration that captures their present view of the time they have spent in this world.

Clients in individual or group therapy can be invited to create a montage that matches a key therapeutic issue that emerges. For example, a middle-aged man I counseled a few years ago, in telling his story, began to focus on the issue of crying. He had become increasingly distressed and perplexed by the way he dissociated from his own feelings and wanted to better understand why he could not cry or experience genuine sadness regarding personal occurrences. For him, a 'crying montage' proved to be quite productive. I asked him to create a collection of words, symbols and images that he associated with crying and to organize these according to stages within his life. I then asked him to capture in writing what he noticed in his collection. This activity summoned up an abundance of vital material regarding this client's past and present life. He highlighted his experience with an abusive father who threatened severe punishment for crying. He also focused on his current role as the passive husband of a controlling wife whose bouts of crying felt very manipulative and left him helpless. More importantly, the combination of collage-making and writing evoked welcome emotion from this client. He found that he could cry in the room with me and not be punished for doing so. He uncovered his emotional self in an atmosphere where he felt safe and grew in understanding of how crying for him was linked not only to terror, shame and loss, but also to self-nurturing and compassion.

Like montage-making, sculpting with clay is another hands-on activity that provides a rich stimulus for meaning-making writing. The very act of molding clay is a relaxing and cathartic experience for most people, if the process rather than the artistic value of the product is emphasized. In an ongoing psychotherapy group for women suffering from depression and anxiety, I and my co-facilitator used the combination of sculpting and writing frequently, to enable participants to explore their self-image and the ways in which they desired to empower themselves. For example during one two-hour session, we invited participants to celebrate a unique skill or talent they possess by creating a clay figure of their choosing. We then asked them to free write on what this figure was 'saying' to them. Through this dual activity, group members were able to access, in a positive framework, physical, emotional and mental aspects of themselves.

Writing in Response to Instrumental Music

Instrumental music is often combined with writing in therapeutic and growth group contexts. Like many facilitators, particularly of groups, I use musical pieces to help create a soothing atmosphere or provide a warm-up. In addition, I invite participants to free write their responses to the sounds and rhythms of the music. Through this activity, the writer often opens up unexpected avenues to explore or discovers new facets of issues that have been uppermost in their minds.

In making choices regarding which music to use, I take into account many different aspects of the therapeutic situation. In general, I find that using musical pieces that are not likely to be known helps to open the doors of imagination. When a work is familiar to the listener, the possibility of exploring new territory is diminished. The tempo of the music is another consideration. While some music tends to calm us, other pieces energize us or even increase anxiety. There have been times when I have deliberately varied the tempo of the music I present, to help create an atmosphere in which a wide range of moods and images is evoked. For instance, as a prelude to a therapeutic discussion of Robert Frost's 'The Armful' (1979a) discussed in Chapter 4, I use a segment of fast-paced music immediately followed by a slow-paced composition. For example, I often play five minutes of such fast-paced pieces as Rossini's 'William Tell Overture,' Rimsky-Korsakov's 'Flight of the Bumblebee' or Khachaturian's 'Sabre Dance.' For music that is soothing and relaxed, I usually offer segments from Steven Halpern's 'Spectrum Suite.' I introduce this juxtaposition in order to set up our later discussion of how we can reduce the stress of a frenetic daily grind.

Integrating Art, Music, Movement and Writing

Personal writing for growth and healing can be very effectively combined with music, artistic expression and movement all in one experience. Years ago, I recall attending a workshop in which all these arts were melded. There was movement to music of varied rhythms after which participants took up crayons or markers to capture their mood and/ or the images summoned up by their self-created dances. The drawing was then followed up with a return to movement, and the culminating activity involved writing for ten minutes. Embodying in words my visceral responses to music-accompanied movement and freestyle drawing resulted in an enriched experience of personal discovery for me and others there. I can still vividly recall how my body, in response to the movement sequence, began bending back and forth from the waist and how the image of an open window's threshold emerged when I began writing. This creative expression took me to a place where I could explore my ambivalence about a transition in my life I felt called upon to make. Writing about it helped me explore my options and the meaning of the change I was contemplating.

The doors to creativity open up for each of us in different ways. It is my belief that the various art forms are compatible with one another and can function synergistically for us. Expressive writing is often stimulated by hands-on visual arts activities, by attentive listening to music and by physical movement. When our bodies and senses are mobilized in ways suggested in this chapter, our writing can assume a whole new look and take us down fruitful avenues of enhanced self-awareness.

CHAPTER 21

The Power of the Group Poem

Cohesion-Building and Communal Pride

The group poem helps build cohesion and a sense of fun in creating something together. I have found that a collaborative written expression increases the energy in the room, as everyone feels a part of what is going on and experiences a sense of pride regarding their participation in the community effort. If each individual is asked to supply only a phrase, word or line, the pressure is minimal. Usually there is wonderful spontaneity to this process, as I continually repeat aloud the lines that have accumulated thus far, in order to stimulate those that will follow. In this way, I maintain a flow of language that helps group members add their contributions. While I usually write the poem as it is generated either on a board or in a notebook, there are some group poems that involve passing a paper around the group, with each person adding a line that seems to follow from the last one written. I do not find this latter method as effective as the first, because the cohesion of the group is less apparent. However, when such a jointly written piece is read aloud for all to hear, surprise and delight often result.

Family and Dyadic Poems: Celebrating Togetherness and Individuality

As I mentioned in the previous discussion of metaphor work with families, the color image is a simple, yet powerful one to use when helping family members articulate their individual identities. When I facilitate a family session in which each family member has mentioned a color that is their favorite and has generated images that embody that color, a good way to bring participants together is to create a 'rainbow poem' to represent this variety in a single entity. This is a playful, but not a trivial activity, because it both inspires family members to cooperate in a joint effort and highlights the respect for difference that is essential to healthy family functioning.

Nicholas Mazza (2003, p.34) describes a 'family collaborative poem' to which 'family members are invited to contribute one or more lines... on a topic relating to the theme or mood of the session.' Mazza provides an example in which the clinician supplies the words, 'I'm most happy at home, when,' inviting family members to complete the sentence. He also refers to a two-line 'dyadic poem' for couples, to which each partner contributes one line describing their relationship (Mazza 2003, pp.36–37).

When family members or couples have the opportunity to juxtapose their voices and their truths, even when these are starkly different from one another, they participate in a team effort that helps reduce tension and facilitates communication. Providing equal space for divergent points of view in a written piece conveys the message that everyone's personhood counts, and we are in the room to hear and better understand one another. For example, one couple in my practice, who had a very different spending philosophy that was the primary source of their conflict, wrote a two-line poem to the following invitation: 'Take the words, "When I spend money," and complete the line in any way that fits for you at this moment.' The resulting two-line poem read something like this:

> Husband: When I spend money, I worry that I will be poor tomorrow and see my father's careworn face;

> Wife: When I spend money on colorful clothes today, I say thank you for this gift to myself.

Hearing their words together as one poem and seeing them combined on the page, both husband and wife could better understand their own and their partner's primary emotions regarding money issues. The wife could recognize how her husband's anxiety had driven his anger over her spending, and the husband could realize how clothes-buying was a source of joy and self-affirmation for his wife, rather than a way to punish him. While this couple still had much work to do before they could generate compromise and find common ground on money issues, they were developing empathy for one another's inner reality and heartfelt experience.

Group Poems as Closure Technique

Group poems provide a very fitting way to conclude a growth or support group. They merge a variety of responses that reflect what each person is taking with them as the group terminates its work. I have frequently used the following three quite different writing prompts for a closing collaborative poem. The first alternative involves asking participants to shout out the word or phrase that comes to mind when they think about their experience in this group. For the second alternative, I suggest a two-stanza group poem with the following framework that I write on a board for all to see: 'I say goodbye to...; I say hello to...' I then invite each person to complete one line in each stanza. As mentioned previously, I repeat aloud the lines already generated, in order to evoke subsequent responses that move the poem along. The third alternative involves writing the word, 'FAREWELL,' vertically as an acrostic on a large board and asking participants to contribute poetic lines beginning with the above letters. I almost always contribute a line or two to these closure collaborative poems and send a copy of our finished product to each group member as a parting gift of remembrance.

Creating a written piece that integrates more than one voice fulfils a number of important therapeutic goals. Collaborative writing experiences usually unite group members and celebrate the unique contributions of everyone in the setting. For this reason, jointly created poems are particularly appropriate at the beginning and ending of group experiences. There is also a kind of democracy in collaboratively written poems that emerge amongst family members and couples, since everyone participating possesses an equal share of the product and can feel counted in the process. In the context of family and marriage counseling, jointly composed poetic expressions result in potent juxtapositions. While the similarities highlight bridges between individuals, the discrepancies in values, needs and expectations provide substance for further discussion.

CHAPTER 22

Concluding Remarks

The therapist or helper who establishes the atmosphere and provides the opportunities for therapeutic reading and writing can be likened to a midwife who assists in bringing forth that which has been gestating and is ready to be born. Both reading and writing are powerful agents of growth and healing at least in part because literary works and our own creative word structuring help make evident personally significant material lying just beneath our consciousness. Our own and others' creative expressions help shape for us in words that which has been nebulous or undefined. We can savor, contemplate and keep for future reference the words that intrigue and surprise us when we read them in printed form, hear them performed aloud or produce them ourselves.

A safe, supportive setting constitutes an essential feature of engagements with creative expressions designed to enhance our clients' therapeutic journeys. As clients respond, in this kind of milieu, to the various features in others' poems and stories, they can trust that their reactions will be taken seriously and heard with sensitivity and openness. When a skilled facilitator encourages spontaneous writing by introducing innovative structures and evocative stimuli, the feelings and insights that are generated can be explored and celebrated in a non-threatening, effective way.

Even though literary expressions have much to contribute to the wellbeing of a great many individuals and surround us on a daily basis, the modality described in this book is not for everyone. There are those who simply do not connect with figurative language of any kind or those whose prejudices or fears regarding literary material are deeply entrenched. While there are individuals who relish opportunities to incorporate literary arts into their quest for a better life, there are many others who know nothing about the therapeutic possibilities of poems or stories. For the growth groups that I facilitate in community and educational settings, I provide ample detail on the poetic approach that we will be taking. When I interview potential participants for these groups, I answer any questions they may have about the work we will be doing. As I begin counseling individuals in my practice as a psychologist, I assess clients' interest in or willingness to engage with poetic expressions before introducing biblio/poetry therapy activities.

As the material presented in this book suggests, there is an abundance of *anecdotal* reports that attest to the benefit of poems, stories and creative writing for individuals from varying age groups and backgrounds and in the context of diverse clinical, educational and medical settings. However, the fields of biblio/poetry therapy and therapeutic writing are still fledglings in the arena of empirical studies, and more remains to be accomplished.

Over the years, measuring, in an objective way, the benefits of any specific mode of therapy has proved elusive, probably because the therapeutic situation and the definition of improved psychological functioning encompass a formidable array of variables. Yet, most researchers studying the effects of therapy have identified the quality of the client-therapist relationship as a particularly significant factor, no matter what the modality. There seems to be widespread agreement that when individual clients or group members perceive their helpers as caring individuals who believe in their ability to heal and grow, they usually rate their experience as beneficial. Jerome Frank (1963), in *Persuasion and Healing*, repeatedly returns to hope and a positive client-therapist connection as two cornerstones of effective therapy, whether it is 'directive' as in short-term behavioral approaches or 'evocative' (Frank 1963, p.147), as is the insight-oriented creative arts approach described in this book. According to Frank (1963), the element of hope involves both the client's 'expectation of help' in the therapeutic encounter and the therapist's 'optimistic outlook' or faith in the client's ability to improve the quality of his or her life. He also indicates that helpers need to be flexible in their approach in order to 'mobilize the patient's expectancy for help.' They need to 'be prepared to modify' their 'approach' in order 'to meet' what they 'discern' are their 'patients' conceptions of therapy' (Frank 1963, pp.214, 115, 233).

Our flexibility as facilitators and our focus on clients' resilience and human potential are integral to the creative arts approach described in this book. As we facilitate the reading and writing processes of others for the purpose of life-enhancement, the work we and our clients do together involves a sense of timing. In his 'Ode: Intimations of Immortality,' William Wordsworth (1965c, p.186) refers to 'a timely utterance' that gave him 'relief' and helped restore his strength. Whether clients discover this particular 'utterance' in a story or a poem written by someone else or created by themselves, its timeliness is of the essence. As facilitators, our timely introduction of literary selections for the individuals we serve and the timing of our interventions as we harness the healing power of creative expressions are crucial.

Helpers who incorporate poetry, story and creative writing in their practice, need to keep front and center the ways in which clients and/ or group members are responding to the reading, writing and sharing processes at any given moment. Those of us who have a literary bent and are enthusiastic about specific creative interventions, need to be careful not to get carried away by our own passions and preferences. It is essential for us, as helpers, to keep in mind that we are not introducing evocative materials and writing invitations merely to unleash emotion and unconscious material. We are presenting these creative opportunities in the interests of the people we serve. We are providing a venue where they can process their initial responses, to make order out of chaos, to cultivate that plot of land where the seeds are planted.

As I reflect upon the client's and helper's joint sense of hopefulness in this fertile therapeutic venture, I call to mind the concluding couplet from Samuel Taylor Coleridge's sonnet, 'Work without Hope' (1950). In the throes of depression, Coleridge's speaker knows and captures, in precise poetic language, exactly what he is missing and most needs: 'Work without hope draws nectar in a sieve,/ And hope without an object cannot live' (Coleridge 1950, p.210). Working as helpers who evince and inspire hope, we can help our clients gather the 'nectar' that will provide both pleasure and an ongoing source of nourishment.

Feedback and Report Forms

There are four forms in this section to use as they are or to modify according to your own preferences and purposes. The first form is a 'Poetry and Story Facilitation Feedback Form,' designed to be used when there is an observing group or individual supervisor who can provide constructive feedback on a facilitator's work in leading a poetry or story session for growth and healing. I use this form when I am teaching introductory and intermediate level courses in poetry/bibliotherapy. I divide the class into two groups, with one set of students acting as observers of my facilitation work and the other set of students functioning as participants in the process. The second form, 'Pre-plan for Biblio/Poetry Therapy Session,' suggests a way for poetry or story facilitators to prepare for their sessions. The third and fourth forms, 'Process Notes for Poetry and Story Therapy Facilitation' (Samples #1 and #2), represent alternative ways to report on a specific session. While these forms are set up for group work, they can easily be adapted to psychotherapy sessions with individuals, couples or families. When facilitators keep clear and thorough records, they can evaluate their work and keep track of how participants are engaging with the reading materials and writing activities.

Poetry and Story Facilitation Feedback Form: A Discussion for Learning

What was your reaction to the materials used?

. . . .

How were the materials introduced?

. . . .

What did you notice regarding the steps in the process?

- Recognition . . . .

. . . .

- Examination . . . .

. . . .

- Juxtaposition . . . .

. . . .

- Application to self . . . .

. . . .

What helped or hindered the process?

. . . .

How was the therapeutic dialogue furthered?

- Open-ended interventions . . . .

. . . .

- Specific interventions . . . .

. . . .

How did you experience the facilitator in relation to yourself?

. . . .

What did you notice about the dialogue between group members and the roles taken on by various participants?

. . . .

What are your observations on the nature of the silences that occurred?

. . . .

What might you have done differently?

. . . .

Pre-plan for Biblio/Poetry Therapy Session

Name of group: . . . .

Name of facilitator: . . . .

Date: . . . .

Location or setting: . . . .

Participants expected to attend: . . . .

. . . .

. . . .

General group goals:

1. . . . .

2. . . . .

3. . . . .

Specific goals for today's session:

1. . . . .

2. . . . .

Warm-up activity: . . . .

. . . .

Reading materials: . . . .

. . . .

How materials will be introduced/presented: . . . .

. . . .

. . . .

Possible questions to invite discussion:

1. . . . .

2. . . . .

3. . . . .

Writing activity: . . . .

. . . .

Idea(s) for closing: . . . .

. . . .

Process Notes for Poetry and Story Therapy Facilitation (Sample # 1) (attach copies of materials used)

Name of group: . . . . Date: . . . . Session # . . . . .

Goals: General and specific:

1. . . . .

2. . . . .

3. . . . .

4. . . . .

Warm-up: . . . .

Material presented: . . . .

How materials were introduced: . . . .

Writing activity: . . . .

Facilitator's major questions and interventions:

. . . .

. . . .

. . . .

Group members' responses to materials and writing activity:
Initial of first name:

H. . . . .

M. . . . .

D. . . . .

F. . . . .

Roles of group members in today's group:

. . . .

Primary themes emerging from today's session:

. . . .

Progress in relation to goals:

. . . .

For you, as facilitator, what worked? What did not work?

. . . .

Process Notes for Poetry and Story Therapy Facilitation (Sample #2)

Facilitator: . . . . Date: . . . . .

Site: . . . . Client population: . . . .

Session #: . . . . Duration: . . . hour(s)

Names of attendees: . . . .

. . . .

Objectives of the session: . . . .

. . . .

Record sequence of activities (including materials introduced, facilitator's interventions, and participants' responses):

Activity #1:

Materials introduced (attach copy with publication information):

. . . .

Facilitator questions or invitations:

. . . .

Specific responses to materials (describe key verbal and nonverbal reactions of individuals): . . . .

. . . .

Activity #2:

Materials introduced:

. . . .

Facilitator questions or invitations:

. . . .

Specific responses to materials:

. . . .

Assessment of group's functioning during this session:

. . . .

Things to consider when planning for upcoming sessions:

. . . .

———◆•◆•◆———

Useful Resources

Selected Poetry and Short Story Anthologies, Film and Web Resources

The following collections provide a rich treasury of materials for therapists, growth group facilitators and educators; however not every poem, story or film included in these books will be therapeutic or appropriate. It is essential to carefully assess each one in terms of the individuals you are serving and the setting in which you are working.

Poetry Anthologies

Alexander, A.L. (ed.) (1956) *Poems that Touch the Heart.* New York: Doubleday.

Astley, N. (ed.) (2002) *Staying Alive: Real Poems for Unreal Times.* Tarset, Northumberland: Bloodaxe.

Banerjee, N., Kaipa, S. and Sundaralingam, P. (eds) (2010) *Indivisible: An Anthology of Contemporary South Asian American Poetry.* Fayetteville, AR: University of Arkansas Press.

Benson, J. and Falk, A. (eds) (1996) *The Long Pale Corridor: Contemporary Poems of Bereavement.* Newcastle upon Tyne: Bloodaxe.

Bly, R., Hillman, J. and Meade, M. (eds) (1992) *The Rag and Bone Shop of the Heart: Poems for Men.* New York: HarperCollins.

Bowen, R., Temple, N., Wienrich, S. and Albery, N. (eds) (2003) *Poem for the Day Two: 366 Poems, Old and New to Learn by Heart.* London: Nicolas Albery Foundation / Random House.

Bowman, T. and Johnson, E.B. (eds) (2010) *The Wind Blows, The Ice Breaks: Poems of Loss and Renewal by Minnesota Poets.* Minneapolis, MN: Nodin Press.

Chavis, G.G. and Weisberger, L.L. (eds) (2003) *The Healing Fountain: Poetry Therapy for Life's Journey.* St. Cloud, MN: North Star Press.

Clifton, L. (1987) *Next: New Poems.* Brockport, NY: BOA Editions.

Cohen, C. and Lorenz, D. (eds) (2005) *Hand-to-Hand, Heart-to-Heart: Children's Poems from Around the World.* Philadephia, PA: Arts and Spirituality Center. Available at www.artsandspirituality.org.

Darling, J. and Fuller, C. (eds) (2005) *The Poetry Cure.* Tarset, Northumberland: Bloodaxe.

Donegan, P. with Ishibashi, Y. (eds and trans.) (2010) *Love Haiku: Japanese Poems of Yearning, Passion and Remembrance.* Boston, MA: Shambala.

Duffy, C.A. (ed.) (1996) *Stopping for Death: Poems of Death and Loss.* New York: Henry Holt.

Esselman, M.D. and Velez, E.A. (eds) (2005) *Love Poems for Real Life.* New York: Grand Central.

France, L. (ed.) (1994) *Sixty Women Poets.* Newcastle upon Tyne: Bloodaxe.

France, L. (ed.) (2008) *Rowing Home.* Newcastle upon Tyne: Cruse Bereavement Care Tyneside.

Fried, E. and Singer, B. (eds) (1985) *Men Talk: An Anthology of Male Experience Poetry.* Eugene, OR: Pacific House.

Gendler, J.R. [1984] (1988) *The Book of Qualities,* 2nd edn. New York: Harper & Row.

Hart, M. and Loader, J. (eds) (1998) *Generations: Poems between Fathers, Mothers, Daughters, Sons.* London: Penguin.

Hass, R. (ed. and trans.) (1994) *The Essential Haiku: Versions of Basho, Buson and Issa.* New York: HarperCollins.

Hirshfield, J. (ed.) (1995) *Women in Praise of the Sacred.* New York: HarperPerennial.

Housden, R. (ed.) (2003) *Risking Everything: 110 Poems of Love and Revelation.* New York: Harmony.

Howe, F. (ed.) (1993) *No More Masks! An Anthology of Twentieth-Century American Women Poets.* New York: HarperPerennial.

Hughes, M.W. (2003) *Flight on New Wings: Healing through Poetry.* St. Cloud, MN: North Star Press.

Keillor, G. (ed.) (2002) *Good Poems.* New York: Penguin.

Keillor, G. (ed.) (2005) *Good Poems for Hard Times.* New York: Penguin.

Klein, P.S. (ed.) (2006) *Treasury of Friendship Poems.* New York: Random House.

Lifshin, L. (ed.) [1978] (1992) *Tangled Vines: A Collection of Mother and Daughter Poems.* San Diego, CA: Harcourt Brace Jovanovich. (First published in 1978).

Lombardo, T. (ed.) (2008) *After Shocks: The Poetry of Recovery for Life-Shattering Events.* Atlanta, GA: Sante Lucia.

Mazziotti, M.G. and Gillan, J. (eds) (1994) *Unsettling America: An Anthology of Contemporary Multi-Cultural Poetry.* New York: Penguin.

Milosz, C. (ed.) (1996) *A Book of Luminous Things: An International Anthology of Poetry.* Orlando, FL: Harcourt.

Mukand, J. (ed.) (1994) *Articulations: The Body and Illness in Poetry.* Iowa City, IA: University of Iowa Press.

Murray, J. (ed.) (2001) *Poems to Live by in Uncertain Times.* Boston, MA: Beacon.

Olds, S. (1984) *The Dead and the Living Poems by Sharon Olds.* New York: Alfred A. Knopf.

Oliver, M. (1992) *New and Selected Poems, Volume One.* Boston, MA: Beacon.

Pastan, L. (1982) *PM/AM: New and Selected Poems.* New York: Norton.

Peacock, M., Paschen, E. and Neches, N. (eds) (1996) *Poetry in Motion: 100 Poems from the Subways and Buses.* New York: Norton.

Perlman, J. (ed.) (1979) *Brother Songs: A Male Anthology of Poetry.* Minneapolis, MN: Holy Cow! Press.

Perlman, J., Cooper, D., Hart, M. and Mittlefehldt, P. (eds) (2009) *Beloved on the Earth: 150 Poems of Grief and Gratitude.* Duluth, MN: Holy Cow! Press.

Reed, I. (ed.) (2003) *From Totems to Hip-Hop: A Multicultural Anthology of Poetry across the Americas, 1900–2002.* Cambridge, MA: Da Capo Press.

Remen, R.N. (ed.) (1994) *Wounded Healers.* Mill Valley, CA: Wounded Healer Press.

Roth, J.B. (ed.) (2002) *We Used To Be Wives: Divorce Unveiled through Poetry.* Santa Barbara, CA: Fithian Press.

Rumi, J. (2006) *Rumi Poems,* edited by P. Washington. New York: Alfred A. Knopf.

Ryan, B. (ed.) (1974) *Search the Silence: Poems of Self-Discovery.* New York: Scholastic Book Services.

Sewell, M. (ed.) (1991) *Cries of the Spirit: A Celebration of Women's Spirituality.* Boston, MA: Beacon.

Shinder, J. (ed.) (1983) *Divided Light: Father and Son Poems.* Riverdale on Hudson, NY: Sheep Meadow Press.

Shinder, J. (ed.) (1992) *First Light: Mother and Son Poems*. San Diego, CA: Harcourt Brace Jovanovich.

Van Den Heuvel, C. (ed.) (1986) *The Haiku Anthology*, revised edn. New York: Simon & Schuster.

van Meenen, K. and Rossiter, C. (eds) (2002) *Giving Sorrow Words: Poems of Strength and Solace*. Pembroke Pines, FL: National Association for Poetry Therapy Foundation.

Williams, J. (ed.) (2010) *It's Not You, It's Me: The Poetry of Breakup*. New York: Overlook Press/Peter Mayer.

Young, K. (ed.) (2010) *The Art of Losing: Poems of Grief and Healing*. New York: Bloomsbury USA.

Story Anthologies

Cahill, S. (ed.) [1975] (2002) *Women and Fiction: Stories by and about Women*. New York: Signet Classic, New American Library. (First published in 1975).

Chavis, G.G. (ed.) (1987) *Family: Stories from the Interior*. St. Paul, MN: Graywolf.

Dow, M. and Regan, J. (eds) (1989) *The Invisible Enemy: Alcoholism and the Modern Short Story*. St. Paul, MN: Graywolf.

Eicher, T. and Geller, J.D. (eds) (1990) *Fathers and Daughters: Portraits in Fiction*. New York: Penguin.

Koppelman, S. (ed.) (1985) *Between Mothers and Daughters: Stories across a Generation*. Old Westbury, NY: Feminist Press.

Koppelman, S. (ed.) (1991) *Women's Friendships: A Collection of Short Stories*. Norman, OK: University of Oklahoma Press.

Kothari, G. (ed.) (1994) *Did My Mama Like to Dance and Other Stories about Mothers and Daughters*. New York: Avon.

Mackay, S. (ed.) (1994) *Such Devoted Sisters*. Wakefield, RI: Moyer Bell.

Muth, J.J. (2005) *Zen Shorts*. New York: Scholastic Press.

Park, C. and Heaton, C. (eds) (1989) *Close Company: Stories of Mothers and Daughters*. New York: Tichnor & Fields.

Remen, R.N. (1996) *Kitchen Table Wisdom: Stories that Heal*. New York: Riverhead.

Sennett, D. (ed.) (1988) *Full Measure: Modern Short Stories on Aging*. St. Paul, MN: Graywolf.

Spinner, S. (ed.) (1972) *Feminine Plural: Stories by Women about Growing Up*. New York: Macmillan.

Strom, R.D. (ed.) (1977) *Parent and Child in Fiction*. Monterey, CA: Brooks/Cole.

Thomas, J., Thomas, D. and Hazuka, T. (eds) (1992) *Flash Fiction: 72 Very Short Stories*. New York: Norton.

Walker, S. (ed.) (1991) *The New Family*. St. Paul, MN: Graywolf.

Washington, M.H. (ed.) (1975) *Black-Eyed Susans: Classic Stories By and About Black Women*. Garden City, NY: Anchor Press/Doubleday.

Anthologies Containing Both Poems and Short Stories

Claman, E. (ed.) (1994) *Each in Her Own Way: Women Writing on the Menopause*. Eugene, OR: Queen of Swords Press.

Hoffman, N. and Howe, F. (eds) (1979) *Women Working: An Anthology of Stories and Poems*. Old Westbury, NY: Feminist Press.

Martz, S.H. (ed.) (1987) *When I Am an Old Woman, I Shall Wear Purple: An Anthology of Short Stories and Poetry*. Manhattan Beach, CA: Papier-Mache Press.

Martz, S.H. (ed.) (1992) *If I Had My Life to Live Over, I Would Pick More Daisies*. Watsonville, CA: Papier-Mache Press.

Martz, S.H. (ed.) (1994) *I Am Becoming the Woman I've Wanted*. Watsonville, CA: Papier-Mache Press.

Moffat, M.J. (ed.) (1982) *In the Midst of Winter: Selections from the Literature of Mourning*. New York: Vintage/Random House.

O'Fallon, A. and Vaillancourt, M. (eds) (2005) *Kiss Me Goodnight: Stories and Poems by Women Who Were Girls When Their Mothers Died.* Minneapolis, MN: Syren.

Wisechild, L.M. (ed.) (1991) *She Who Was Lost Is Remembered: Healing from Incest through Creativity.* Seattle, WA: Seal Press.

Film Resources: Books on Film Therapy Containing Lists of Therapeutic Films

Engstrom, F. (2004) *Movie Clips for Creative Mental Health Education.* New York: Wellness Reproductions & Publishing.

Hesley, J.W. and Hesley, J.G. (1998) *Rent Two Films and Let's Talk in the Morning: Using Popular Movies in Psychotherapy.* New York: Wiley.

Kalm, M.A. (2004) *The Healing Movie Book (Appendix A & B).* Self-Published.

Solomon, G. (1995) *The Motion Picture Prescription.* Santa Rosa, CA: Aslan.

Recommended Websites

Arts and Spirituality Center
www.artsandspirituality.org/we_the_poets

'We the Poets' is a program of the Arts and Spirituality Center, which creates a forum where children from different cultures write and share their poetry. A non-sectarian organization, the Center empowers and transforms individuals and communities through spiritual and creative expression. It is located at 3723 Chestnut Street, Philadelphia, Pennsylvania 19104-7701. Telephone #: 215 386-7705.

Cinematherapy Film Index
www.cinematherapy.com/bibliography.html

This site, inspired by Birgit Wolz, psychotherapist and grief counselor in Oakland, California, provides a bibliography of cinema therapy books and articles for personal and clinical applications.

www.cinematherapy.com/filmindex.html

The Cinema Therapy Film Index provides an extensive list of film titles dealing with a wide variety of issues.

Google (for locating poems and stories by author and/or title)
www.google.com

There is a large number of both contemporary and traditional poems available in full text here.

Healing Words Productions
www.healingwordsproductions.com/poems.html

This site focuses on the link between medicine and the expressive arts, and its goal is to produce documentaries in poetry and healing. It features a selection of poems pertaining to physical and emotional illness, health and wellbeing. The contact person is Joan Baranow, Tel. # 415 381-8641.

Lapidus: UK Organization for Creative Writing and Reading for Well-Being and Health

www.lapidus.org.uk

Lapidus is an organization of writers, poets, educators, therapists, medical and health care professionals, complementary practitioners, survivors and artists working for wellbeing. The site features reading suggestions, notices of conferences, readings and workshops and information on practitioners in the field. Address: BM Lapidus, London WC1N 3XX. info@lapidus.org.uk.

Library of Congress Poetic Resources

www.loc.gov/rr/program/bib/lcpoetry/

This Library of Congress (Washington D.C.) website provides a comprehensive guide to locating poetry resources, including full text of poems, audio recordings, webcasts and news on poetry readings.

National Association for Poetry Therapy

www.poetrytherapy.org

The National Association for Poetry Therapy (NAPT) is an organization based in the U.S. but with members all over the world. Promoting growth and healing through language, story and symbol, NAPT consists of mental health professionals, health care professionals, pastoral counselors, poetry therapists and other creative arts therapists, occupational and recreational therapists, educators, writers, poets and storytellers. The site provides an on-line 'Museletter' and information on conferences and other educational opportunities in biblio/poetry therapy. Address of NAPT: 3365 Wildridge Drive NE, Grand Rapids, Michigan 49525. Telephone #: 866 844-NAPT. Administrator address: contact@ poetrytherapy.org.

National Federation for Biblio/Poetry Therapy (for training and certification information)

www.nfbpt.com

This organization provides training and certification information for practitioners in the field of biblio/poetry therapy and serves as a clearinghouse for questions about professional training requirements. It approves training applications and confers credentials on qualified trainees. Its site provides a list of mentor/supervisors with contact information. Administrator address: 1625 Mid Valley Drive, #1, Suite 126, Steamboat Springs, Colorado 80487. admin@nfbpt.com.

Poetry 180: A Poem a Day for American High Schools

www.loc.gov/poetry/180/p180-list.html

Operated by the Library of Congress, Washington D.C., 'Poetry 180' provides access to printable versions of 180 selected poems by a wide variety of authors.

Poetry Foundation

www.poetryfoundation.org/archive/poetrytool.html

This very practical and useful site contains printable versions of a variety of poems organized by subject categories as well as by occasion, titles and first lines. Contact information: mail@poetryfoundation.org.

The Responsibility Project

www.responsibilityproject.com/resources/11-life-lessons-from-animated-movies

Sponsored by Liberty Mutual, this site is a place to reflect upon and discuss ethical issues and decision-making. It contains synopses and reviews of full-length animated films that inspire and teach lessons of hope, courage and love.

www.responsibilityproject.com/resources/best-family-movies

This site contains summaries of films that provide an effective way to begin conversations on the ways our values affect our choices. The films featured here portray characters that show responsibility, integrity, compassion and courage.

Stories of Recovery

www.storiesofrecovery.org.uk

This site contains the full text of 30 stories (copyrighted 2009-2010) of recovery from addiction that offer hope and inspiration. The Greater Glasgow and Clyde Drug Action Team, along with Lapidus writing and storytelling service, worked with recovering drug users who wrote about their recovery process.

Therapeutic Themes and Relevant Movies by Ofer Zur and Birgit Wolz

www.zurinstitute.com/movietherapy.html

Sponsored by Zur Institute, which provides innovative resources and on-line continuing education, this site is designed for mental health professionals using films in their practice. It provides an extensive list of films organized by a wide array of categories.

References

Adams, C. (ed.) (1996) *The Soul Unearthed: Celebrating Wildness and Personal Renewal through Nature* . New York: Jeremy P. Tarcher/G.P. Putnam's Sons.

Adams, K. (1990) *Journal to the Self: Twenty-Two Paths to Personal Growth*. New York: Warner.

Aesop (1912) *The Hare and the Tortoise: A New Translation by V.S.V. Jones*. New York: Avenel.

Aesop (2005a) 'The Hare and the Tortoise' in M. Morpurgo (ed.) *The McElderry Book of Aesop's Fables*. New York: Margaret K. McElderry.

Aesop (2005b)'The Town Mouse and the Country Mouse' in M. Morpurgo (ed.) *The McElderry Book of Aesop's Fables*. New York: Margaret K. McElderry.

Aesop (2006) *The Hare and the Tortoise*, edited by L. Zwerger. New York: North-South.

Anderson, H.C. (1998) *The Little Mermaid and Other Fairy Tales*, introduced by N. Philip. New York: Penguin.

Anderson, S. (1987) 'Unlighted Lamps' in G.G. Chavis (ed.) *Family: Stories from the Interior*. St. Paul, MN: Graywolf.

Angelou, M. (1978) 'Phenomenal Woman' in M. Angelou, *And Still I Rise*. New York: Random House.

Anonymous (2009) 'Love the Winter' in *Winter Oak: Super Awesome Poem of the Week, 21 December, 2009*. Available at www.facebook.com/note.php?note_id=240563340578. Site visited February 2010.

Anonymous (n.d.) 'The Cracked Pot.' Available at www.lovethissite.com/crackedpot and www.story-lovers.com/listscrackedpotstory.html. Sites visited May 2007 and November 2009.

Avnet, J. (director) (1991) *Fried Green Tomatoes*. Los Angeles, CA: Act III Communications.

Bass, E. (2002) 'The Thing Is' in K. van Meenen and C. Rossiter (eds) *Giving Sorrow Words Poems of Strength and Solace*. Pembroke Pines, FL: National Association for Poetry Therapy Foundation.

Bentley, P. (1987) 'Mother and Daughter' in G.G. Chavis (ed.) *Family: Stories from the Interior*. St. Paul, MN: Graywolf.

Benton, R. (director) (1979) *Kramer vs. Kramer*. Burbank, CA: Columbia Pictures Industries.

Berenstain, S. and Berenstain, J. (1986) *The Berenstain Bears and the Trouble with Friends*. New York: Random House.

Bergh, K.S. (1997) *She Would Draw Flowers: A Book of Poems*. St. Cloud, MN: Sentinel.

Berry, W. (1980) 'The Peace of Wild Things' in W. Berry, *Openings: Poems by Wendell Berry*. San Diego, CA: Harcourt Brace Jovanovich.

Bettelheim, B. [1978] (1986) 'Foreword' to H. Dieckmann, *Twice-Told Tales: The Psychological Use of Fairy Tales*, translated by B. Matthews. Wilmette, IL: Chiron.

Bishop, E. (1983) 'One Art' in E. Bishop, *Elisabeth Bishop: The Complete Poems 1927–1979*. New York: Farrar, Straus & Giroux.

Blake, W. (1968) 'Proverbs of Hell' in D.V. Erdman (ed.) *The Poetry and Prose of William Blake*. Garden City, NY: Doubleday.

Blumenthal, M. (2006) 'The New Story of Your Life' in M. Blumenthal, *Against Romance: Poems*. New York: Pleasure Boat Studio: A Literary Press.

Bobotek, H. (2003) 'Reflections [inspired by Wisława Szymborska's poem, "Possibilities"].' *Journal of Poetry Therapy, 16*, 3, 189–190.

Boden, H. (2006) 'Footnotes.' *Lapidus Quarterly, 2*, 1, 8–12.

Bolton, G. (1999) *The Therapeutic Potential of Creative Writing: Writing Myself.* London: Jessica Kingsley Publishers.

Bolton, G. (2004) '"Every Poem Breaks a Silence that Had to Be Overcome": The Therapeutic Role of Poetry Writing' in G. Bolton, S. Howlett, C. Lago and J.K. Wright (eds) *Writing Cures: An Introductory Handbook of Writing in Counseling and Therapy.* Hove: Brunner-Routledge.

Bolton, G. (2006) 'My Magical Mystery Tour.' *Lapidus Quarterly, 2*, 1, 4–7.

Boyum, J.G. (1985) *Double Exposure: Fiction into Film.* New York: Universe.

Brown, C.R. (1974) 'We Are Not Hen's Eggs' in B. Ryan (ed.) *Search the Silence: Poems of Self-Discovery.* New York: Scholastic Book Services.

Browne, M.D. (1998) 'Poetry and Walking.' *Gettysburg*, winter, 605–612.

Campbell, J. (1986) *The Inner Reaches of Outer Space: Metaphor as Myth and as Religion.* New York: Harper & Row.

Canfield, J., Hansen, M.V., McCarty, H. and McCarty, M. (eds) (1997) *A 4th Course of Chicken Soup for the Soul: 101 Stories to Open the Heart and Rekindle the Spirit.* Deerfield Beach, FL: Health Communications.

Cattaneo, P. (director) (1997) *The Full Monty.* Los Angeles, CA: Fox Searchlight Pictures.

Chavis, G.G. (ed.) (1987) *Family: Stories from the Interior.* St. Paul, MN: Graywolf.

Cisneros, S. (1992a) 'Eleven' in S. Cisneros, *Woman Hollering Creek and Other Stories.* New York: Vintage/Random House.

Cisneros, S. (1992b) 'Woman Hollering Creek' in S. Cisneros, *Woman Hollering Creek and Other Stories.* New York: Vintage/Random House.

Clifton, L. (1987) 'what the mirror said' in L. Clifton, *Next: New Poems.* Brockport, NY: BOA Editions.

Clifton, L. (1991) 'to my friend, jerina' in L. Clifton, *Quilting: Poems 1987–1990.* Brockport, NY: BOA Editions.

Coleridge, S.T. (1950) 'Work without Hope' in I.A. Richards (ed.) *The Portable Coleridge.* New York: Viking.

Crooker, B. (2005) 'In the Middle' in G. Kiellor (ed.) *Good Poems for Hard Times.* New York: Penguin.

Daldry, S. (director) (2000) *Billy Elliot.* Universal City, CA: Universal Studios.

Darnell, C.P. (1994) 'The Lesson of Texas' in R.N. Remen (ed.) *Wounded Healers.* Mill Valley, CA: Wounded Healer Press.

DeSalvo, L. (2001) 'How Telling Our Stories Transforms Our Lives.' *Poets and Writers Magazine, 29*, 3, 48–50.

de Wit, M.D. (writer/director) (2000) *Father and Daughter.* UK: Cloudrunner; Netherlands: CinéTé Filmproductie BV.

Dickinson, E. (1961a) 'Much Madness is Divinest Sense' in T.H. Johnson (ed.) *Final Harvest: Emily Dickinson's Poems.* Boston, MA: Little, Brown.

Dickinson, E. (1961b) 'This was a Poet—It is that' in T.H. Johnson (ed.) *Final Harvest: Emily Dickinson's Poems.* Boston, MA: Little, Brown.

Dieckmann, H. [1978] (1986) *Twice-Told Tales: The Psychological Use of Fairy Tales*, translated by B. Matthews. Wilmette, IL: Chiron.

Dowrick, S. (1993) *The Intimacy and Solitude Workbook: Self-Therapy for Lasting Change.* New York: Norton.

Draper, N. (2009) 'Teens Craft Hope in Prose.' *Star Tribune*, 15 July, B.

Drew, E. (1959) *Poetry: A Modern Guide to Its Understanding and Enjoyment.* New York: Dell.

Eastwood, C. (director) (2009) *Invictus.* Burbank, CA: Warner Bros. Pictures.

Fainlight, R. (1983) 'Handbag' in R. Fainlight, *Fifteen to Infinity.* London: Hutchinson.

Fargnoli, P. (1999) 'Going' in P. Fargnoli, *Necessary Light: Poems by Patricia Fargnoli.* Logan, UT: Utah State University Press.

Feinstein, E. (1977) 'Marriage' in E. Feinstein, *Some Unease and Angels: Selected Poems.* University Center, MI: Green River Press.

Ferber, E. (1947) 'Sudden Sixties' in E. Ferber, *One Basket: Thirty-One Short Stories by Edna Ferber.* Chicago, IL: People's Book Club.

Ferrary, J. (2004) 'Parsley' in J. Ferrary, *Out of the Kitchen: Adventures of a Food Writer.* McKinleyville, CA: John Daniel.

Fisher, D.C. (1997) 'Sex Education' in D.C. Fisher, *The Bedquilt and Other Stories*, edited by M.J. Madigan. Columbia, MI: University of Missouri Press.

Fonda, J. (2010) 'On Golden Pond.' Available at http://janefonda.com/on-golden-pond, site visited on 24 November 2010.

Frank, J.D. (1963) *Persuasion and Healing: A Comparative Study of Psychotherapy.* New York: Schocken.

Frankel, D. (director) (2006) *The Devil Wears Prada.* Los Angeles, CA: 20th Century Fox Studios.

Franklin, C. (director) (1998) *One True Thing.* Universal City, CA: Universal City Studios.

Freud, S. (1933) 'The Psychology of Women' in S. Freud, *New Introductory Lectures on Psycho-Analysis*, translated by J.H. Sprott. New York: Norton.

Frost, R. (1972) 'The Figure a Poem Makes—Introduction' in E.C. Lathem and L. Thompson (eds) *The Robert Frost Reader: Poetry and Prose.* New York: Henry Holt.

Frost, R. (1979a) 'The Armful' in E.C. Lathem (ed.) *The Poetry of Robert Frost: The Collected Poems, Complete and Unabridged.* New York: Holt, Rinehart & Winston.

Frost, R. (1979b) 'The Road Not Taken' in E.C. Lathem (ed.) *The Poetry of Robert Frost: The Collected Poems, Complete and Unabridged.* New York: Holt, Rinehart & Winston.

Gendler, J.R. [1984] (1988) 'Fear' in J.R. Gendler, *The Book of Qualities*, 2nd edn. New York: Harper Perennial.

Gibbs, A. (1987) 'Father Was a Wit' in G.G. Chavis (ed.) *Family: Stories from the Interior.* St. Paul, MN: Graywolf.

Gibran, K. [1926] (1971a) 'On Children' in K. Gibran, *The Prophet.* New York: Alfred A. Knopf.

Gibran, K. [1926] (1971b) 'On Marriage' in K. Gibran, *The Prophet.* New York: Alfred A. Knopf.

Giovanni, N. (2003a) 'A Certain Peace' in N. Giovanni, *The Collected Poetry of Nikki Giovanni 1968–1998.* New York: William Morrow.

Giovanni, N. (2003b) 'Poetry' in N. Giovanni, *The Collected Poetry of Nikki Giovanni 1968–1998.* New York: William Morrow.

Gladding, S.T. (1994) 'Teaching Family Counseling through the Use of Fiction.' *Counselor Education and Supervision, 33*, March, 191–199.

Goedicke, P. [1978] (1992) 'Circus Song' in L. Lifshin (ed.) *Tangled Vines: A Collection of Mother and Daughter Poems.* San Diego, CA: Harcourt Brace Jovanovich.

Gold, J. (1988) 'The Value of Fiction as Therapeutic Recreation and Developmental Mediator: A Theoretical Framework.' *Journal of Poetry Therapy, 1*, 3, 135–148.

Goldberg, N. (1986) *Writing Down the Bones.* Boston, MA: Shambala.

Gonzalez, R. (1994) 'Praise the Tortilla, Praise the Menudo, Praise the Chorizo' in M.M. Gillan and J. Gillan (eds) *Unsettling America: An Anthology of Contemporary Multicultural Poetry.* New York: Penguin.

Green, K. (1983) 'Don't Make Your Life Too Beautiful' in K. Green, *If the World Is Running Out: Poems by Kate Green.* Minneapolis, MN: Holy Cow! Press.

Hayden, R. (1985) 'Those Winter Sundays' in F. Glaysher (ed.) *Robert Hayden: Collected Poems.* New York: Liveright.

Henley, W.E. (1965) 'Invictus' in J.H. Buckley and G.B. Woods (eds) *Poetry of the Victorian Period*, 3rd edn. Chicago, IL: Scott, Foresman.

Hesley, J.W. and Hesley, J.G. (1998) *Rent Two Films and Let's Talk in the Morning: Using Popular Movies in Psychotherapy.* New York: Wiley.

Holub, M. (1990) *Miroslav Holub: Poems Before and After. Collected English Translations* by I. Milner, J. Milner, E. Osers and G. Theiner. Newcastle upon Tyne: Bloodaxe.

Howard, G. (1990) 'Sally Forth.' *Star Tribune*, 8 July, 7.

Howard, R. (director) (1989) *Parenthood*. Los Angeles, CA: Universal Pictures.

Hughes, L. [1994] (2001) 'Island[1]' in A. Rampersad and D. Roessel (eds) *The Collected Poems of Langston Hughes*. New York: Alfred A. Knopf.

Hunnicutt, E. (1992) 'Blackberries' in J. Thomas, D. Thomas and T. Hazuka (eds) *Flash Fiction: 72 Very Short Stories*. New York: Norton.

Hynes, A. and Hynes-Berry, M. [1986] (1994) *Biblio/Poetry Therapy: The Interactive Process. A Handbook*. St. Cloud, MN: North Star Press.

Johnson, C. (1986) 'Afterwords' in R. Shapard and J.T. Layton (eds) *Sudden Fiction: American Short-Short Stories*. Salt Lake City, UT: Peregrine Smith/Gibbs Smith.

Jordan, J. (1977) 'Ah, Momma' in *Things that I Do in the Dark*. New York: Random House.

Keats, J. (1990a) *The Fall of Hyperion: A Dream* in E. Cook (ed.) *John Keats: The Major Works*. Oxford: Oxford University Press.

Keats, J. (1990b) 'Letter to George and Tom Keats, 21/27 December, 1817' in E. Cook (ed.) *John Keats: The Major Works*. Oxford: Oxford University Press.

Keats, J. (1990c) 'Letter to J.H. Reynolds, 19 February, 1818' in E. Cook (ed.) *John Keats: The Major Works*. Oxford: Oxford University Press.

Keats, J. (1990d) 'To Autumn' in E. Cook (ed.) *John Keats: The Major Works*. Oxford: Oxford University Press.

Kipling, R. (1989) 'If' in R. Kipling, *Rudyard Kipling, Complete Verse: Definitive Edition*. New York: Random House.

Kopp, R.R. (1995) *Metaphor Therapy: Using Client-Centered Metaphors in Psychotherapy*. New York: Brunner/Mazel.

Kottler, D.B. (1979) 'LIST For My Father' in M. Kriel (ed.) *The Selby-Lake Bus: A Collection of Minneapolis-St. Paul Poets*. Minneapolis, MN: Lake Street Review Press.

Lamott, A. (1994) *Bird by Bird: Some Instructions on Writing and Life*. New York: Anchor/Random House.

Lardner, R. (1963) 'Old Folks' Christmas' in M. Geismar (ed.) *The Ring Lardner Reader*. New York: Charles Scribner's Sons.

Lavin, M. [1951] (2003) 'The Widow's Son' in A. Charters (ed.) *The Story and Its Writer: An Introduction to Short Fiction, Compact Sixth Edition*. Boston, MA: Bedford/St. Martin's Press.

Lawrence, D.H. (1962) 'Letter to A.W. McLeod, 26 October, 1913' in H.T. Moore (ed.) *The Collected Letters of D.H. Lawrence, Volume I*. New York: Viking.

Lazarsfeld, S. (1949) 'The Use of Fiction in Psychotherapy.' *American Journal of Psychotherapy, 3*, 26–33.

Lehmann, M. (director) (1996) *The Truth about Cats and Dogs*. Los Angeles, CA: 20th Century Fox Corporation.

Lepore, S.J. and Smyth, J.M. (eds) (2002) *The Writing Cure: How Expressive Writing Promotes Health and Emotional Wellbeing*. Washington, DC: American Psychological Association.

Lerner, A. and Mahlendorf, U.R. (1992) 'Introduction' in A. Lerner and U.R. Mahlendorf, *Life Guidance through Literature*. Chicago, IL: American Library Association.

Levertov, D. (1987) 'Variation on a Theme by Rilke [The Book of Hours, *Book I, Poem 1, Stanza 1*]' in D. Levertov, *Breathing the Water*. New York: New Directions.

Levertov, D. (2002) 'Talking to Grief' in P.A. Lacey (ed.) *Denise Levertov: Selected Poems*. New York: New Directions.

Lindbergh, A.M. (1955) *Gift from the Sea*. New York: Vintage.

Luckey, B. (writer/director) (2003) *Boundin'*. Pixar Animation Studios in *The Incredibles Collector's Edition*. Burbank, CA: Pixar/Disney.

McCarty, H. (1997) 'Permission to Cry' in J. Canfield, M.V. Hansen, H. McCarty and M. McCarty (eds) *A 4th Course of Chicken Soup for the Soul*. Deerfield Beach, FL: Health Communications.

McCullers, C. (1987) 'A Domestic Dilemma' in C. McCullers, *Collected Stories of Carson McCullers*. Boston, MA: Houghton Mifflin.

MacLeish, A. [1956] (1987) 'Ars Poetica' in L. Perrine (ed.) *Sound and Sense: An Introduction to Poetry*, 7th edn. San Diego, CA: Harcourt Brace Jovanovich.

Maguire, I. (2004) 'Origins' in I. Maguire, *Shout If You Want Me to Sing*. Kilcar, Donegal: Summer Palace Press.

Mazursky, P. (director) (1974) *Harry and Tonto*. New York: 20th Century Fox Corporation.

Mazza, N. [1999] (2003) *Poetry Therapy: Theory and Practice*. London: Routledge.

Merton, T. (2005) 'Love Winter When the Plant Says Nothing' in L.R. Szabo (ed.) *In the Dark Before Dawn: New Selected Poems of Thomas Merton*. New York: New Directions.

Mill, J.S. (1993) 'A Crisis in My Mental History. One Stage Onward' (Chapter 5 of *Autobiography*) in M.H. Abrams (ed.) *Norton Anthology of English Literature, Volume 2*, 6th edn. New York: Norton.

Myers, L. (2003) *Becoming Whole: Writing Your Healing Story*. San Diego, CA: Silver Threads Press.

Nelson, G.M. (1992) 'Growing Up with Fairy Tales' in K. Vander Vort, J.H. Timmerman and E. Lincoln (eds) *Walking in Two Worlds: Women's Spiritual Paths*. St. Cloud, MN: North Star Press.

O'Brien, T. (2010) 'The Things They Carried' in L.G. Kirszner and S.R. Mandell (eds) *Portable Literature: Reading, Reacting, Writing*, 7th edn. Boston, MA: Wadsworth.

Oliver, M. (2006) 'Heavy' in M. Oliver, *Thirst: Poems by Mary Oliver*. Boston, MA: Beacon.

Oliver, M. [1990] (1992) 'The Summer Day' in M. Oliver, *Mary Oliver: New and Selected Poems, Volume One*. Boston, MA: Beacon.

Ornish, D. (1996) 'Foreword' in R.N. Remen, *Kitchen Table Wisdom: Stories that Heal*. New York: Riverhead.

Parker, D. [1944] (1973a) 'A Telephone Call' in D. Parker, *The Portable Dorothy Parker*, introduced by B. Gill. New York: Penguin.

Parker, D. [1944] (1973b) 'The Waltz' in D. Parker, *The Portable Dorothy Parker*, introduced by B. Gill. New York: Penguin.

Pastan, L. (1982) 'Marks' in L. Pastan, *PM/AM: New and Selected Poems by Linda Pastan*. New York: Norton.

Pastan, L. (2003) 'Why Are Your Poems So Dark?' *Poetry, 182*, August, 249.

Pastan, L. (2009) 'Keynote Poetry Reading.' National Association for Poetry Therapy Conference, Washington, DC, 17 April.

Peacock, M. (1999) *How to Read a Poem…and Start a Poetry Circle*. New York: Riverhead/Penguin.

Pennebaker, J.W. [1990] (1997) *Opening Up: The Healing Power of Expressing Emotions*. New York: Guilford.

Perlman, H.H. (1987) 'Twelfth Summer' in G.G. Chavis (ed.) *Family: Stories from the Interior*. St. Paul, MN: Graywolf.

Peterson, L. (2005) 'Wounded Healers and Flawed Heroes: Growing through Our Stories of Imperfection.' Workshop presented at 'Healing through Stories' Conference, Minnesota.

Philipp, R. and Robertson, I. (1996) 'Poetry Helps Healing.' *Lancet, 347*, February, 332–333.

Portnoy, M. (1987) 'Loving Strangers' in G.G. Chavis (ed.) *Family: Stories from the Interior*. St. Paul, MN: Graywolf.

Reiter, S. (1998) 'Palm-of-the-Hand Stories in Bibliotherapy.' Workshop presented at Conference of the National Association for Poetry Therapy, San Jose, CA.

Reiter, S. with Contributors (2009) *Writing Away the Demons: Stories of Creative Coping through Transformative Writing*. St. Cloud, MN: North Star Press.

Remen, R.N. (1996a) 'Introduction' in R.N. Remen, *Kitchen Table Wisdom: Stories that Heal*. New York: Riverhead.

Remen, R.N. (1996b) 'I Never Promised You a Rose Garden' in R.N. Remen, *Kitchen Table Wisdom: Stories that Heal*. New York: Riverhead.

Remen, R.N. (1996c) 'A Room with a View' in R.N. Remen, *Kitchen Table Wisdom: Stories that Heal*. New York: Riverhead.

Remen, R.N. (1996d) 'Three Fables on Letting Go' in R.N. Remen, *Kitchen Table Wisdom: Stories that Heal*. New York: Riverhead.

Roethke, T. (1966) 'Dolor' in *The Collected Poems of Theodore Roethke*. Garden City, NY: Doubleday.

Rosenblatt, L. [1938] (1968) *Literature as Exploration*, 3rd edn. New York: Noble & Noble.

Roth, J.B. (2002) 'From the Threshold' in J.B. Roth (ed.) *We Used To Be Wives: Divorce Unveiled through Poetry*. Santa Barbara, CA: Fithian Press.

Rumi, J. (2006) 'The Guest House' translated by C. Barks, in P. Washington (ed.) *Rumi Poems*. New York: Alfred A. Knopf.

Rydell, M. (director) (1981) *On Golden Pond*. Los Angeles, CA: Universal Pictures.

Sandburg, C. (1969a) 'Definitions of Poetry' in *Good Morning, America*, in C. Sandburg, *The Complete Poems of Carl Sandburg*. New York: Harcourt Brace Jovanovich.

Sandburg, C. (1969b) 'Different Kinds of Good-by' in C. Sandburg, *The Complete Poems of Carl Sandburg*. New York: Harcourt Brace Jovanovich.

Schneider, P. (1990) 'Irma' in I. Zahava (ed.) *Word of Mouth: 150 Short-Short Stories by 90 Women Writers*. Freedom, CA: Crossing Press.

Scott-Maxwell, F. (1975) 'The Measure of My Days' in M.J. Moffat and C. Painter (eds) *Revelations: Diaries of Women*. New York: Random House.

Sendak, M. [1963] (1991) *Where the Wild Things Are*. New York: HarperCollins.

Shapard, R. (1986) 'Introduction' in R. Shapard and J.T. Layton (eds) *Sudden Fiction: American Short-Short Stories*. Salt Lake City, UT: Peregrine Smith/Gibbs Smith.

Shapard, R. and Layton, J.T. (eds) (1986) *Sudden Fiction: American Short-Short Stories*. Salt Lake City, UT: Peregrine Smith/Gibbs Smith.

Shelley, P.B. (1967) *A Defence of Poetry* in B.R. McElderry, Jr. (ed.) *Shelley's Critical Prose*. Lincoln, NE: University of Nebraska.

Shelley, P.B. (1993) 'Ode to the West Wind' in P.B. Shelley, *Shelley's Poems*. New York: Alfred A. Knopf.

Shrodes, C. (1949) *Bibliotherapy: A Theoretical and Clinical Experimental Study*. Unpublished doctoral dissertation. Berkeley, CA: University of California.

Silko, L.M. [1977] (2006) *Ceremony*. New York: Penguin.

Skeen, A. (1994) 'The Woman Whose Body Is Not Her Own' in S. Martz (ed.) *I Am Becoming the Woman I've Wanted*. Watsonville, CA: Papier-Mache Press.

Slattery, D.P. (1999) 'Poetry, Prayer and Meditation.' *Journal of Poetry Therapy, 13*, 1, 39–45.

Sobiloff, H. (1954) 'My Mother's Table' in H. Sobiloff, *Dinosaurs and Violins*. New York: Farrar, Straus & Young.

Solari, R. (1996) 'The Sound of What Matters.' *Common Boundary*, January/February, 24–32.

Solomon, G. (1995) *The Motion Picture Prescription*. Santa Rosa, CA: Aslan.

Somerville, R.M. (1964) *Family Insights through the Short Story: A Guide for Teachers and Workshop Leaders*. New York: Bureau of Publications, Teacher's College, Columbia University.

Spielberg, S. (director) (1985) *The Color Purple*. Burbank, CA: Amblin Entertainment.

Stageberg, N.C. and Anderson, W.L. (1952) *Poetry as Experience*. New York: American Book Company.

Stegner, W. (1987) 'The Blue-Winged Teal' in G.G. Chavis (ed.) *Family: Stories from the Interior*. St. Paul, MN: Graywolf.

Tan, A. [1957] (2003) 'Two Kinds' in A. Charters (ed.) *The Story and Its Writer: An Introduction to Short Fiction, Compact Sixth Edition*. Boston, MA: Bedford/St. Martin's Press.

Thomas, D. (1957) 'Do Not Go Gently' in D. Thomas, *The Collected Poems of Dylan Thomas*. New York: New Directions.

Thoreau, H.D. (1975) 'Walking' in W. Harding (ed.) *The Selected Works of Thoreau*. Boston, MA: Cambridge Edition, Houghton Mifflin.

Timpane, J. and Watts, M. (2001) 'Introduction' in J. Timpane and M. Watts, *Poetry for Dummies*. NewYork: Hungry Minds.

Tolstoy, L. [1960] (2003) 'Family Happiness' translated by J.D. Duff in L. Tolstoy, *The Death of Ivan Ilych and Other Stories*. New York: Signet Classic, New American Library.

Townsend, A. (2005) 'My Mother's Pastels' in A.M. O'Fallon and M. Vaillancourt (eds) *Kiss Me Goodnight: Stories and Poems by Women Who Were Girls When Their Mothers Died*. Minneapolis, MN: Syren.

Turner, A. (1990) *Responses to Poetry*. New York: Longman.

Ueland, B. [1938] (1987) *If You Want to Write*. St. Paul, MN: Graywolf. (First published in 1938).

Van Sant, G. (director) (1998) *Good Will Hunting*. New York: Miramax Film Corporation.

Varley, S. (1984) *Badger's Parting Gifts*. New York: Lothrop, Lee & Shepard/William Morrow.

Viorst, J. (1971) *The Tenth Best Thing about Barney*. New York: Aladdin/Simon & Schuster.

Viorst, J. (1972) *Alexander and the Terrible, Horrible, No Good, Very Bad Day*. New York: Atheneum/ Simon & Schuster.

Vodges, N.L. (1980) 'Snowbound.' *Social Work, 1,* 25.

Walcott, D. (1986) 'Love after Love' in D. Walcott, *Collected Poems 1948–1984*. New York: Noonday Press/Farrar, Straus & Giroux.

Waldman, A. (1996) 'Fast Speaking Woman' in A. Waldman, *Fast Speaking Woman: Chants and Essays*. San Francisco, CA: City Lights.

Walker, A. (1975) 'A Sudden Trip Home in the Spring' in M.H. Washington (ed.) *Black-Eyed Susans: Classic Stories by and about Black Women*. Garden City, NY: Anchor Books/Doubleday.

Wang, W. (director) (1993) *The Joy Luck Club*. Burbank, CA: Hollywood Pictures.

Wellington, G. (1977) 'I Wanted to Be a Cauliflower' in J. McDowell and M. Loventhal (eds) *Contemporary Women Poets: An Anthology of California Poets*. San Jose, CA: Merlin Press.

Whitman, W. (1993) 'Song of Myself' in W. Whitman, *Leaves of Grass*. New York: Modern Library/ Random House.

Whyte, D. (2009) 'David Whyte—*The Journey*.' Available at www.youtube.com/ watch?v=6PK3GhnHOJc, accessed on 24 November 2010.

Wiegner, K. (1974) 'Autobiography' in K. Wiegner, *Country Western Breakdown*. Trumansburg, NY: Crossing Press.

Winnicott, D.W. (1988) 'The Tree' in A. Phillips, *Winnicott*. London: Fontana.

Wolz, B. (2009) *Guidelines for Watching Films: Watching Movies with Conscious Awareness*. Available at www.cinematherapy.com/watching.html. Site visited 3 June 2009.

Woolf, V. (1976) 'A Sketch of the Past' in J. Schulkind (ed.) *Moments of Being: Unpublished Autobiographical Writings*. New York: Harcourt Brace Jovanovich.

Wordsworth, W. (1965a) 'Expostulation and Reply' in J. Stillinger (ed.) *William Wordsworth: Selected Poems and Prefaces*. Boston, MA: Riverside Editions/Houghton Mifflin.

Wordsworth, W. (1965b) 'I Wandered Lonely as a Cloud' in J. Stillinger (ed.) *William Wordsworth: Selected Poems and Prefaces*. Boston, MA: Riverside Editions/Houghton Mifflin.

Wordsworth, W. (1965c) 'Ode: Intimations of Immortality from Recollections of Early Childhood' in J. Stillinger (ed.) *William Wordsworth: Selected Poems and Prefaces*. Boston, MA: Riverside Editions/ Houghton Mifflin.

Wordsworth, W. (1965d) 'Preface to the Second Edition of Lyrical Ballads' in J. Stillinger (ed.) *William Wordsworth: Selected Poems and Prefaces*. Boston, MA: Riverside Editions/ Houghton Mifflin.

Wordsworth, W. (1965e) 'The Prelude, Book 12' [1905 edition] in J. Stillinger (ed.) *William Wordsworth: Selected Poems and Prefaces*. Boston, MA: Riverside Editions / Houghton Mifflin.

Wordsworth, W. (1965f) 'Tables Turned' in J. Stillinger (ed.) *William Wordsworth: Selected Poems and Prefaces*. Boston, MA: Riverside Editions/Houghton Mifflin.

Wordsworth, W. (1965g) 'The World Is Too Much with Us' in J. Stillinger (ed.) *William Wordsworth: Selected Poems and Prefaces*. Boston, MA: Riverside Editions/Houghton Mifflin.

Yamamoto, H. (1985) 'Seventeen Syllables' in S. Koppelman (ed.) *Between Mothers and Daughters: Stories across a Generation*. Old Westbury, NY: Feminist Press.

Yeats, W.B. (1996a) 'The Lake Isle of Innisfree' in R.J. Finneran (ed.) *The Collected Poems of W.B. Yeats, Revised Second Edition*. New York: Scribner/Simon & Schuster.

Yeats, W.B. (1996b) 'Sailing to Byzantium' in R.J. Finnerman (ed.) *The Collected Works of W.B. Yeats, Revised Second Edition*. New York: Scribner/Simon & Schuster.

Zahava, I. (1990) 'Preface' in I. Zahava (ed.) *Word of Mouth: 150 Short-Short Stories by 90 Women Writers*. Freedom, CA: Crossing Press.

Zelvin, E. (1981) 'Coming Apart' in E. Zelvin, *I Am the Daughter*. Moorhead, MN: New Rivers Press.

Subject Index

Author Index